The Never-dying Fire

The Life and Thought of Sri Aurobindo

Luc Venet

ink | kāli

Title: The Never-dying Fire: The Life and Thought of Sri Aurobindo
Author: Luc Venet

ISBN: 978-93-92209-65-9

First published in India 2023
This edition published 2023

Published by:
BluOne Ink LLP
A-76, 2nd Floor, Noida Sector 136,
Uttar Pradesh 201305

Website: www.bluone.ink
Email: publisher@bluone.ink

Printed in India.

Kali, Occam and BluPrint are all trademarks of BluOne Ink LLP.

The Never-dying Fire

Contents

Part II: The Life Divine

Preface

Paris, May 1968

As tear gas wafted through the air, legions of young people rallied from all sides. The metro station at Place of the Odeon poured out an exalted human tide. Paris was preparing for a revolution.

Among the groups densely clustered under Danton's statue, someone stood out: 'Pierre!' He looked up, stepped forward towards me with open arms; we embraced. What a surprise to run into this old friend who had left France months ago to explore the world. I was eager to hear his account.

In the air of gravity on his face, I read this was no time to chat. Scribbling a few words on a piece of paper, he drew me aside and whispered: 'Listen, read this book, and we'll talk later.' By way of clarification, he added: 'The young people here dream of a revolution that will change the world, but they are deluded. In a few weeks or months, things will return to what they were. The only enduring revolution is one that changes what we are, the human beings, from inside out. That's what I learnt in India, at the Ashram of Sri Aurobindo in Pondicherry.'

The author of the book suggested by Pierre was a Frenchman named Satprem. From French Guiana to Africa and India, he had travelled the world in search for the truth of his life. By the late 1940's, he ended up in Pondicherry, at the Ashram of Sri Aurobindo, where he was privileged to attend a *Darshan*—when the disciples, joined by a few guests, marched past in front of the Master to receive his look. In the radiance of this look, Satprem intuited that his quest would soon find an answer.

Thereafter, living in Pondicherry and practicing the 'integral yoga' under the guidance of the Mother, Sri Aurobindo's companion, he had chronicled in his essay, *Sri Aurobindo or the Adventure of Consciousness,* the radical inward transformation resulting from Sri Aurobindo's teaching.

Some 20 years later, as I read his book—and despite my background in mathematics—I was spontaneously conquered by the 'logic' of the yoga. The challenge of a new paradigm, a new way of living life, attracted me. For example, when the aspirant begins treading what Satprem calls the 'path of silence', he faces singular paradoxes, such as this one:

'If the ability to think is a remarkable gift, the ability *to stop thinking* is a greater one yet; let the seeker try for five minutes to realise how tough it is.'[1]

This challenge is particularly demanding for the Western mind whose intellect is the pre-eminent attribute and who follows the dictates of reason since kindergarten.

Yet for Sri Aurobindo, 'the power of silence is a capacity and not incapacity, a power and not a weakness'.[2] Silence opens the way to another mode of being, a transcendence, which transforms the core relationship of a person. What I sensed in Satprem's book motivated me to try to experience this other mode of being. In July 1969, I left Paris for India and arrived at the Sri Aurobindo Ashram in Pondicherry.

At that time, charters from Paris to Bombay stopped over in Cairo, and I found it a good omen to contemplate the Sphinx before landing in India: the riddle prior to the revelation. When I reached the former French colony of Pondicherry, I was astounded by the contrast between the town's bustling activity and the haven of tranquility and peace pervading the Ashram compound. In the shade of the gigantic 'Service' tree surmounting Sri Aurobindo's flowery tomb,[3] clusters of disciples and visitors were absorbed in meditation.

The Mother had accepted to receive me—by fortune of the calendar—on Bastille Day. I did not know that this day would usher me in the revolution of my life.

A short wait on a small shaded terrace on the second floor. And the door opened. A slim, still indistinct figure was facing a large bay window overlooking the 'Service' tree. I approached in total silence, held out my flowers.... She looked at me. I felt swept up into an immensity of sweetness and love unknown to this earth, and this immensity smiled at me. I did not know where I was. I did not who I was. I had cast off the old moorings of myself: no words could account for this other Luc sitting on the golden carpet. It had taken 30 seconds to get a glimpse of an unknown 'me', to become aware of a vaster, deeper existence. Thirty seconds to call into question 26 years of lifetime.

Back in the street, I kept pacing the waterfront to the heartbeat of this one question: 'What happened to me?' 'What happened to me?' Embedded in my chest, throbbing with its own life, that interrogation felt like a warm afterglow. Everything in me had disappeared but that question.

A few days later, the poignancy of the experience dissipated, its fervour declined; I became 'normal' again. But the memory remained. I felt an aching *need* to re-activate 'That' which had miraculously blossomed in me, thanks to Mother's presence.

After eight weeks in Pondicherry and before going home to my teaching job in Paris, I wanted to meet Satprem, who had opened my understanding through his book. I had prepared a few questions, but the smile in his steady blue eyes was the best answer he could give me, as it prompted me to recall what I had glimpsed with Mother.

I returned to Paris with a new heart. My teaching life took a different turn. To impart the discipline of mathematics to my students was no longer enough. By chance, I stumbled on the following line of Sri Aurobindo's:

'All life is only a lavish and manifold opportunity given us to discover, realise, express the Divine.'[4]

In other words, practical life, daily life, however trivial or inadequate, was the ground upon which to exercise the highest truth. This orientation would liberate us from the slavery of all externality and open us to the supreme meaning. The revelation within would then fulfil its aim of converting life without.

I soon realised that my first stay in Pondicherry was to be the prelude of a much vaster change. My thoughts, my emotions, my everyday reactions—all that seemed the very nature of my life up until now—were becoming opportunities for reflection and questioning; the least activity introduced unusual perspectives, instinctive knowledge, a comprehension that dealt with the inwardness of things and people, rather than their mechanical activities. This introspection became each day more concrete, significant and natural. Without knowing it, I was entering the reality of Sri Aurobindo's teaching, the 'yoga'—this Indian discipline whose aim is to free the soul from its existential burden by union with the 'Absolute'. The West knows mostly the physical aspect of this yoga, that is, the practice of *asanas*, postures in which the main aim is relaxation and well-being, eluding the deeper signification of the discipline.

In 1972, I left for Pondicherry to get my life attuned with what Mother had revealed in me—and to attempt to practice Sri Aurobindo's yoga.

Notes

1 Satprem, *Sri Aurobindo ou l'Aventure de la Conscience*, Paris, Buchet/Chastel, 1964, p. 36-37.

2 *The Synthesis of Yoga, Complete Work of Sri Aurobindo*, CWSA, vol. 23-24, p. 316.

3 Sri Aurobindo had passed away 19 years earlier, in 1950.

4 *The Human Cycle*, CWSA, vol. 25, p. 148.

Introduction

> Spirituality is the master key of the Indian mind;
> the sense of the infinite is native to it.
>
> —Sri Aurobindo

At a large political rally for the French presidential election of 2017, one of the presidential candidates surprised his audience by reading aloud a political pamphlet written more than a century ago by Sri Aurobindo. Usually known to English-speaking readers for his *Letters on Yoga* or *The Life Divine*, two of the many books he wrote on yoga, Sri Aurobindo created an Ashram in Pondicherry where many people come today to pay their homage upon his memorial.

What is largely unknown is that before becoming a yogi and moving to Pondicherry from his native Bengal, Sri Aurobindo played a major role in the Indian independence against British colonialism. Between 1893 and 1910, while Gandhi was still far away in South Africa, Sri Aurobindo, through his writing and his action in the political field, opened the way to India's freedom.

His political struggle—the subject of this essay—is part of India's organic evolution in which the founding texts of her spirituality and the dramatic invasions she was subjected to, have been the leaven of her civilisation.

The Beginnings

Between 5000 BC and 4000 BC, in the days of ancient Egypt, Mesopotamia and the early Chinese Neolithic culture, a little-known civilisation occupied the valley of the Indus, extending from what is known today as Pakistan to north-western India. Archaeological findings have revealed a rational culture spread over a complex urban landscape—the Manhattan of the Bronze Age, as some archaeologists put it.

At the end of the second millennium BC, this first civilisation was lost in the following period, called Vedic Age, which produced a corpus of sacred texts in Sanskrit, the Veda or 'Book of Knowledge', couched in metaphorical language and meant to help humankind to face 'the Great Falsehood' of mortal existence. The Vedic sages or rishis composed these texts with the aim of opening humanity to its own powers of interiority.

A 1,000 years later, in the continuity of the Veda, appeared the Upanishads, another corpus of aphorisms, which left the symbolic style for that of spiritual philosophy. A few centuries later, two great epic tales were born: the Ramayana and the Mahabharata (of which the renowned Bhagavad Gita was the centerpiece), tales of bravery and heroism depicting spiritual and 'significant' social ideals.

For a few centuries, India's civilisation soared into a mosaic of states, some of which operated under a regime of republic comparable to the cities of ancient Greece. Large dynasties, at times encompassing almost all the regions of the subcontinent, guided her destiny. Three centuries before Christ, Ashoka's imperial regime championed religious tolerance, treated its subjects irrespective of castes and beliefs, built hospitals and granted rights to animals.

The Invasions

But taking advantage of the weaker periods of the central authority, invaders from Europe or Central Asia entered India through the high passes of the Hindu Kush. Alexander inaugurated this period of invasions in 327 BC. Emboldened by his recent Persian conquests, he marched into Afghanistan and let his troops spread out through the Indus Valley. After several lightning conquests, the mutiny of his army eventually forced him to withdraw and return to Babylon.

Until the 5th century AD, Scythians, Parthians and White Huns thus found the way Alexander had discovered over the mountains; they conquered and settled in parts of the north-western territories and Punjab, sometimes spreading further south or east into Bengal. When these invaders were not quickly defeated and forced to retreat, they were, after a few generations, assimilated into Indian society. Contrary to what happened to the Roman Empire, where the Barbarians imposed their inferior political system, these first invaders of India could neither destroy nor undermine the civilisation—they integrated it.

The Muslim Invasions

Mahomet was born in 570. As the future prophet of Islam, he enforced his revelation of the Koran over a tribal Arabic peninsula. In less than a century after his death, the followers of Islam strove to propagate the new faith. Muslim armies spread over Asia Minor and laid siege to Constantinople; they invaded Persia (present-day Iran) where Zoroastrianism was eradicated or its worshippers converted; they seized Egypt and subjected much of North Africa; they conquered the entire Iberian Peninsula.

As a desirable prey with great human and territorial potentials, India received the first Islamic strikes in the middle of the 7th century, as maritime incursions on the Bombay coast and armed raids in the Sind province. In 712, just as the Iberian Peninsula wrestled with the first Muslim armies, a 17-year-old Arab general, Mohamed Bin Qasim, marched onto the Sind province, where the ancient civilisation of the Indus had flourished.

Testimonies differ as to the vicissitudes of his military campaign and his treatment of the occupied territories, but the instructions he had received from his paternal uncle (who taught him the art of war and supervised his conquests) were blunt: 'Here are my orders: kill all belligerents; take hostage and imprison their sons and daughters. Grant freedom to non-combatants and organise their submission under the rule of the Sharia [Islamic law].' Ensuing violence broke out throughout the province: large temples were razed and replaced by mosques; priests and civilians paid the heaviest tributes of blood; one-fifth of the captured booty, including slaves, was shipped to the Caliph in Damascus.

Once the province was subdued, the young general sought to establish a Muslim rule. But before reaching his 20th year, his star paled when his protector uncle died, soon followed by the Caliph. Recalled to Damascus, accused of treason, he was put to death by the new regime. Muslim presence in the Sind province collapsed under his successors, and Arab advances in the region were discontinued for three centuries—until the next wave.

What the Arabs did not accomplish by sea, other Muslim armies achieved through the Hindu Kush passes. It may not be necessary to detail these 'conquests' of which the young Bin Qasim would not have been ashamed, except to say that in the space of two centuries, from 1000 to 1206 AD, the face of India would be scarred forever, the entire northern and central parts of the country given over to pillage and destruction.

The two masterminds behind this carnage were Mahmoud of Ghazni and Muhammad of Ghor. Of the first, the Persian scholar Al-Biruni (who followed his campaigns) said: 'Mahmoud completely ruined the prosperity of the country and accomplished singular exploits, reducing the Indians to atoms of dust. Their scattered remains naturally keep the strongest aversion towards Muslims.'[1] From his Ghazni stronghold in Afghanistan, Mahmoud launched no fewer than 17 incursions against India between 1001 and 1027. Then, loaded with his booty and his slaves, he returned to Ghazni to embellish the city, build palaces and mosques, open an immense library and act the part of a patron of the arts. Encouraged by the Caliph in Baghdad, he spent his last years ransacking the temples of Ajmer and Somnath, personally smashing the idols to steal the gold and jewels in them.

After a 150-year respite, the second assailant took the stage. Born into a Persian family converted to Islam, Muhammad of Ghor was even more fearsome, adding shrewdness to a cool, murderous determination. Not only did he plunder and destroy everything in his path, but he calculatedly expanded his empire to include all the territories he had conquered. In Delhi, he raised the highest minaret in India, Qutb Minar, building its vast complex with material seized from the demolition of 27 'idolatrous' Hindu temples, as may be read on an inscription visible to this day.

It is almost inconceivable to imagine the Tarain battlefield (north of Delhi) where Muhammad of Ghor had lined up 1,000,000 men against King Prithviraj Chauhan's 3,000 elephants and 300,000 horsemen and infantry. The entire battle was decided in a single day of carnage in which 100,000 men were slain. With luck and cunning, Muhammad routed the Hindu army, then took the king to his Afghan stronghold to execute him. The defeat of Tarain (1192) foreshadowed the huge territorial losses conceded by India during the next six centuries; it opened to Muhammad the Ganges Valley and secured for him a series of conquests from Delhi (1193) to Bengal (1202) through Benares (1194) and the Buddhist cultural centres of Nalanda and Vikramashila (1199). Everywhere, universities and temples were razed to the ground and monks slaughtered, while a handful of trusted men and troops were left to hold the conquered areas.

After Muhammad of Ghor's death in 1206 (he was assassinated in his sleep), one of his generals, mandated to hold and administer Delhi, proclaimed himself sultan, thus establishing what history would record as the Delhi Sultanate. A few centuries later, this would pave the way for the Mughal Empire to seize control of practically the entire Indian subcontinent until the beginning of the 18th century.[1]

But before arriving at a relative peace and stability, India had yet to suffer further devastation. There were the Mongols, initially led by Genghis Khan, who annexed Kashmir (1235) and attempted to supplant the Delhi Sultanate. Then the infamous Tamerlane (1370-1405), another 'Patron of the Arts', the most blindly savage of all, whose Turko-Mongol troops ravaged Delhi and slaughtered people as far as Nagarkot and Jammu, before finally leaving India in 1399. His lightning-fast assault had left the Delhi Sultanate in tatters, but no fewer than 90 elephants were needed to transport his personal booty of precious gems to his lair of Samarkand.

There would also be reprieves—periods of reason and reconstruction when a rare Muslim leader would attempt to consolidate and administer instead of destroying. This was the case of Firuz Shah (1309-1388), who was keen on education and culture, undertook irrigation works and built hospitals with the support of Hindu Brahmins. In the 16th century, after the establishment of the Mughal Empire by Babur, this would also be the case of Humayun, who founded the famous Mughal school of miniature painting, and of Sher Shah (1486-1545), a great conqueror but also a talented administrator, the first Muslim monarch to establish a truly Indian commonwealth recognising both Muslims and Hindus as equal subjects—who died by falling from the stairs leading to his library roof, where he was making astronomical observations. Later still, this would be the case of the great Akbar, who combined his zeal and energy to bring together the Muslim and Hindu communities and to establish a common patriotism. His reign (1556-1605) marked the climax of the Mughal Empire, opening a period of liberalism and religious tolerance reminiscent of the best moments of the great Hindu empires of ancient India. There was also Shah Jahan (1592-1666), who loved the arts and protected the artists—and who had the magnificent Taj Mahal mausoleum built in memory of his favourite wife.

Despite the determination of Muslim conquerors and the autocratic management of their empires, 16th- and 17th-century India was far from being a monolithic, prostrate nation. Led by no less determined Rajput princes, the Hindus put up a fierce resistance and maintained their independence in small Rajput kingdoms of Rajasthan. Only Akbar succeeded in attaching the Rajputs to his empire by making them his advisors and generals. In South India, under the Sangama and Tuluva Dynasties, the great Hindu kingdom of Vijayanagar formed a barrier against Muslim expansion until 1565. Sanskrit as well as Dravidian cultures flourished; literature, music, architecture and science developed away from the Persian influence of northern Muslim states. In Bengal, whose submission to the Delhi Sultanate always remained nominal, part of the population converted to Islam under the influence of Sufi missionaries, giving rise to a unique cultural blend and a rich and abundant literature in vernacular.

Finally, in the mid-17th century, as the Mughal Empire had begun to lose its prestige during the reign of the fanatical emperor Aurangzeb, south-western India saw the rise of armed groups of peasants, the Marathas, led by a daring and charismatic leader, Shivaji, who emerged as a defender of Hinduism to lead a guerrilla warfare against Mughal forces. Competent and disciplined, Shivaji spoke to the Hindu sentiment and rallied the support and dedication of an entire people. In 1674, he founded the Maratha Empire, which gradually extended to most of the Deccan until 1818, and greatly contributed to the Mughal Empire's downfall after Aurangzeb.

The British Colonisation

There would remain one ultimate ordeal for India to endure. The new invader did not destroy her temples and idols, her palaces and gardens. It was a 'civilising' colonialism, adorned with economic liberalism and parliamentary practices, which was to try to replace the glory of her past and the genius of the Veda.

In 1498, with the landing of Vasco da Gama on the Malabar Coast, the Portuguese had secured the monopoly of maritime trade with India, which they maintained for a century from their base in Goa. But in 1612, this monopoly was challenged when the British East India Company negotiated with Emperor Jahangir (the son of Akbar) the settlement of a trading post on the Gujarat Coast, at Surat. Using daring and ruthless trading practices, this private British company would eventually expand its dominion to practically the whole of India, running the country as its commercial property.

In a recent article in *The Guardian* newspaper, the Scottish historian William Dalrymple summarised the East India Company's achievements: 'In many ways, the EIC was a model of corporate efficiency: 100 years into its history, it had only 35 permanent employees in its head office. Nevertheless, that skeleton staff executed a corporate coup unparalleled in history: the military conquest, subjugation and plunder of vast tracts of southern Asia [Japan and China in addition to India]. It almost certainly remains the supreme act of corporate violence in world history. For all the power wielded today by the world's largest corporations—whether ExxonMobil, Walmart or Google—they are tame beasts compared with the ravaging territorial appetites of the militarised East India Company.'[2]

By recruiting mercenary troops, the Sepoys, and bribing local administrators, the East India Company managed to eliminate its main commercial rivals (the Dutch and the French) and to settle in Calcutta in the east, Madras in the south and Bombay in the west. But it was by ensuring its military supremacy over the declining Mughal Empire that the balance of power was radically tipped in favour of the British company. After its armed forces won the crucial Battle of Plassey against the Nawab of Bengal and his French allies in 1757, then the Battle of Buxar against the emperor himself in 1764, the East India Company was granted the right to levy property taxes in Bengal, Bihar and Orissa. At the end of the 18th century, thanks to further victories won against the Kingdom of Mysore and the Maratha Empire, it dominated almost all of Southern India. While the Mughal Empire was now virtually confined to its capital Delhi, it was the East India Company which governed India de facto, organising its alliances and relations with local governments, Hindu princes or Muslim moguls.

Although the British Parliament had tried, repeatedly, to control the East India Company and its rapacious practices, the exorbitant profits it garnered allowed it to deal on an equal footing with the political power in Westminster, even to the point of lending money to the Treasury. While the world was about to enter an era of hard-core colonialism, a new god by the name of 'economy', burst onto the human scene. An uncontrollable appetite took hold of people and institutions: all the resources of imagination and creativity were mobilised to maximising instant profit. No doubt the individuals who exploited India for the most mercantile purposes were not the same who had conceived the writ of habeas corpus, but that difference was not immediately discernible in the practices engaged in by Britain over the three and half centuries of her presence in the country.

Politically, the Mughal Empire was about to expire; the East India Company would soon end the pretence of managing India in the name of the Emperor. The proud Mughal army was dissolved in 1805 and the Emperor renamed 'King of Delhi', before being deposed a few years later and sent off to finish his days in Burma.

In 1857, this booming capitalist system experienced its first setbacks when the Sepoy army mutinied. The demands of the mutineers, mostly class- and status-related, brought about a civil rebellion by the Indian feudal nobility, landowners and peasants. Shortly after the mutiny was quelled and the Sepoys returned to their barracks, Westminster quickly seized the opportunity to draft a series of organic laws revamping the relationship with India: in the strictest colonial tradition, the country would now come under London's direct rule. The British Raj was born, and Queen Victoria, who assumed the title of 'Empress of India', proclaimed: 'We hold ourselves bound to the natives of our Indian territories by the same obligations of duty which bind us to all our other subjects.' It was now a 'Secretary of State for India', based in London, who would frame India's destiny, while a Governor General, also called 'Viceroy', would rule over the government from his official residence in Calcutta.

The East India Company was to be dissolved a few years later. The Indian Army was reorganised as 60,000 British officers and troops were mobilised to supervise 130,000 indigenous soldiers.

It is without much illusion about their 'civilising' influence that the British brought some measures of participation in administering the country—a pious wish, largely ineffective. A 'Legislative Council' sat alongside each provincial governor and included one half of Indian residents, in an advisory capacity, while the other half, made up of members of the government, voted the laws.

With all the administration devoted to encouraging economic exploitation, the country was now in the hands of a disillusioned and moralising British elite, most often displaying an attitude of superiority towards an indigenous society considered too 'backward', rigidly trapped in its primitive customs and obscure traditions from another age. Whereas many previous 'invaders', even the most belligerent, had often settled in India and become assimilated, with very few exceptions, the British would never be able to understand the Indians or to feel attuned with them.

As the Viceroy was busy distributing property rights among a new Indian class, the Zamindars, now responsible for making the land profitable and levying taxes, a special school, the *Indian Civil Service*, was created in London to attract the elite of the British and Indian youth to administrative professions. As early as 1880, India had no fewer than 20,000 miles of railway tracks; new canals, bridges, roads and a telegraph system were being built—mostly to facilitate the transportation of goods, especially cotton, to the ports. With this industrial fever were born the ills afflicting modern societies: the interdependence of markets. Almost overnight, India became vulnerable to the vagaries of the British economy, while England expected Indian vitality to dispose of some of its finished goods.

In 1893, Sri Aurobindo arrived in Bombay….

Notes

1 Cited by Éric Paul Meyer, *Une histoire de l'Inde: les Indiens face à leur passé*, Albin Michel, Paris, 2007, p. 133.

2 William Dalrymple, *The Guardian*, 4 March 2015.

Part I
POLITICS

1893: Arriving in India

Apollo Bunder, Bombay

Aurobindo contemplated the liquid darkness about him. At long last, a pale line ruptured the horizon. India was drawing near. To the throbbing of its engines, the steamer headed towards the growing light. Burning off the last shreds of morning mist, an enormous sun soared into the sky, revealing the outlines of a city. The day dawned on Bombay.

Aurobindo Ghose was 20. He was returning from England, where he had spent 13 years steeped in Western classical culture. A Greco-Latin scholar and erudite in several European languages, he spoke refined English and wrote in a style that had earned him praise from his professors at Cambridge.

After a month at sea, he stepped ashore onto the Apollo Bunder, the long harbour pier of Bombay, amidst the hustle and bustle of a large colourful Indian crowd. Happy memories from his childhood flashed in his mind as he made his way through the jumble of porters and zigzagging handcarts, children and dogs, heavily laden donkeys and placid cows.

As he absorbed this flood of colours and clamour, a strange sensation gradually overcame him. An immense calm pervaded his entire being. All feelings and thoughts became utterly still and vanished into an extraordinary silence as if his very individuality had dissolved into an unlimited blank Self. Boundaries abolished, every object and living creature around him became part of this vaster Self.

> A momentless immensity pure and bare,
> I stretch to an eternal everywhere.

The whole world breathed within him. He abandoned himself to the fullness of the moment.

Nothing had prepared Aurobindo for such an experience, even though, only a few weeks earlier, in England, he had read a text of which every word had remained engraved in his mind:

> He who understands all and who knows all, he to whom all this glory in the world belongs, the Self, is placed in the ether, in the heavenly city of Brahman.
>
> That immortal Brahman is before, that Brahman is behind, that Brahman is right and left. It has gone forth below and above; Brahman alone is all this, it is the best.

Intrigued by these lines, he had attempted to 'comprehend' this Self (also called *Atman*), the cornerstone of India's ancestral explanation of the universe as set in the Upanishads.

He had even studied the explanations of the Sanskrit translator, an Oxford professor named Max Müller: 'Beyond the aham or ego, with all its accidents and limitations, such as sex, senses, language, country and religion, the ancient sages of India had realised, from time immemorial, the Atman or Self, independent of these accidents.'

In other words, the Atman stood for what would be left of a human being if one could magically do away with the randomness of his birth and all his atavistic traits: a person's own indefectible, unconditional existence.

Now, Aurobindo could relate these explanations to the mute sense of infinity still pervading his being.

His steps led him to Bombay Central Station, bringing him back to ordinary consciousness.

Aurobindo would not breathe a word about what he had felt upon his arrival in Bombay. On that day of 6 February 1893, he did not know that this was the first of many spiritual experiences his future held. Many years later, he would write:

> Since I set foot on Indian soil on the Apollo Bunder in Bombay, I began to have spiritual experiences, but these were not divorced from this world but had an inner and intimate bearing on it, such as a feeling of the Infinite pervading material space and the Immanent inhabiting material objects and bodies. At the same time, I found myself entering supraphysical worlds and planes with influences and an effect from them upon the material plane, so I could make no sharp divorce or irreconcilable opposition between what I have called the two ends of existence and all that lies between them.

Arriving at the station, he boarded a train to Baroda, a princely state north of Bombay. The Maharajah awaited him.

Cambridge Scholarship

Thirteen years earlier, in 1880, Krishnadhan Ghose, a medical graduate from Aberdeen University, had sent his three sons to study in Britain as he had done. The youngest, Aurobindo, was not yet eight years old.

A native of Bengal, where he held the post of medical officer in charge of Rangpur District, Dr Ghose admired the British system. It was the time of the great Darwinian debate on *The Origin of Species,* and Dr Ghose's medical education incited him to champion a world governed by reason. To immerse his family in English culture, he banned the use of the Bengali language in his household. 'We know the English are a superior race and can teach us much,' he proclaimed.

Through a friend, he had come into contact with William Drewett, an Anglican clergyman in Manchester who had agreed to take in his three sons and guide their education. For the doctor to send his sons to the other end of the earth in quest of an uncertain diploma must have been emotionally wrenching, but he felt it his duty.

He accompanied his sons to England, along with his daughter, Sarojini, and his wife, Swarnalotta. He planned to take advantage of the trip by having his wife examined by a neurologist, as she suffered from a mental disorder.

After escorting his sons to Drewett's home in Manchester and before returning to India, he took the time to have a portrait taken of his family. The photo shows a man with a quiet determination standing between his two older startled sons, a chubby Sarojini sitting on her mother's lap, and in the foreground, seated with his hands on his knees, seven-year-old Aurobindo, whose eyes shine with intense curiosity.

A few months later, before leaving England, Swarnalotta gave birth to the couple's fourth son, Barin, whose revolutionary impetuosity would play a leading role in Aurobindo's life and the future emancipation of India.

One can visualise the three young boys concentrating for hours on the five Latin declensions as Pastor Drewett tried to bring the ancient world to life in their heads while the new world of the industrial revolution opened before their eyes. In this bleak suburb of England's largest industrial centre, they could see the grey smoke of the smelting furnaces obscuring the skyline and hear the roar of the boilers and the accompanying sharp metallic clanging.

After two years of this austere regime, the two older boys were ready to enter grammar school. Aurobindo, who had just turned nine, continued to receive private lessons: Latin and history with the pastor, French, geography and arithmetic with his wife.

However, he had a clear preference for poetry. By the age of 10, he fell in love with Shelley, the great romantic English poet, who inspired him to compose his first poem, *Light*, modelled on the versification of Shelley's poem *The Cloud*. Another work of Shelley's drew his interest, *The Revolt of Islam*, in which two young heroes instigated a bloodless coup against the Sultan of the Ottoman Empire. Although not yet formulated as a political awakening, this was the onset of an attraction for the works involved in changing the world.

Aurobindo more than fulfilled his father's expectations. At 17, he won prizes in classical and modern literature and ranked first at the entrance examination for King's College Cambridge. He was also awarded a scholarship to study for the Indian Civil Service (ICS), the academic requirement for entering government service in India. He became a 'gentleman'. For two years, he waded through the legal jungle of doctrines in force in India. From the Code of Justinian to Jeremy Bentham's *An Introduction to the Principles of Morals and Legislation*, not to mention Hindu law, Muslim law and British India's Penal Code, nothing must elude the erudition of the future administrators of the British Raj. He even attended John Neville Keynes's classes on political economy.

His thirst for knowledge was insatiable, and his curiosity was seemingly boundless. Devouring French and English novels and European history, he remained indifferent to modern philosophy. He did not share in the enthusiasm of his time for Hegel and Kant, but he read Plato, whose *Republic* and *Symposium* he placed among humanity's 'highest points of thought and literature'. At 18, he was so impressed by these two works that he began writing, in the Platonic mode, *The Harmony of Virtue*, 'an explanation of the cosmos on the foundation of the principle of Beauty and Harmony'. His interest in Plato predisposed him to a nuanced agnosticism.

Over the years, Krishna Ghose had ceased admiring the British system. He now called it 'a heartless government', and he sent in his letters *The Bengalee's* clippings chronicling the mistreatment of Indians by the British authorities.

At Cambridge, there was no question of mistreatment, only of mutual affinity and common interest. Yet the mindset, sports and activities of his English classmates did not appeal to the young Indian student. Aurobindo remained distant and spontaneously chose his comrades among his compatriots. He, thus, befriended Keshav Deshpande, with whom he would share his revolutionary ideals. In London, the two friends had keenly followed the repeated failures of Prime Minister Gladstone in introducing the Irish Home Rule in Parliament. Aurobindo's sympathy went to Charles Stewart Parnell, the Irish nationalist leader and former Cantabrigian, whose courage and convictions drew admiration even in the British Parliament (After Parnell's death in 1891, he would dedicate two poems to his memory.).

Emerging from his reserve, the young Aurobindo began displaying his nationalist feelings and delivering impassioned speeches at meetings of the Indian Majlis, a student organisation he headed for a time, before enlisting briefly in a 'secret society', romantically called 'Lotus and Dagger'.

While he brilliantly passed the academic tests for the entrance examination to the ICS, he neglected an ultimate requirement: to display his skill in horsemanship. For this seemingly insignificant reason, he was denied final admittance. His influential friends rallied. One of his tutors at Cambridge wrote, 'That a man of this calibre should be lost to the Government of India merely because he failed in sitting on a horse or did not keep an appointment appears to me, I confess, a piece of official short-sightedness which would be hard to beat.' The Secretary of State for India was urged to intercede in his favour, but he pronounced that 'no candidate ought to be allowed to go to India who cannot ride'.

Deep down, however, Aurobindo was not displeased with this setback. For months, he had been developing an instinctive aversion to the administrative system introduced under the

British rule. He could not see himself adopting the lifestyle expected of him in the Indian Civil Service. His disqualification exempted him from having to reject the Service, which his family would not have allowed. For the first time in his life, Aurobindo had challenged paternal wishes.

It was Henry Cotton, a long-time friend of the Ghose family and a member of the ICS, who found a way out of the predicament. Having learned that the Maharajah of Baroda was visiting London, he solicited an interview for Aurobindo. The Maharajah received the young man and, seizing upon the opportunity to secure a fresh ICS academic graduate without paying the high price of a full-fledged qualification, he offered to hire him in the administration of his principality. The proposal suited Aurobindo, as he presumed the Baroda environment to be less rigid than the British administration. The modest salary offer (₹200 per month) could not dampen the hope of a promising future.

At the Baroda Government

India was under British rule. In 1858, following the Indian Mutiny, Queen Victoria's government took the reins from the East India Company, a commercial enterprise that had run India as its private property for two and a half centuries. India had become the British Raj and Queen Victoria, the 'Empress of India'. To control a territory 10 times the size of England and populated by 300 million people, the British had divided it into 'presidencies' (large provinces), administered by British-appointed governors under the supervision of a Governor-General, or Viceroy, who shared the responsibility of running the country with the Secretary of State in Westminster. Some 600 Princes and Maharajahs, who had pledged allegiance to Victoria in matters of defence and foreign policy, had retained control of their princely estates.

Baroda was the capital of one of these semi-independent enclaves. Three hundred miles north of Bombay, this principality of about a 1,000 square miles, headed by Maharajah Sayaji Roa Gaekwar III, was one of the Raj's most prosperous. Educated from childhood by English tutors, the sovereign was known for his liberalism, and his reign (1875– 1939) is regarded as the Golden Age of Baroda. During his third trip to Europe, the 30-year-old monarch met Aurobindo.

Four times the size of Buckingham Palace and in the middle of a 500-acre park, the residence of the Maharajah stood like an apparition worthy of *The Thousand and One Nights*.

In a recent publication, Gayatri Devi, the Maharajah's granddaughter, describes the life of her brothers and sisters in this fairyland edifice of a 1,000 rooms:

> Lakshmi Vilas was a huge building surrounded by marble verandas with scalloped arches supported by arrays of thin columns. The interior of the palace was a curious blend of Victorian and traditional Indian styles, with here and there touches of English or French craftsmanship. Persian rugs ran along endless corridors. The salons were crowded with French furniture, photographs in silver frames, ornaments and trinkets placed on low tables. [...] Contrasting with our impeccable bearing and the courtesy everyone extended towards us, long-tailed monkeys moved about everywhere. It took very little to make them angry, and they would chase after us through the corridors, shrieking and snarling in a terrifying way.

The Maharajah had learned under British example how to rule his people, and these standards challenged his new appointee's natural inclinations. Initially assigned to the Settlement Department, Aurobindo spent the first year exploring the labyrinth of land assessment. He was then transferred to the Revenue Department, where he became acquainted with the tax code and the intricacies of tax collection. He had learned enough Gujarati (the language of the principality) and Marathi (used at court) to communicate easily with everyone. It was only after three years of this tedious apprenticeship that the Maharajah entrusted Aurobindo with tasks more attuned to his skills.

Despite the monotony of his work, every moment reinforced his conviction that he had made the right choice in turning down the material advantages of a Western career: here was the appointed place of his destiny, bringing out 'a natural attraction to Indian culture and ways of life and a temperamental feeling and preference for all that was Indian'. He adopted Indian dress habits, and, although he donned the obligatory three-piece suit during the day, in private, he wore a white *dhoti* along with a coarse Ahmadabad cotton shawl and old-fashioned slippers with upturned toes.

In his spare time, he wrote or pursued the study of Sanskrit, which he had begun in England as an autodidact, by reading the Mahabharata, the great epic text of Indian mythology. To daily translate some 40 lines of this monumental poem was demanding, but after a month of practice, he felt ready to tackle the more esoteric Sanskrit of the Upanishads. He longed to explore the philosophical treatises of ancient India, to discover the source of their insight, to understand what ushered in this primaeval thought, 'this true Being or true Substance' (in the words of the Upanishads).

Although his intellectual background favoured a relativistic reading of existence, and while the Industrial Revolution exploded in feverish expectations in the world around him, Aurobindo aspired for some unalterable course of life, an innermost absolute.

His experience in Bombay remained vivid. He could recall the sovereign state of awareness which had seized him beyond all contingencies, outside the world's mental or sensory experience. To his astonishment, the stamp of the hushed silence had lingered within him: some indefinable presence remained in the background of his activities. Whenever he checked his thoughts and withdrew within himself, the silence came back like a bedrock of unshakeable peace, an impersonal stillness that dissolved the world's agitation. He had grown accustomed to flowing into this space in the midst of his work, always emerging from these moments of disconnection with renewed energy.

Yet Aurobindo had no plan to turn to spiritual life. Outside his work, his mind was focused on poetry and on what seemed the extreme opposite of poetry: politics.

First Chronicles

Now he was face to face with the reality of British occupation in India: the crudeness of the philistine and the hypocrisy of big business interests beneath calculated liberalism.

In the government offices, where the Maharajah deliberately addressed him as *Aurobindo Babu*, on account of his scholarship and Bengali origin, he had become *Mister Aurobindo Ghose* to his colleagues. However, to the British, despite his impeccable accent, he remained a 'native'. His status as a gentleman, which had transcended race in London and Cambridge, seemingly vanished after crossing an invisible frontier at the Suez Canal. Here, a gulf divided the two races.

The British controlled the country with practically no use of force but rather through tacit agreement. Some hypnotic spell seemed to work its magic on Indian society, empowering fewer than 100,000 men from a distant island to impose their system on 300 million people. For Aurobindo, this spell—'the artificial glare of English prestige', as he called it—was the crux of the problem. His historical readings on revolutionary movements, which resulted in establishing a national identity (from Joan of Arc in France to the American Revolution to the Unification of Italy), had taught him that it would be futile to expect a radical transformation of society to emerge from parliamentary debates. He was silently contemplating another prospect for change: the forcible expulsion of the British.

Some months after arriving in Baroda, an opportunity arose to make his voice heard. Keshav Deshpande, his comrade from Cambridge, had been appointed editor-in-chief of a Bombay literary and political weekly, the *Indu Prakash,* and asked him to contribute an article. Aurobindo accepted on the condition of keeping the anonymity required by his employment in the government.

The British Parliament had recently allowed the ICS examination to be held simultaneously in England and India. For an enthusiastic Indian press, this measure was further proof of British benevolence.

To this tide of euphoria, Aurobindo replied:

> This chorus of jubilant paeans arising from the Press resembles nothing so much as the joyful chorus of ducks when the monsoon arrives.

Aurobindo pointed out that, in reality, the vote in the British Parliament was a surprise and that it was due to the sole presence in the House of a handful of liberal members favourable to India. Castigating a press that 'seems eager to accept even the flimsiest excuse for deluding itself', he proceeded to give a rundown of the voting blocs and prevailing influences in the House of Commons, where India was chronically under-represented, before launching into an incisive indictment of his countrymen's attitude:

> We constantly find it asserted that the English are a just people and only require our case to be clearly stated in order to redress our grievances. It is more than time that some voice should be raised to tell the Press and the public that this is a grave and injurious delusion, which must be expunged from our minds if we would see things as they really are.... If we are indeed to renovate our country, we must no longer hold out supplicating hands to the English Parliament, like an infant crying to its nurse for a toy, but must recognise the hard truth that every nation must

> beat out its own path to salvation with pain and difficulty, and not rely on the tutelage of another.

A 20-year-old urges his countrymen to break the yoke of their illusions and confront the humiliation of their servitude! He shines an unwavering light on the resignation that ended up in the capitulation of an entire people. This first address to his country forecasts what would become the hallmark of his action: a call for catharsis, for the requirement to find the cause of the ills and their remedy in *oneself.*

Delighted with this first article, his friend Deshpande asked for more of these. A month later, Aurobindo submitted the beginning of a series of essays entitled *New Lamps for Old*, devoted to examining the nature and workings of the Indian National Congress.

The Indian National Congress, consisting of an anglophile Indian elite tolerated by the Raj government, met once a year, in December, to approve and validate the pre-eminence of the colonial system. Since its foundation in 1885 by Allan Hume, an English theosophist, this Congress had proffered dozens of resolutions, only one of which had elicited a tepid response from the Government. The Indian National Congress' yearly displays of pomposity were greeted with complete indifference by the Indian population.

Although the Congress was the only Indian political forum, Aurobindo denounced its subservience to colonialism and its deluded optimism in the British parliamentary system. To one of the leaders who referred to 'the class' represented by Congress members as 'the thinking portion of the population', Aurobindo retorted:

> If I were asked to describe this class by a single name, I should not hesitate to call it our new middle class. For here, too, English goods have

> driven out native goods: our society has lost its old landmarks and is being demarcated on the English model.

Aurobindo argued that the activities of the Indian National Congress could be summarised in one word: failure. It was now high time that Indians confronted the problems besetting them and abandoned their servility and naivety about the supposed selflessness of English politicians. Then he grew bolder:

> I say, of the Congress, then, this—that its aims are mistaken, that the spirit in which it proceeds towards their accomplishment is not a spirit of sincerity and whole-heartedness, and that the methods it has chosen are not the right methods, and the leaders in whom it trusts, not the right sort of men to be leaders—in brief, that we are at present the blind led, if not by the blind, at any rate by the one-eyed.

The reaction would not be long in coming. No sooner was Aurobindo's text made public than one of the Congress leaders informed the publisher of the *Indu Prakash* that he would be prosecuted for sedition should future essays continue in the same vein. Deshpande asked his bold writer to tone down his criticisms by coating them in 'academia'. Aurobindo complied for a while before losing interest. Not until 1950, almost 60 years later, was the series *New Lamps for Old* exhumed from the *Indu Prakash* archives, published verbatim, and its author hailed by historians as a precursor of the militant nationalism, which eventually reshaped the Indian National Congress into a democratic political institution.

The Being of Light

In Baroda, Aurobindo moved about town in a horse-drawn carriage. One day, in a busy street, the usually placid animal became startled and reared up. Aurobindo felt the carriage was about to overturn. But all of a sudden, from within, a completely different sensation emerged: a 'Being of Light'.

> I sat behind the dance of Danger's hooves
> In the shouting street that seemed a futurist's whim,
> And suddenly felt, exceeding Nature's grooves,
> In me, enveloping me the body of Him.
> Above my head a mighty head was seen,
> A face with the calm of immortality [...]
> His hair was mingled with the sun and breeze;
> The world was in His heart and He was I.

The horse calmed down. All returned to normal. The 'Being of Light' had prevented the accident. No one had noticed anything in the busy street. For the second time since his arrival in India, Aurobindo had experienced a world beyond the world.

Gandhi

In this notable year, 1893, Bombay witnessed both the arrival of Aurobindo and, two months later, the departure of Mohandas Gandhi.

Three years older than Aurobindo, Gandhi had also studied in England for his law degree. After his admission to the Bar, he returned to his country in 1891, but was forced to abandon the practice of law in Bombay because he suffered panic attacks during public hearings. Resigned to work as a clerk in his brother's law practice, he settled in his hometown of Porbandar, in Gujarat. When his brother, Laxmidas, was implicated in an obscure case of theft in the court of the local Maharajah, Gandhi tried to help him by petitioning the English magistrate in charge of the case. Rebuked by the magistrate, Gandhi lost his temper, refusing to admit the impropriety of his request. Weeping and foaming with rage, he further aggravated the situation by demanding an apology from the magistrate. For Gandhi, the incident, which stood to jeopardise his legal career, illustrated the racial arrogance of the English. Sickened to the core, he jumped at an offer from a prosperous law firm in Johannesburg, South Africa, and left India. He was not to return until 22 years later. Gandhi sailed from Bombay to South Africa in April 1893, exactly two months after Aurobindo's arrival in India.

On 15 August 1893, Aurobindo celebrated his 21st birthday.

1894–1899: At Home in India

Family Visit

In February 1894, Aurobindo made his first visit to Bengal to meet his family. The Indian railway system was fast expanding, and some 30,000 miles of tracks connected almost all major cities. Crossing the country from west to east took fewer than four days. After climbing the Rajasthan Plateau and travelling onward through the fertile northern plains, the train descended towards the Ganges Valley and Calcutta. In Bihar, Aurobindo took a branch line to Deoghar, where his maternal grandfather, Rajnarayan, had retired to the dry and temperate climate south of the Himalayan Range. The presence of a well-known temple dedicated to Lord Shiva made it a favourite stopover town for pilgrims, who sometimes called in to pay their respects to Rajnarayan, the old Brahmo Samaj militant. The whole family gathered around Rajnarayan for the Puja season, to escape the heat of Calcutta and South Bengal.

The arrival of the young traveller from Baroda aroused great curiosity. As he alighted from his coach, Aurobindo was surrounded by a group of women and young girls, amongst whom he felt at a loss to recognise his aunts, cousins and sister. His grandfather enveloped him in his arms. Aurobindo's sister, Sarojini, five years his junior, remembered: 'A delicate face and a long mane of hair cut in the English fashion.' She found him very shy: 'It was hard to penetrate his reserve and communicate with him.' His younger brother, Barin, whom he had never met, found in his *Sejda* [elder brother] 'a strange friend… at once a playmate and a guide, with a quiet and absorbed look and almost always lost in deep studies'.

For his cousin, Basanti, the most intriguing was the content of his steamer trunks, which she imagined filled with sumptuous costumes and rare perfumes. 'What? A few ordinary clothes and books, only books! We are all here to have fun on vacation and chat pleasantly. Is Auro-dada going to spend all his time reading, and then take pleasure in it?' She was only reassured when she realised that her 'Auro-dada' was quite capable of holding his place in the family circle and participating in the fun.

A man of convictions, a scholar and a lover of the Upanishads, Grandfather Rajnarayan welcomed this grandson whom he knew loved poetry. The two shared a habit of bursting into laughter at the slightest provocation. However, perhaps, because the Brahmo Samaj movement sought to reform certain practices of Hinduism by aligning with Western Christianity, Aurobindo never adhered to his grandfather's religious conceptions. Rajnarayan, nevertheless, supported his grandson's struggle against the colonial regime and offered his love and a place to rest when needed.

Among the other adults, Aurobindo soon identified his Aunt Lilavati, his mother's younger sister, and her husband, Krishna Kumar Mitra. Both would play a crucial role over the next 15 years, participating in his struggle, sometimes risking their safety and offering their home in Calcutta to shelter him. A university professor and editor of a political weekly (*Sanjivani*), Krishna Mitra was a leading critic of the regime, denouncing instances of unbridled capitalism, notably among Bengal's indigo plantations and Assam's tea estates. Friends of Rabindranath Tagore and Vivekananda, Lilavati and Krishna Kumar personified the class of educated Bengalis whom the British could never seduce nor subjugate.

Another uncle whom Aurobindo learnt to appreciate was his mother's younger brother, Jogen, to whom he affectionately bestowed the distinction 'Prophet of Isabgol' (a medicinal plant purported to soothe upset stomachs, which Jogen recommended for daily use). Jogen took the youngsters climbing the Nandam Hills nearby or exploring the banks of the Daroa river. Only the subject of India's destiny brought gravity to Aurobindo's voice when he evoked 'her glorious past, her present degradation and her possible deliverance'. 'A dream, far above my young mind,' sighed Barin.

Besides Aurobindo's two elder brothers, Manmohan and Benoybhusan, both still detained in England, two people were missing from this joyful family reunion: Krishna and Swarnalotta Ghose, Aurobindo's father and mother.

Krishna Ghose had passed away a year earlier, scarcely two months before Aurobindo's return home. He who had been so anxious to secure his sons' success, who had sacrificed his paternal interests to ensure their accomplishment in England, was snatched from life before he could embrace the fruit of his labours. In a dramatic turn of events, his demise seemed to have been caused by erroneous information concerning the fate of his favourite son, Aurobindo: Doctor Ghose mistakenly believed his son to have boarded a ship that sank off Portugal, and the shock of the news, compounded with the tensions in his personal life, broke him. That evening a neighbour found him in a state of extreme prostration, from which he never recovered. He was 48.

In Khulna, Bengal, where Dr Ghose had practised medicine whilst assuming well-rewarded administrative responsibilities, he was revered by everyone. He lived in a comfortable European-style house with domestic staff. However, for many years, his life had been undermined by his wife's mental health.

On her return from London, Swarnalotta's bipolar storms had redoubled, and the doctor had to resign himself to parting from her. He had found a comfortable bungalow in a village near Deoghar and had left her in charge of their two youngest, Sarojini and Barin. But shortly thereafter, the first signs of ill-treatment appeared, and the children had to be removed from their mother and reunited with the rest of the family.

Before leaving Deoghar, Aurobindo visited Rohini, the village where his mother lived. Swarnalotta did not recognise the seven-year-old child she had left in England. A scar on his finger convinced her that he was her son. From then on, in addition to the portion of his wages devoted to Sarojini's education, Aurobindo would contribute to Swarnalotta's monthly maintenance.

Bankim, Ramakrishna, Vivekananda

Barely back to his desk from the family visit, Aurobindo received a letter from his sister asking him to return in a few months. He replied: 'It will be, I fear, quite impossible to come to you again so early as the Puja season, though if I only could, I should start tomorrow. Neither my affairs nor my finances will admit of it. Indeed it was a great mistake for me to go at all; for it has made Baroda quite intolerable to me.'

To keep the hours of office boredom at bay and feel closer to his family, at least in thought, he set about tutoring himself in his mother tongue. He turned to the works of the greatest Bengali contemporary writer, Bankim Chandra Chatterjee, who had passed away in April 1894. Enthused after studying his novels, Aurobindo decided to pay tribute to his talent by publishing a series of articles in Deshpande's *Indu Prakash*. Referring to Bankim's 10 novels and critical essays as 'pure gold', he added: 'Of his style I shall hardly trust myself to speak. To describe its beauty, terseness, strength and sweetness is too high a task for a pen like mine. I will remark this only that what marks Bankim above all, is his unfailing sense of beauty.'

But Bankim was not only a peerless prose stylist. Through his historical novels, 'the desire for a nobler and more inspiring patriotism is growing more intense'. In his master-piece, *Anandamath* (*Monastery of Bliss*, 1882), which narrates the struggle of a group of *sannyasins* taking up arms against British tax collectors who starve the people, Bankim caught the imagination of the young, who had become weary of the current political climate. In them, Aurobindo foresaw 'the embryo of a new generation soon to be with us… a generation national to a fault, loving Bengal and her new glories'.

These words would come alive a few years later, on the occasion of the partition of Bengal, when the Bengali youths drew from *Anandamath* their cry of devotion to the mother-land: *Bande Mataram* (I bow to you, O Mother), which would become the battle cry of the Nationalist Movement throughout the country and the title of the opposition newspaper published by Aurobindo and his friends. *Bande Mataram* is now the national song of India.

Bankim's novels were rooted in the Bhagavad Gita. His characters modelled their actions on Krishna's teaching to Prince Arjuna, and Aurobindo was particularly touched by this spiritual influence. Like Bankim, he felt that the 'liberation' of India was not only about freeing the country from a foreign grip but also about restoring her spirit from the source of her ancient wisdom.

> We must learn to swim and use that power to reach the good vessel of unchanging truth; we must land again on the eternal rock of ages.

Another influence affecting these early years of reconnection with Bengali culture came from the great Yogi Paramhansa Ramakrishna, who had died eight years earlier. Aurobindo pored over Ramakrishna's life, his thoughts and aphorisms, as well as the works of his main disciple, Vivekananda, who had recently given his famous speech at the Parliament of the World's Religions in Chicago (September 1893). 'The first visible sign to the world that India was awake not only to survive but to conquer,' thought Aurobindo. With Vivekananda, the philosophy of the Upanishads had made a memorable entrance into the West, fascinating American and European audiences and attracting many followers.

Ramakrishna had incarnated the flame which rekindled the consciousness of his contemporaries. He had inspired 19th-century Bengal to preserve its identity despite the alien forces of disintegration:

> There were always indications, always great forerunners, but it was when the flower of the educated youth of Calcutta bowed down at the feet of an illiterate Hindu ascetic, a self-illuminated ecstatic and 'mystic' without a single trace or touch of the alien thought or education upon him that the battle was won.

Life in Baroda

Aurobindo had befriended an officer in Baroda's army, Madhavrao Jadhav, who shared his political views. The two of them, together with Madhavrao's older brother, Khaserao, a senior government official, formed a small casual circle of friends, hosting lively exchanges late into the night. Khaserao owned a spacious house in Baroda's residential quarter and, after his return from Deoghar, Aurobindo often stayed there. It, eventually, became his permanent residence.

One year, Aurobindo brought back from Bengal a young Bengali writer, Dinendra Kumar Roy, whom he had hired to help improve his penmanship skills in his mother tongue. Compiled 10 years later, Dinendra's *Memoirs* provide a rare glimpse into Aurobindo's life in Baroda.

At their first encounter, Dinendra was disconcerted by his employer's unassuming figure, the cotton shawl flung over the shoulder, the long Indian dhoti, the mass of black hair and soft dreamy eyes. He justly appreciated the affability and composure of this 'slight and unobtrusive figure', but could not fail to notice the air of gravity and the 'firm set' of his lips, the mark of an 'inflexible will'.

In Khaserao's house, Aurobindo led a sober and frugal existence, monitored by a pocket watch he frequently consulted. He spent most of his free time writing and reading, motionless, eyes glued to the page, 'like an ascetic rapt in contemplation'. In England, he had acquired a taste for cigars in which he indulged freely. After dark, he worked by the light of a kerosene lamp, unruffled by mosquito bites. He went to bed late and slept on a thin cotton mattress without complaining of the scorching summers or the cold winters. He began the day at his desk. Before his bath, he took the time to re-read what he had written the previous evening, then left for the office at around 11.

Dinendra was also perplexed by Aurobindo's generosity and casual attitude towards money, which he kept visibly on his table, drawing from it according to his needs (including the money orders to his family, which often left him penniless by the quarter's end). To a visitor expressing surprise at these bank notes lying in full view, he replied with a smile: 'Well, it is proof that we are living in the midst of good and honest people!'

The Maharajah had, finally, assigned Aurobindo a delicate mission: to unravel a controversial incident of corruption, tarnishing the reputation of the principality as well as disturbing the sleep of its ruler. After collecting incriminating evidence and testimonies, Aurobindo drafted a digest for his employer to see through the tangle of abuse perpetrated by his state officials, and he suggested judiciary measures to strengthen the State's credibility.

His sleep restored, His Highness was so impressed by these recommendations that he decided to move Aurobindo into the Prime Minister's Office, right next to his own, and to increase his salary by 50 rupees. Aurobindo was now frequently summoned to write official State letters or the Maharajah's speeches and was sometimes invited to share His Highness's table. The sovereign seemed to enjoy his company as he praised his sagacity. He may have thought of assigning him to a higher government position, but Aurobindo had made no secret of his desire to teach rather than seek bureaucratic advancement.

In early 1898, he obtained satisfaction. The Maharajah was persuaded to assign Aurobindo a teaching position at the College, perhaps at the insistence of the principal, who was eager to attach the new Cantabrigian to his faculty. Aurobindo was appointed as acting professor of English literature, a position he would hold until 1901 before returning to administrative assignments. For three years, he prepared undergraduates for Bombay University examinations and tutored older students in French.

Indian education was no more than a drab reproduction of the British scholastic curriculum, the result of an impersonal administration rigidly fitting an exemplary model onto a subject society. Aurobindo felt that 'it tended to dull and impoverish and tie up the naturally quick, brilliant and supple Indian intelligence, to teach it bad intellectual habits and spoil by narrow information and mechanical instruction its originality and productivity'. To a student who asked how to improve his literary style, he replied:

> Do not be anybody's slave, but be your own master. Therefore you may read any good author carefully, but should think for yourself and form your own judgement. It is likely you may differ from the views of the writer. You should think for yourself and cultivate a habit of writing and in this way you will be the master of your style.

He improvised special courses, soon attended by students of nearby colleges; he wrote articles for the school newspaper and moderated school debates.

To his own reading list, he had now added works assigned to his students. From booksellers in Bombay and Calcutta, he received his provision of books by rail, in enormous wooden crates, 'which lasted from 8 or 10 days' until the next consignment. On his shelves, Dinendra identified 'collections of all the English poets from Chaucer to Swinburne', while innumerable novels were heaped up in 'every corner of the room, in cupboards and steel trunks'.

After College, Aurobindo was often on call for the Maharajah's correspondence. On such occasions, an armed Turkish horseman presented himself at his door, bearing a letter from the Maharajah's secretary: 'The Maharajah would be particularly pleased if you could join him for lunch.' Claiming a work overload, Aurobindo sometimes declined the invitation, and it was no small wonder to Dinendra to see 'this ordinary schoolmaster regarding his own duty as more important than a visit to the Maharajah's palace, while countless noblemen cherished for months on end the vain hope of obtaining even a single interview with the Maharajah'.

In reality, Aurobindo pursued his research and took advantage of every moment of free time to indulge in poetry.

The Atman experience in Bombay and the unexplained event of his carriage in a Baroda street had challenged his analytical approach to the world. On two occasions, mental logic had gone off the rails while an unusual phenomenon took over the normal determinism of existence. What *was* this different 'law', this different Force which seemingly belied gravity and even causality? Maybe poetic creation, the exploration of areas of intuition beyond the intellect, could open the way to another type of awareness.

> All poetry is an inspiration, a thing breathed into the thinking organ from above; it is recorded in the mind, but is born in the higher principle of direct knowledge or ideal vision, which surpasses mind. It is in reality a revelation.

With Dinendra's help, Aurobindo endeavoured to master the rules of Bengali poetic expression in order to compose an epic poem in that language. During a stay in Deoghar, Barin was amazed to see him cover page after page of Bengali script. Aurobindo's older brother Manmohan, who had evolved into a skilful English poet, believed he was wasting his time. After several months of toil, Aurobindo conceded: 'To be original in an acquired tongue is hardly feasible.' He returned to writing English verse.

Towards the middle of 1899, while reading the Mahabharata, he came across the story of Ruru and his wife, Princess Priyumvada. Bitten by a snake, the young bride died on her wedding day but was allowed to regain her life in exchange for half of her husband's. Inspired by the subject: '….during 14 days of continuous writing', Aurobindo composed a 1,000 lines, 'in the mornings only, of course, for I had to attend office the rest of the day and saw friends in the evening', his body becoming for a time 'the harp of the spirit' (in the image of the Upanishads).

> There is a sudden exaltation, a glow… the mind itself becomes illuminated as with a rush of light and grows like a crowded and surging thoroughfare in some brilliantly lighted city, thought treading on the heels of thought faster than the tongue can express or the hand write or the memory record them.

This surrender of his mental substance and his increasing subjection to the powers of intuition above the intellect were the precursors to a long solitary work of inner transformation.

Framework of Protest

At the end of the day, Aurobindo and his friends gathered outside Khaserao's house to talk about the country's political situation and to comment on the latest news. They spoke of Bal Gangadhar

Tilak, the man whose reputation had spread beyond the borders of his native Maharashtra (the province around Bombay), the man who defied liberal British order and openly criticised the submissiveness of Congress of which he was a member.

Born into a traditional Hindu family and the son of a Sanskrit scholar, Tilak had pursued brilliant scientific studies before teaching Mathematics. Soon revolted by the Western domination of his country, his political militancy led him to journalism. His popular newspaper, the *Kesari*, rapidly became the main voice of Indian nationalism in Maharashtra.

As a Congress delegate from the Poona District, this charismatic man with a commanding presence had gathered around him a handful of nationalist sympathisers, who were promptly stigmatised by Congress as 'extremists'. To challenge the fawning passivity of Congress and summon the courage of his countrymen, Tilak promoted the celebration of Shivaji, the great Maratha hero. He was accused, in 1896, of having incited the assassination of a local government official through his writing and was sentenced to 18 months imprisonment. Aurobindo and his friends followed Tilak's trial with keen attention since Deshpande was one of his defence lawyers. When Tilak was released from prison in September 1898, he became a national hero.

Another seminal event stimulated the discussion in Baroda: the fierce resistance of South Africa's Boer community against the British Empire. Between October 1899 and May 1902, an entire population rose up to protect its land and its independence, waging guerrilla warfare against the occupying British. It would take several months of engagement, the commitment of considerable armed forces and the internment of thousands of Boer families in the first 20th-century concentration camps for England to finally subdue the Boers. Aurobindo praised their courage and bravery in a long poem composed during the conflict.

Contrary to the South African situation, however, Indians enjoyed overwhelming superiority in numbers. Moreover, British forces were so scattered throughout the land that they often called upon local mercenaries to maintain their supremacy. The main issue was, therefore, to transform the apparently submissive attitude of the people and gather its strength to a level comparable to the Boers' after two centuries of subjugation.

To take on the entrenched political status quo and embolden his countrymen, Aurobindo devised a three-pronged comprehensive strategy: first, creating a secret revolutionary organisation capable of engaging in armed insurrection; next, establishing a country-wide propaganda drive to bring Indian society around to the ideal of independence; and finally, setting up a broad-based popular movement of passive resistance and refusal to cooperate with the British regime.

This programme was considered utterly unrealistic, an 'almost insane chimera', by most of Aurobindo's interlocutors. They argued that a mere generation would never suffice for the Indian lamb to metamorphose into a lion. But no abstract argument could deter Aurobindo, and he continued to assess the prospects of an insurrection. Guerrilla warfare backed by a popular uprising could defeat the British army: it would be enough to procure arms shipments from foreign sources to tip the scales of firepower. Moreover, it was not unthinkable that the Indian Armed Forces, which now supported the Raj, might one day turn against their British masters.

From his trips to Bengal, Aurobindo had learned that a climate of defiance was crystallising around certain personalities. In Calcutta's educated circles, people now spoke openly of rebellion. Sarala Devi Ghosal, Rabindranath Tagore's niece, promoted the training of young men in the use of the *lathi* (bamboo cane) as a weapon. Sister Nivedita, following the precepts of her spiritual master, Vivekananda, advocated extreme measures against the British. She was in touch with Russian anarchists and with the Japanese nationalist artist Okakura Kakuzo, who spoke in Calcutta:

> You are such an educated race. Why do you let a handful of Englishmen tread you down? Do everything you can to achieve freedom, openly as well as secretly. Japan will assist you.

Present at the meeting was P. Mitra, a Bengali attorney, who decided to take up Okakura's challenge by creating the first samiti (cultural society), which could then become a youth recruiting and training centre. Nivedita warmly supported the idea.

In 1899, in this atmosphere of incipient revolt, Baroda saw the arrival of a young sannyasin clad in orange: Jatin Banerjee. This disciple of Vivekananda travelled throughout India in search of a personal commitment to the cause of his country. He sought to learn the art of war, but a British regulation prohibited Bengalis from enlisting in the Raj's army. Aurobindo asked his friend, Madhavrao, to help the young man enrol in Baroda's armed forces. Jatin thus learnt to handle weapons and to perfect himself in the martial arts. Simultaneously, he received from Aurobindo his first lessons in political science.

It seemed an auspicious occasion to embark on Aurobindo's 'strategy' and gather the scattered threads of Bengal's protest into a secret organisation extending to the entire province. Under cover of samitis, the Bengali youth would be introduced to the idea of a future uprising against the British regime and get the opportunity to train themselves. Covertly financed by progressive elements among the adult population, these samitis were to be set up in every Bengali town and village. Everything had to be organised from the ground up.

But Aurobindo was realistic. He estimated that 30 years might be necessary to set up an effective war machine, the indispensable armed wing of a national liberation movement. The important thing was to begin.

Jatin seemed the perfect choice for this first phase of communication and coordination. In 1901, having completed his military training in Baroda, he left for Calcutta, carrying with him a letter of introduction addressed by Aurobindo to Sarala Devi (Rabindranath Tagore's niece).

1901–1903: Engagement

Famine

Did Aurobindo sense the calamities that would befall the twentieth century? This note scribbled in 1901, seemed remarkably premonitory.

> The last century of the second millennium after Christ has begun; of the 20 centuries, it seems the most full of incalculable possibilities and to open the widest door on destiny. The mind of humanity feels it is conscious of a voice of a distant advancing Ocean and a sound as of the wings of a mighty archangel flying towards the world, but whether to empty the vials of the wrath of God or to declare a new gospel of peace upon earth and goodwill unto men, is as yet dark to our understanding.

The death of Queen Victoria in January 1901 ended the longest reign of the British Monarchy. Edward VII, her son, succeeded her. Nothing changed for India. Except for a few gusts of defiance limited to the educated classes of Bengal, Maharashtra and Punjab, the colonial system remained the unchallenged authority in India.

In 1899 and 1900, famine devastated the entire central and western parts of the country. It affected about 60 million people (from Rajasthan to Maharashtra, an area three times the size of England). In rural areas directly under British control, more than 1 million Indians had died of starvation—the worst death rate of the century (38 per 1,000 inhabitants). In the 40 years from 1870 to 1910, recent studies put the number of deaths by starvation in India at 30 million.

The instinctive reaction is to attribute these tragedies to natural causes: irregular rainfall can turn arable fields into deserts from one year to the next. But a deeper examination reveals another explanation: that of human interference with the ancestral cycle of land use.

In India (as in all of Southeast Asia), it was customary to maintain flexible borders among the three major types of land: forests, pastures and cultivated fields. This flexibility was part of a fluid synergy among nomadic people, forest dwellers and farmers. But one of the first tasks of the British administrators was to survey and register the land for the purpose of tax collection. With the fallow land becoming administratively arable, nomadic communities were forced into sedentary practices, thus disrupting the organisation of rural life in order to bring it in line with modern rules of land management—but at variance with the climatic irregularities. The adaptability, which, in the past, had enabled people to absorb weather irregularities and survive droughts, had been replaced with a deadly straitjacket.

To make matters worse, a new tax-enforcement system, inaugurated mid-century, threatened Indian farmers with confiscation of their land if property taxes could not be paid on time. At the same time, the British had closed their eyes to the notorious practices of 'local bankers' (*Baniya* and *Sahukar*) who lent farmers to pay their taxes in drought years, then proceeded to use the new British courts to strip them of their land when they could not meet their financial commitments. The injustice of this unregulated capitalism was accentuated by the new railroads, which enabled traffickers to move stocks of grain from one region to another to accommodate market demands, further depleting drought-affected areas.

Faced with this indecent speculation, the British administrators had buried their heads in the sand. Emphasising the 'natural' character of the disasters, they refused any assistance to the affected populations—some officials even privately justified this do-nothing policy by echoing Malthusian pronouncements that famines are part of a 'natural regulation of the population'. Meanwhile, the government did its utmost to hide the statistics of these human tragedies, so the nascent nationalist opposition would not denounce them. Its only concern was to guarantee the peaceful exploitation of the country in the name of liberal efficiency.

Aurobindo was profoundly affected by the suffering he saw around him. He wrote:

> In these hard days, the whole country is seeking refuge at my door, I have 300 million brothers and sisters in this country—many of them die of starvation, most of them weakened by suffering and troubles are somehow dragging on. They must be helped.

Marriage

At this time, he learnt that his teaching duties were soon to end. The Maharajah, who was travelling abroad, informed him that he wished to begin writing his memoirs for which the services of his favourite wordsmith were indispensable. Before stepping down from the College, Aurobindo was granted leave of absence for an event he had so far kept to himself: his marriage.

He was 28. For years, his friends had urged him, as was the custom in India, which his two older brothers had already undertaken, to begin a family whilst still in the prime of life. He, undoubtedly, had the desire to experience the feeling of love so often evoked in his poetry, to find his 'other-half':

> The wife is the Shakti of the husband; that means that the husband sees his reflection in the wife, finds the echo of his own noble aspiration in her and thereby redoubles his force.

As was customary, he had published a matrimonial advertisement in the *Calcutta Press*, which earned him no fewer than 50 replies. After visiting the prospective fathers-in-law, he chose his future bride from a traditional Hindu family. Her father, Bhupal Chandra Bose, was an agricultural engineer. His bride-elect was 14-years-old and her name was Mrinalini.

The wedding took place in late April in Calcutta, according to Hindu traditions. After a short stop in Deoghar to introduce Mrinalini to her new family, the newlyweds, accompanied by Sarojini, Aurobindo's sister, travelled to Nainital. The Maharajah, who spent the hot summer months in this Himalayan resort, offered them a lodge on the lake. Returning to Baroda in early July, they moved into the cottage arranged for them. Sarojini's presence reassured the young bride and left Aurobindo free to attend to his work during the day.

At the palace, he resumed supervision of the Maharajah's official correspondence and began compiling material for the royal memoirs (which never reached beyond the planning stage). He also took over the education of the Maharajah's children while their regular tutor was on leave. It was with no great enthusiasm that he fulfilled this latter task as, apart from Princess Indira (who would later be in the news for defying her parental choice for her marriage), the royal children showed little interest in their studies. Aurobindo concomitantly gave private English lessons to the Maharajah himself.

At home, he spent part of the evenings with his wife and sister or else renewed his conversations with his friends Madhavrao and Deshpande. But above all, night after night, he returned to his reading and solitary studies.

India's Bedrock

Eight years had passed since Aurobindo had returned to India, eight years during which he had observed the colonial machinery holding the country in bondage, eight years that he had suffered India's submissiveness to what he called 'the artificial glare of English prestige' and eight years that he had dreamed of stirring his people into revolt by setting up an army of young volunteers to train for war. His countrymen's self-denial and resignation filled him with dismay. First, there were those who, out of self-interest or cowardice, collaborated with the colonial authorities. Then there were those who were afraid to take a stand. Finally, there was the vast majority who, conscious but distraught, resigned themselves to the political expediency of a puppet Congress and an alien government.

Aurobindo wondered. What miracle could bring about the rebirth of a sovereign civilisation after centuries of foreign occupation, first Muslim, then European? What force could break the yoke of oppression, awaken 300 million people and instil the flame of rebellion into them?

As he had experienced in a Baroda street, a Force could perform what seemed to be physically impossible, what looked like a miracle. But how to mobilise this Force to help liberate the country just as it had righted his carriage? Since this Force seemed to abide in India, to be closely associated with India's very existence, it made sense to investigate what gave birth to this civilisation. Pursuing his idea, Aurobindo decided to go back in time to the Sanskrit origins of ancient India to penetrate the epic works that shaped this humanity.

> Out of the infinite silence of the past… a few voices arise which speak for it, express it and are the very utterance and soul of those unknown generations, of that vanished and now silent humanity. These are the voices of the poets.

Aurobindo immersed himself in the works of three legendary poets who incarnated India's ancestral history: Valmiki, Vyasa and Kalidasa. All three dominated Indian classical literature, just as Homer, Shakespeare and Dante dominated Western literature. 'Their works are pictures at once minute and grandiose of three moods of our Aryan civilisation of which the first was predominately moral, the second predominately intellectual, and the third predominately material.'

In his Ramayana, written five to eight centuries before Christ, Valmiki depicted an idealised society. Prince Rama, the virtuous heir apparent, and Ravana, who abducted Rama's wife, personified the emblematic collision between good and evil. Valmiki seized on this conflict to paint a world where the social system would exist in the service of Beauty and Good.

After all sorts of incidents, the epic culminated in a paradigm of morality and virtue, promoting and uniting society around a 'meaningful tradition' in which tales of bravery and courage contributed to moulding the minds of people. The Ramayana reflected the standards of India's early ages, the heroic character of the Hindu spirit.

The second masterpiece of ancient India after the Ramayana, the Mahabharata (25,000 stanzas in its original version), depicted a more complex thought. Its author, Vyasa, the poet of action, differed from Valmiki in his realism. He did not deny the code of violence prevalent in society, provided it be purified and transfigured by a commitment to action free from desire. Morality and material development were powerfully influenced by intellectual considerations. Mental activity was sovereign.

The core of the Mahabharata, the Bhagavad Gita, was a plea for the establishment of the Empire of the Righteous (*Dharmarajya*), a practice of government based on righteousness, purity and selfless dedication to the common good. For Krishna, its protagonist and supreme authority in spiritual matters, although attaining peace in God remained the ultimate goal of existence, it must be sought *through action.*

> Not by refraining from actions can a man enjoy actionlessness nor by mere renunciation does he reach his soul's perfection; for no man in the world can even for one moment remain without doing works; everyone is forced to do works, whether he will or not, by the primal qualities born of Prakriti (Nature).

Aurobindo contrasted this ancient rule of action, as exemplified by Krishna, with India's subsequent subservience and self-denial before the oppressive colonial yoke. He speculated that already several centuries before Christ, India, rather than following the Gita's exhortations in favour of a deliberate commitment to the works of the world, had sided with passivity and indolence in her search for 'liberation'. He attributed this historic abdication to Buddhism:

> Before the Bhagavad Gita with its great epic commentary had time deeply to influence the national mind, the heresy of Buddhism seized hold of us. Buddhism with its exaggerated emphasis on quiescence and the quiescent virtue of self-abnegation, its unwise creation of a separate class of quiescents and illuminati, its sharp distinction between monks and laymen implying the infinite inferiority of the latter, its all too facile admission of men to the higher life and its relegation of worldly action to the lowest importance possible stands at the opposite pole from the gospel of Sri Krishna and has had the very effect he deprecates; it has been the author of confusion and the destroyer of the peoples. Under its influence half the nation moved in the direction of spiritual passivity and negation, the other by a natural reaction plunged deep into a splendid but enervating materialism. As a result our race lost three parts of its ancient heroic manhood, its grasp on the world, its magnificently ordered polity and its noble social fabric.

Aurobindo proceeded to draw a parallel between some precepts of Buddhism and Christianity: both encouraged a form of political passivity to the detriment of action. For him, only a completely unselfish zeal in public affairs, as advocated by Vyasa in the Gita, could advance the cause of social progress. He did not mince his words:

> The Christian and Buddhistic doctrine of turning the other cheek to the smiter, is as dangerous as it is impracticable. The disinterested and desireless pursuit of duty is a gospel worthy of the strongest manhood.

After Valmiki and the Ramayana, after Vyasa and the Mahabharata (and the Bhagavad Gita) came Kalidasa, whose poetry reflected yet another aspect of India's soul. His works emerged in the 4th to the 5th century after Christ, when the great Emperor Chandragupta II ruled over a civilisation at its zenith—a material exuberance extolling the beauty and the life of the senses where architecture, painting, music, theatre, the art of gardens and jewellery reached their peak.

Kalidasa appeared in the city of Ujjayini, the capital of the Gupta Dynasty. Of privileged birth, moving in the best circles of this brilliant city, fluent in the arts and sciences, philosophy and law, he incarnated the ethos of his time. Contrary to Valmiki and Vyasa, Kalidasa's characters were not captivated by the nobility of character or the ideal of heroism but reflected the vital and material civilisation to which they belonged. In their actions and words, they revealed the hedonism that drove them. A supreme poet of the emotions, Kalidasa was unrivalled in his ability to endow each form, each poetic object, with harmonious and sensual beauty.

Such was the Age of Kalidasa, when India, having exhausted the possibilities of spiritual experience through intellectual effort and rational inspiration, attempted to seek God through the senses.

In his exploration, completed in July 1902, Aurobindo took stock of his journey by publishing his essay on Kalidasa in the *Madras Indian Review*:

> It was the supreme misfortune of India that before she was able to complete the round of her experience and gather up the fruit of her long millenniums of search and travail... the inrush of barbarians broke in finally on her endless solitary *tapasya* (rigorous discipline) of effort and beat her national life into fragments.... Will she yet arise, new combine her past and continue the great dream where she left it off, shaking off, on the one hand, the soils and filth that have grown on her in her period of downfall and futile struggle, and reasserting on the other her peculiar individuality and national type?

First Samiti

Mrinalini and Sarojini, Aurobindo's young wife and sister, did not adjust well to their new environment. The language, the local customs, the cooking, everything was different from Bengal. They endured their discomfort, according to their Hindu education, with fortitude but in a silence that spoke volumes. Aurobindo had little time to spend with the two young women. On several occasions, he explained his predicament to his stepfather:

> I am afraid I shall never be good for much in the way of domestic virtues. I have tried, very ineffectively, to do some part of my duty as a son, a brother and a husband, but there is something too strong in me which forces me to subordinate everything else to it.

Refusing to subject them to an unsuitable life, Aurobindo decided to take Mrinalini and Sarojini back to Bengal. In April 1902, he took advantage of his annual leave to accompany them to Calcutta. Mrinalini travelled back home to her parents in Assam, where she would remain for several months.

In Calcutta, Aurobindo visited Jatin who, with the help of the attorney P. Mitra, was organising a samiti to recruit Bengali youth. The movement had gathered momentum. Aurobindo and the two men discussed the implementation of similar samitis throughout Bengal, and set out discreetly to inform the youth of neighbouring areas about the budding movement of rebellion. Immediately after Aurobindo's departure, Jatin left on a propaganda tour from town to town, notably in Midnapore, where he visited young members of a group founded by Jogen, Aurobindo's uncle.

Once again, Aurobindo made the long journey back to Baroda. The summer of 1902 was particularly trying for the Principality. In his correspondence to Mrinalini, he described the effects of the drought devastating the region:

> The wells are all nearly dried up; the water of the Ajwa Reservoir which supplies Baroda is very low and must be quite used up by next November; the crops in the fields are all parched and withering. This means that we shall not only have famine; but there will be no water for bathing and washing up, or even, perhaps for drinking. Besides, if there is famine, it is practically sure that all the officers will be put on half-pay.... For you to come to Baroda and endure all the troubles and sufferings of such a state of things is out of the question.

Overworked by the Maharajah, who considered that 'every use should be made of his talents', he turned a deaf ear to the request for yet another report on the 'Management of the State' demanded by the British authorities.

In August, he was 30 years old.

The Pulse of Rebellion

In October, Sister Nivedita visited Baroda for talks with the Maharajah. As her master, Vivekananda, had died a few months earlier, she had decided to leave her monastic order to devote herself to the revolutionary cause. She set off on a tour of Western India to take the pulse of the country and raise funds. From the Maharajah, known for his independence and (veiled) criticism of the British, she hoped to obtain tacit encouragement and perhaps some material help. Aurobindo went to meet her at the station. Even though this was their first encounter, she had heard of him and knew they supported the same cause. A political friendship was instantly born between them, which would last until Nivedita's death in 1911.

Her meeting with the Maharajah, who prudently refrained from displaying any opposition to the British regime, was not so gratifying, and Nivedita could not hide her disappointment. She had failed to sway the one Indian ruler most likely to side with the rebellion.

A month later, Barin appeared at Khaserao's house. Now 22 years old, he had spent 4 years after school wandering across Northern India: a few months with his older brothers, Manmohan in Dhaka and Benoybhusan in Cooch Behar, then a business venture in Patna and finally Baroda, where he turned up unannounced. Aurobindo gave him some political books to read. In the evenings, Barin attended the discussions among his brother's small circle of friends and discovered their secret involvement in a nationwide uprising against the British. Barin could barely contain his excitement. In December, he escorted his brother to Bombay to meet a revolutionary sympathiser, a member of the ICS who had pledged funds for sending Madhavrao to Japan to train in modern techniques of guerrilla warfare.

As happened every December, this was also the annual Congress meeting. This session took place in Ahmedabad, the capital of Gujarat, and was preceded by an industrial conference where the Maharajah was to deliver the dedicatory address. Written by Aurobindo, the two-hour speech spelled out the country's ills: its increasing poverty and its plight of endemic disease and famine—all of which contrasted with Europe's prosperity. It was in the hijacking of India's political power by the East India Company, followed by the absorption of India into the British Empire, that one had to seek the causes of these glaring inequalities, underscored the speaker. Only a social revolution, '.... a great national movement in which each man will work for the nation and not for himself or for his caste' would enable India to regain her place in the world. Destined for an audience of business leaders and politicians, this remarkable balancing act closed with wishes of long life and prosperity to 'His Gracious Majesty, the Emperor of India' (Edward VII).

The contrast between the Maharajah's bold speech at the industrial conference and, just a week later, the fawning palaver of Congress's so-called moderate leaders was startling: 'It is for our benefit that the British power should continue to be supreme in our land,' one of them proclaimed. 'We plead for the permanence of the British rule in India,' amplified the year's chairman. Alongside the Maharajah, Aurobindo attended for the first time the proceedings of the institution he had castigated a decade earlier in his *Indu Prakash* articles. He was there only to meet with the delegate from the Poona District: Tilak.

Once introduced, Tilak drew Aurobindo outside the conference '.... and talked to him for an hour in the grounds expressing his contempt for the Reformist movement and explaining his own line of action in Maharashtra'. Aurobindo emerged from this meeting with the conviction that Tilak was 'the one possible leader for a revolutionary party'.

Aurobindo then travelled to an undisclosed location in the Bombay area, where he was formally introduced (probably by Tilak) to the five-member board of the secret society planning a country-wide revolt against British rule. Little is known about this network except that it was founded several years earlier by a Rajput noble. The Maharashtra branch, headed by Tilak, included prominent political leaders. Aurobindo, thus, became the link between the educated liberal circles in the Bombay region and the old anti-establishment tradition of Bengal.

Back in Baroda, he put down on paper a few reflections inspired by recent events. In both the pompous inanity of the Congress debates and the ostentation of the Bombay Industrial Conference, he saw the signs of an ebbing past:

> Behind and under cover of this failure and falling back there has been slowly and silently gathering another and vaster wave the first voices of which are now being heard, the crests of whose foam are just mounting here and there into view. Soon it will push aside or assimilate its broken forerunner, occupy the sea and ride on surging and shouting to its predestined failure or triumph.

In February 1903, Aurobindo again left for a short trip to Calcutta to visit Barin, who he had sent two months earlier to help Jatin recruit young men for the fledgling samiti.

Barin's easy-going demeanour contrasting with Jatin's strapping build arose considerable curiosity. 'Brother,' Barin said to a young visitor, 'if it makes your heart ache to see India in bondage, don't waste any time, join us, this very moment!'

The young man grabbed his hand: 'Right, Brother! From now on I'm with you.' His name was Abinash Bhattacharya, and he was the first recruit.

Aurobindo was introduced to Abinash, who related this encounter in his memoirs:

> With his eyes fixed on me, Aurobindo Babu gazed at me for a long time. I almost lost my balance—it seemed perhaps he was wringing out the depths of my heart? I could neither close nor avert my eyes. My chest was heaving heavily. Then he examined my forehead, pressed it a number of times, then the eyelids, later turned the eyelids to examine them. Swiftly he turned my head down and started examining it by tapping gently. Then he said, 'Your first selection is good—firm in determination, a faithful and silent worker.'

Before leaving, Aurobindo travelled to Midnapore, where Uncle Jogen proudly presented him with the local recruits. He and Barin were invited to a target-shooting practice in a deserted canyon nearby.

Meanwhile, Mrinalini languished at her parents', but Aurobindo could not take her with him because, for the second consecutive year, drought had ravaged Baroda, and outbreaks of the plague had appeared. It was agreed that Mrinalini would find shelter at grandfather Rajnarayan's.

The Throne of Solomon

The Maharajah spent the summer months with his family and his court at his summer residence in Kashmir. He asked Aurobindo to join him. Aurobindo would reside for almost five months in this 'earthly paradise', tasting 'the charm of its mountains and rivers and the ideal life dawdling along in the midst of a supreme beauty in the slowly moving leisure of a houseboat'. He composed poetry, and even 'the over-industrious Maharajah, whose idea of Paradise was going through administrative papers and making others write speeches for which he got all the credit', did not lessen his enchantment.

One day, he set up climbing the Throne of Solomon, a rocky peak above the capital Srinagar, from where one overlooked the Kashmir Valley and the majestic Himalayan crests. Alone at the top, he found himself on a terrace supporting a small 7th-century temple dedicated to God Shiva. Legend has it that Adi Shankara, the great architect of the *Advaita Vedanta*, visited the small temple sometime in the 9th century. Gazing at the boundless panorama before him—as in Bombay on the Apollo Bunder, as with the runaway horse in the Baroda street—Aurobindo was seized with a vision beyond this world. Once again, he would not mention to anyone that he had had a glimpse of the Absolute, the Brahman. Only 30 years later, he would write:

> All had become one strange Unnameable,
> An unborn sole Reality world-nude,
> Topless and fathomless, for ever still.
> A Silence that was Being's only word,
> The unknown beginning and the voiceless end
> Abolishing all things moment-seen or heard....

1903–1906: The Partition of Bengal

British Schemes

October 1903.

Accompanied by one of Jatin's recruits, a young Bengali writer and lecturer by the name of Debavrata Bose, Aurobindo journeyed to East Bengal. At Khulna, where his father had practised medicine, a cheering crowd welcomed the son of the doctor whose dedication to his patients was still vividly remembered. Yet, whenever Debavrata mentioned the colonial rule, faces clouded over, and everyone fell silent. The situation was heartbreaking: only a handful of Indians aspired for independence. The whole country seemed to be covered with 'a black veil of darkness', felt Aurobindo.

In the samitis they visited, the young recruits did not seem to comprehend the stakes of their engagement: 'Are these the men who will take up the fight?' wondered Aurobindo. As he travelled through the country, he came to realise that 'a secret action or preparation by itself was not likely to be effective if there was not also a wide public movement of patriotic fervour which would popularise the idea of independence as the ideal and aim of Indian politics'. People's minds needed to be awakened. This was the primary task to undertake.

Almost at the same time, the government revealed a plan to proceed with the long-coveted intention of partitioning Bengal—a singular administrative reform that was to precipitate the popular catharsis Aurobindo had hoped for.

With a territory the size of England, and a population of 80 million, Bengal had always been a thorn in the side of the

British. Its dazzling culture had overflowed its borders to as far afield as Malaysia, Thailand and Cambodia. Greek and Roman historians suggested that it was when Alexander the Great discovered Bengal's army with its 4,000 elephants that he was persuaded to curb his ambitions in India and return home. From the 12th century onward, Muslim invasions and Hindu retaliations divided Bengal's territory. It eventually fell to the Mughal Dynasty before being replaced by the British East India Company two centuries later. After the takeover of India by Queen Victoria's government in 1858, Calcutta became the capital city of the Raj and the residence of the Viceroy.

Hindus and Muslims now lived in peace in Bengal. More concentrated in the east of the province, Muslims considered themselves as being Bengali before being Muslim. Centuries of coexistence had eroded communal tensions, reconciled the cultures and mitigated religious singularities. But peace was suddenly threatened by scheming British administrators who, for years, had toyed with the idea of dividing the province.

Lord Curzon, the new Viceroy appointed in 1899, would put his name on record on the most egregious decision of the British Empire in India: the Partition of Bengal.

Curzon considered that 'Bengal was too large a charge for any single man'. In a memo, the then-current governor of Bengal concurred, adding his prescription: 'I believe that Dhaka and Mymensingh (two Eastern districts) would give less trouble if they were under Assam.' At the end of 1903, Curzon endorsed the proposed transfer of these districts to the province of Assam and undertook a tour of the region. During this trip, he realised the political benefit he could derive from the plan. As H.H. Risley, his Secretary of the Interior, put it: 'It would split up and thereby weaken a solid body of our opponents to our rule.'

The 'opponents' were the educated Hindu Bengalis, the most politically conscious group in India, who, under the scheme, would become a linguistic minority in West Bengal in contrast to non-Bengalis, and a numerical minority in East Bengal in contrast to Muslims.

Curzon belonged to that long line of British administrators who, nourished by a sense of superiority in all things, did not hesitate (when necessary) to assert themselves through violence.

He never hesitated to voice British aspirations aloud: 'As long as we rule India, we are the greatest power in the world. If we lose it, we shall drop straight away to a third-rate power.'

Before Curzon, in 1862, Viceroy Elgin had been no less bold: 'India was conquered by the sword and by the sword it shall be held.'

A storm of protests engulfed Bengal as the project of Partition was disclosed. In *The Bengalee*, Surendranath Banerjee, the main Bengali leader in Congress, did not mince his words: 'We object to the proposed dismemberment of Bengal and we are sure the whole country will rise as one man to protest it.' Even the English-language Press in India (*The Englishman*, *The Statesman*, *The Pioneer*), usually very accommodating with the colonial government, took exception to the plan.

Another warning from Congress's year-end session—when a surprising number of delegates expressed 'opposition to a project that breaks up India's unity'—failed to arouse any reaction among English strategists. Even some Muslims, choosing to ignore the benefits they would derive from the Partition, asked the government to reconsider its decision; such was the case of Nawab Syed Amir Hussain, who felt that 'the partition is neither necessary nor desirable'. Yet all these signs fell short of affecting the determination of the men in power.

At Baroda, informed by a telegram from Barin, Aurobindo recorded his first reaction in a notebook:

> This measure is no mere administrative proposal but a blow straight at the heart of the nation.

Then he drafted an article, which he sent at once to Calcutta, asking Barin to print it clandestinely and to disseminate it by hand. This anonymous pamphlet, *No Compromise*, was distributed by Samiti members to all the major newspapers as well as to political and intellectual leaders in the city.

In February 1904, Curzon set off for Dhaka (East Bengal), the planned capital of the new province. There he met the Muslim leader Nawab Salimullah Khan, granted him a £100,000 loan (about 50 million pounds today), and swayed the Muslims in attendance by declaring that 'the Mohammedans of Eastern Bengal will regain a unity which they have not enjoyed since the days of the old Musalman Viceroys and Kings'. There was no easier way to stir Muslims than to evoke their past domination of India. With utter recklessness, Curzon chose to ignore that reawakening the memory of Muslim invasions was playing with fire. Satisfied that their position was enough justification to redraw borders and territories where people had tended to the earth for centuries, senior British officials were about to open the way to a long period of political convulsion in Bengal, and to the awakening of the Indian people.

'Build a Temple'

Meanwhile, the Minister of Education in Baroda had pleaded with the Maharajah: would His Majesty consent to lend his 'Cantabrigian' to the College, where his past tenure had left such excellent memories? About to embark on a lengthy European tour, the Maharajah acquiesced, and after a four-year break, Aurobindo resumed his teaching at Baroda College. His salary was increased to 550 rupees, and he was promoted to the post of vice-principal.

Before assuming this office, he made another trip to Calcutta to arbitrate a dispute in the Samiti. It was not uncommon that Jatin and Barin quarrelled, the disciplinarian outlook of the former clashing with the spontaneity of the latter. On previous occasions, Barin had asked his older brother to intervene, but Aurobindo had invariably invited him to solve his problems by himself. This time, however, the conflict seemed more profound. Aurobindo tried to reconcile the two young men by reminding them of the cause they shared for India's liberation—but in vain. Their egos were in control. Jatin left Calcutta while Barin followed his brother back to Baroda. The first Calcutta samiti had broken up.

By late October 1904, Aurobindo and Barin were settled in Khaserao Jadhav's residence in Baroda, where Mrinalini could finally join them. It was the first time in three years that the couple was reunited.

While the Maharajah packed his countless steamer trunks and gave his final instructions to his ministers, Aurobindo prepared the College programmes for the next year's curriculum. A rare period of domestic serenity prevailed in the hospitable mansion housing the future vice-principal and his family as well as the Jadhav brothers' respective families. Barin tended the garden, wrote poetry and played the *esraj*, an Indian violin. In the evenings, the entire household convened to share the news of the day, but Mrinalini did not join in the general conversation. She was so shy, remembered Barin, that not once had she dared speak to him directly since their arrival in Baroda.

In December, Aurobindo was in Bombay to attend the annual Indian Congress assembly. This session was chaired—an exceptional occurrence—by an Englishman, Henry Cotton, a senior official of the Indian Civil Service and faithful friend of the Ghose family (it was he who had introduced Aurobindo to the Maharajah). From the presidential chair, Henry Cotton declared himself in favour of Indian autonomy and against the Partition of Bengal. This uncompromising position would, no doubt, cause him serious problems with his superiors, though unfortunately, it would have no effect upon the Congress majority, which, as it did every year, voted to register its obsequious reverence to the colonial authorities.

In January, at Baroda College, in a quiet voice, his eyes lowered as in meditation, Aurobindo resumed his literary courses with his method of 'throwing light on the subject in an all-round way which went to the roots'. A reading programme found in a notebook of the time included Goethe's *Iphigenia in Tauris*, Molière, Ernest Renan, Octave Feuillet's *Roman d'un jeune homme pauvre*. To the list were now added more Sanskrit works. The wooden cases of books from Bombay and Calcutta reappeared. In his memoirs, Barin described this familiar scene:

> A table, a sofa, a few chairs, all heaped pell-mell with books and a revolving bookcase groaning under their weight—all thinly covered with dust; a quiet small unassuming man buried there for hours in a trance of thought and very often writing page after page of poetry.

Aurobindo had translated several short Upanishads before turning to study the most aphoristic, *Isha*, which holds in 18 verses the essence of Vedantic philosophy. Over the centuries, the *Isha Upanishad* had generated a wealth of scriptural commentaries, including the great Shankara's, which Aurobindo was impatient to confront with the original text.

Since Shankara, it was professed that the Upanishads postulated the principle of illusion (Maya) as inseparable from material existence; the solidity of the world around us was but a creation of Maya, only real in our space-time continuum. Once we attain Knowledge, we realise that this material universe is but a fallacious distortion of consciousness. Therefore, there is no fundamental reason for a man to invest himself in terrestrial life and its illusory formation—a shadow of the Brahman. By identifying with the Self or Atman, a person's soul merges with the immutable existence of the Brahman, thus escaping the involvement with the world and its dualities.

However, by researching the original Sanskrit, Aurobindo was to understand that Maya did not entail 'illusion', as Shankara had asserted. Instead, according to the Upanishads, it stood for the 'principle of phenomenal existence', that is, the power by which the world of phenomena comes into existence. Hence Aurobindo's interpretation of Maya integrated the material universe within the All that is the Brahman. Rather than a sterile deception of consciousness, the world about us was another mode of the Absolute. Such was the fundamental divergence with Shankara's interpretation.

By bridging the metaphysical chasm between God 'above' and God 'below', Aurobindo laid the ground for an argument challenging Brahmanic thought and breaking away from the age-old legacy of detachment in India. Life on earth was as much a measure of the ultimate realisation as life in the Beyond. Instead of fleeing the difficulties of existence by retreating into a blank enlightenment, the realised Yogi was to accept the earthly burden and work to embrace and better the material world through the divine Force that stimulated him.

> If we find out this Divine within us, if we know ourselves as this spirit which is of one essence and being with the Divine, that is our gate of deliverance and in it we can remain ourselves even in the midst of this world's disharmonies, luminous, blissful and free.

Aurobindo's long periods of study wore out Barin's patience. Though his older brother may have been revolutionising centuries of metaphysical delusion, Barin ached for a more material revolution. He had devoured Bankim Chatterjee's historical novel *Anandamath* (*The Monastery of Bliss*): the story of Sannyasins who, during the great famine of 1770 in Bengal, had taken up arms against the occupying British. He yearned to follow their example and express his worship of *Bharat Mata* (Mother India) in everyday life. Impulsively, he decided to go in search of a spiritual guide and a place to build a temple, a rallying point for revolutionary monks. He carried out a thorough investigation of the Vindhya Mountains of Central India and explored the headwaters of the sacred River Narmada, only to return with a severe case of jungle fever.

In Khaserao's residence, political discussions were sometimes replaced by séances of automatic writing at which Barin showed a remarkable gift in communicating with the Beyond. During such a séance, his pen, guided by a spirit, predicted Viceroy Curzon's imminent departure from India before the end of his term.

Aurobindo also tried his hand at automatic writing, soon to realise the uncertain character of this technique and its ultimate unreliability.

During one of the séances at Khaserao's, the spirit of Ramakrishna, dead for 19 years, suddenly manifested and conveyed this message through Barin's pen: '*Arabindo, mandir karo, mandir karo*' (Aurobindo, build a temple, build a temple). To Barin, this was the clear validation of his project of warrior monks, and this prompted Aurobindo to write a 20-page pamphlet (*Bhawani Mandir*, the Temple of the Mother) profiling a religious congregation devoted to the worship of Mother India:

> What is our mother country? It is not a piece of earth, nor a figure of speech, nor a fiction of the mind. It is a mighty *Shakti* (Energy). The Shakti we call India, Bhawani Bharati, is the living unity of the Shaktis of 300 million people.... Many of us utterly overcome by tamas, the dark and heavy demon of inertia, are saying nowadays that it is impossible;

> that India is decayed, bloodless and lifeless, too weak ever to recover; that our race is doomed to extinction.... We have to change our natures, and become new men with new hearts, to be born again.

However, he warned against a spirituality disconnected from life: 'Adoration will be dead and ineffective unless it is transmuted into Karma (action).' His text evinced the teachings of the Bhagavad Gita.

Although Aurobindo was prompted by Barin's intuition, he was not convinced of the necessity of adding yet another physical temple to the multitude already existing in India. Ultimately, Barin's plan 'fizzled out'. Not a new community of monks, but a new attitude was the pressing necessity. Such was the meaning of Ramakrishna's communication as he understood it: 'Build the temple of the spirit *within thyself*.'

From time to time, Aurobindo travelled to Chandod, 40 miles away on the Narmada river, to visit his friend, Deshpande, who now held the post of district officer in this pilgrimage town. In the temples, Aurobindo watched the ascetics and sadhus performing their age-old Tantric rituals. Before his eyes, a sannyasin, while chanting a mantra, had cured Barin of his fever by offering him to drink a glass of water he had cut with a knife. Despite his Western education, Aurobindo did not feel inclined to doubt or disbelieve what he had seen.

> Abnormal, otherwise supra-physical experiences and powers, occult or Yogic, have always seemed to me something perfectly natural and credible. Consciousness in its very nature could not be limited by the ordinary physical human-animal consciousness; it must have other ranges.

Occasionally, he and Deshpande travelled upriver to Ganganath, the monastery of Swami Brahmananda, who was rumoured to have lived for more than 200 years. The practice of *Raja* and *Hatha yoga* had transformed him into 'a man of magnificent physique showing no signs of old age except white beard and hair, extremely tall, robust, able to walk any number of miles a day and tiring out his younger disciples'. His eyes half-closed, the Swami blessed the visitors who bowed before him to receive his blessings. But his eyes were wide open as he greeted Aurobindo, who returned his gaze and felt the effect of this look as 'simply electric and magnetic, bringing a great sense of peace within'.

Despite the many promptings from his friends, Aurobindo had not felt like engaging in any yogic discipline: 'a solitary salvation leaving the world to its fate was felt as almost distasteful'. But he now sensed that such discipline could help him in his political activities:

> I took up (yoga) seriously when I learnt that the same Tapasya (yogic discipline) which one does to get away from the world can be turned to action—I learnt that yoga gives power and I thought: why should I not get power and use it to liberate my country?

One of Brahmananda's disciples taught him to inhale and exhale consciously, to hold his breath and make it flow through the body. Soon, Aurobindo began practising *pranayama* (control of the breath) with the same intensity he put into everything he did:

> I used to practise five to six hours a day, three hours in the morning and two in the evening.

The results were not long in coming:

> Formerly I used to write with difficulty. For a time the flow would increase; then again it would dry up. Now it revived with astonishing vigour and I could write both prose and poetry at tremendous speed.

His health improved, his body grew stronger:

> Earlier I was very thin. My skin also began to be smooth and fair and there was a peculiar new substance in the saliva.

He noticed that whenever he sat for pranayama, 'not a single mosquito would bite (him), though plenty of mosquitoes were humming around'. Most surprisingly, internal visions began arising in him:

> When I first began to see inwardly (and outwardly also with the open eye), a scientific friend of mine began to talk of after-images—'these are only after-images!' I asked him whether after-images remained before the eye for two minutes at a time—he said, 'no', to his knowledge only for a few seconds; I also asked him whether one could get after-images of things not around one or even not existing upon this earth since they had other shapes, another character, other hues, contours and a very different dynamism, life-movements and values—he could not reply in the affirmative.

Three Cases of Madness

Mrinalini had now turned 18. She still could not adjust to life in Baroda. After a few months, she left again to return to her parents, and in a long letter dated August 1905, Aurobindo blamed his own 'madness' for the difficulties of their relationship. He asked: 'Will you try to become the mad wife to match the mad husband?'

As he declared it, he felt afflicted with three cases of madness. His first madness was to feel that none of the talents he had received from God belonged to him. It also applied to what he earned:

> I have the right to spend only so much as is necessary for the maintenance of the family and on what is absolutely needed. Whatever remains should be returned to the Divine. Until now, I have been giving only one-eighth

> of my money to God and have been spending the rest of it on my personal happiness. I have been pursuing the life of the animal and of the thief.

His second madness concerned his desire to have the direct experience of God:

> If the Divine is there, then there must be a way of experiencing His existence, of meeting Him; however hard be the path, I have taken a firm resolution to tread it. Hindu Dharma asserts that the path is there within one's own body, in one's mind.

His third madness related to his love for India:

> Whereas others regard the country as an inert piece of matter and know it as the plains, the fields, the forests, the mountains and the rivers, I know my country as the Mother, I worship her and adore her accordingly. What would a son do when a demon, sitting on his mother's breast, prepares to drink her blood? Would he sit down content to take his meals or go on enjoying himself in the company of his wife and children, or would he rather run to the rescue of his mother?

Then he added:

> I know I have the strength to uplift this fallen race; not a physical strength, I am not going to fight with a sword or a gun, but with the power of knowledge.... This is not a new feeling in me, not of recent origin, I was born with it, it is in my very marrow.

It was a moment of truth for Mrinalini. Her husband's declaration might well have frightened her. Aurobindo understood her fears:

> You might reply: 'What could a simple woman like me do in all these great works? I have neither will power, nor intelligence, I am afraid even to think of these things.' There is a simple solution for it—take refuge in the Divine, step on to the path of God-realisation. He will soon cure

> all your deficiencies; fear gradually leaves the person who takes refuge in the Divine. You will get that strength from your devotion to God. In the beginning, you won't have to do anything more than to devote half-an-hour every day to meditate on God. You should put before Him your strong aspiration in the form of a prayer: 'May I not come in the way of my husband's life, and his ideals, and in his path to God-realisation; may I become his helper and his instrument.' Will you do it?

Aurobindo hoped to inspire her to embrace the inner life. In reply to his: 'Will you try to become the mad wife to match the mad husband?' she wrote in the margin of his letter: 'a very sweet word!'

In reply to his: 'I have been pursuing the life of the animal and of the thief,' she scribbled: 'Admirable! Admirable!' Stereotypic reactions from a very young woman who was not in the least ready to follow the 'madness' of her husband.

Boycott and Swadeshi

For more than a year, Bengali agitation had mounted over the government's Partition project while the Viceroy's men put the final touches to their scheme. Even in Baroda, Aurobindo could feel the rising tension. In one sense, the letter about the three cases of madness was addressed as much to himself as to Mrinalini: the time of open action had arrived.

On 7 July 1905, the government promulgated the decree of the dismemberment of Bengal. A new province, East Bengal, was to be created by combining Assam with the easternmost districts of Bengal, which was thus divested of a substantial portion of its population.

The news sent a shock wave across the country. In his *Bengalee* editorial, Surendranath Banerjee predicted:

> *A Grave National Disaster.* We are on the threshold of an agitation which for its intensity and universality will be unrivalled in the annals of this province.

The High Court of Calcutta described the plan as a 'harmful approach'. While spontaneous demonstrations erupted across Bengal, speaker after speaker urged the crowds to boycott British goods.

Boycott! The word spread like wildfire. Krishna Kumar (Aurobindo's uncle) wrote in his *Sanjivani* that until the Partition decree was rescinded, 'the use of articles of foreign make would be regarded as the greatest sin'.

On 7 August, a huge crowd assembled in Calcutta with the cry of 'Boycott! Boycott!' It solemnly proclaimed that, henceforth, products of Indian origin would be used instead of English products. This initiative, known as 'Swadeshi', was masterly in its simplicity, as it contributed to returning substantial economic leverage to Indian control while dealing a severe blow to British exports. 'India appears to be waking up in these days.... I think Curzon has broken the British Empire,' Sister Nivedita bluntly declared while encouraging students to devote themselves to the national cause.

Bengali leaders urged the boycott of fabrics from Manchester and salt from Liverpool. Students took to the streets, chanting slogans and extending the boycott to schools and colleges. British-made textiles were burned in public squares; in September, they had diminished by 90 per cent. With samitis beginning to appear in many towns and villages, it was naturally with the song *Bande Mataram* that the young expressed their aspiration. It rapidly became the rallying cry of those demanding economic independence and yearning for political freedom.

On 16 October, when the Partition came into effect, it was a day of mourning and general strike throughout Bengal. People fasted, bathed in the Ganges and walked barefoot in long processions, chanting *Bande Mataram*. At the initiative of the poet Rabindranath Tagore, Hindus and Muslims alike attached colourful *rakhi* threads around one another's wrists as a sign of unity. Many Muslim leaders joined in the protest. On his arrival in the capital Dhaka, the freshly-appointed governor of the new province, an obscure bureaucrat by the name of Bampfylde Fuller, was greeted by a sparse crowd chanting *Bande Mataram*.

Judging the situation to be out of control, Fuller requested and obtained the application of emergency powers: the new province was to be ruled by decrees. Meetings and public processions were prohibited; singing *Bande Mataram* was declared seditious. Non-Bengali police tracked down students and patrolled the towns and villages, applying the boycott.

On 7 November, in Barisal (a port city in East Bengal), a violent clash was narrowly avoided. As leaflets supporting Swadeshi had been printed and distributed in the streets, Fuller, surrounded by a strong police detachment, arrived on the scene and denounced this distribution as seditious, even though it was perfectly legal. He demanded that the perpetrators withdraw their leaflets at once. Fearing that their arrest might trigger a riot, local Bengali leaders agreed to the governor's injunction.

The scale and suddenness of the protests were surprising for a people who, until now, had always docilely obeyed. Although boycott attempts had been launched before, they had never reached this intensity. Begun as a demand for economic independence, Swadeshi would quickly rise to mean far more than the origin of the clothes people wore. As Tilak put it, 'Like the bodies, our minds should also become Swadeshi.... Swadeshi thoughts should always reign in our hearts.' Under the leadership of Tilak, soon joined by Aurobindo and a handful of other 'extremists', Swadeshi would become the symbol of India's independence in addition to being the most effective answer against the British economic steamroller.

Viceroy Curzon would be the first casualty of the outburst he had set in motion. He continued to display an abysmal incomprehension of Indian society and a narrow-minded reliance on the merits of 'his' reform, but behind the posturing, his personal situation must have been rather more precarious. He used the pretext of an administrative dispute with Field Marshal Kitchener (Commander-in-Chief of the Indian Army) to offer his resignation, which was immediately accepted by the India Office in London.

Despite his affectation, his departure bore all the stigma of political disgrace. The fruit of his misguided 'labour' was dismantled in 1911, when Bengal was reunited 'to facilitate its administration'. Lord Curzon was replaced on 18 November 1905 by Lord Minto. Barin's stint at automatic writing had been right.

Call to Passive Resistance

Twelve hundred miles away in Baroda, Aurobindo savoured the last moments of the calm before the storm. His daily practice of pranayama, combined with his vegetarian diet, nurtured his sense of lightness and purity. At the college, where he replaced the incumbent principal, he was engrossed in organising the end-of-year examinations. In the evenings, a visitor would often find him sitting 'in a contemplative mood, calm and serene, with the gravity of a man of ripe old age'.

If he read less, he still wrote profusely, and his notebooks were filled with draughts of ambitious writing projects. Among them, a comment on the *Isha Upanishad* showed that he reflected on the primacy of human action liberated from the ego, which the human worker of yoga—the *Karmayogin*—was supposed to carry out in the world.

> Whatever others may do, the *Karmayogin* must not remove himself from the field of action and give up work in the world... He must, therefore, be ready to live out his life and work out his work calmly and without desire,

> seeking only through his life and actions to get nearer to Him who is the Lord of life and Master of all actions.

Together with his friends, he organised a local association promoting Swadeshi products and, on that occasion, took the floor in support of the campaign. This was his first public partisan speech.

He had been outraged by the capitulation of the Indian leaders in Barisal. 'No Bengali can read the account of the interview between Mr Fuller and the Barisal leaders, without a blush of shame for himself and his nation,' he wrote as an introduction to an article where he warned the government:

> Let the authorities remember this, that when a government breaks the Law, by their very act the people are absolved from the obligation of obeying the Law.

Hostilities had begun. Aurobindo advocated the approach of *passive resistance*, which would become the classic technique used later by Gandhi and his followers. It was incumbent upon Indians to respond firmly to the foreign occupier by circumventing strategies rather than by frontal assault.

> The words *Bande Mataram* must be written—printed, would be better—on every door in Barisal. Public meetings must be held as before and if they are dispersed by the police, the people must assemble in every compound where there is room for even 50 people to stand and record an oath never to submit or crouch down before the oppressor.

Aurobindo boldly called the protest movement taking the country by storm as 'new Nationalism'. He concluded his article with a reminder of the spirit that united the people of India:

> What use to cry day and night Adoration to the Mother if we have not the courage to suffer for the Mother?

National College of Bengal

The youth was on the front lines. Defying police pickets of students prevented the selling of British goods and proclaimed their defiance by chanting the *Bande Mataram*. In an attempt to muzzle their voice, a new government directive prohibited students from attending political gatherings. A further injunction threatened principals with the revocation of government grants if their pupils were caught supporting the boycott. Undaunted, the young then called for an outright boycott of all government institutions, and the Bengali intelligentsia resolved to revisit the long-cherished project of an independent educational system. This intention came unexpectedly into effect with the help of two individuals whom Aurobindo had met a few months earlier.

The first, Charu Chandra Dutt, was born with revolution in his blood. Although he graduated from the ICS and held the office of a judge in Maharashtra, this did not prevent him from mixing with Irish revolutionaries and being involved with a secret society to liberate India. He had met Aurobindo almost by accident at the Baroda Railway Station, and the two had become fast friends.

During one of his visits to Thana, where Charu Chandra Dutt was posted, Aurobindo was introduced to the second individual, Subodh Mallik, Charu's brother-in-law and heir to a shipping fortune in Calcutta. The three men had shared their feelings about the oppressive British yoke borne by their country. When Aurobindo read out his text on *Bhawani Mandir* and outlined his ideas on the spiritual dimension he perceived behind India's liberation, the two friends were left in no doubt that this man should be supported: he embodied the light capable of guiding the struggle for independence.

On 9 November 1905, every intellectual and pedagogue in the province was invited to a large rally in support of a new Bengali educational system. Subodh Mallik chaired the meeting. During his speech, to everyone's surprise, he pledged to commit 100,000 rupees as initial funding for the 'Bengal National College', adding, 'the call of the Mother is clear; whether big or small, we have to respond'. The one condition he attached to this gift was that his friend Aurobindo be appointed as the first principal of the new institution.

The New Party

Aurobindo was, of course, attracted by the educational proposal made possible by Subodh Mallik's gift. He fully intended to participate in it, but this was not the main purpose of his visit to Calcutta, his first since the Partition had come into effect.

> I entered into political action and continued it with one aim and one alone, to get into the mind of the people a settled will for freedom and the necessity of a struggle to achieve it.

He stayed at 12 Wellington Square, the elegant mansion of Subodh's family. The residence was a favourite gathering place of Calcutta's liberal elite. Rabindranath Tagore called round to read his poems in the presence of the Aga Khan, while the Maharajah of Baroda rubbed shoulders with members of Congress. It was in this unexpected setting that Aurobindo had his first important encounter: Bipin Chandra Pal.

A small group of Bengali intellectuals, recently converted to a more assertive brand of nationalism by the Swadeshi campaign, aspired to distance themselves from the conciliatory reflexes of the Bengali political class, and especially from its old 'moderate' leader, Surendranath Banerjee, the publisher of the *Bengalee*. With their leader Bipin Chandra Pal, they wanted to form a 'New Party' centred on a nationalist agenda and to carry their orientation into the Congress arena (of which Bipin was already a member). For Bipin, as for Aurobindo, the primary task was, therefore, 'to capture the Congress and to make it an instrument for revolutionary action'. That would strengthen the force of the boycott and Swadeshi and compel an irreversible change in Indian society.

The Congress, however, was in the hands of the so-called moderate party, a loose aggregation of members federated around the objective of preserving British hegemony. Aurobindo distinguished two trends among these members: the loyalists—'who regard the rule of the British bureaucracy as a dispensation of Providence and preach therefore a gospel of faith in the foreigner, distrust of our countrymen'; and the actual Moderates—'a hybrid species, emotionally nationalist, intellectually loyalist. It is owing to this double nature that their delusions acquire an infinite power for misconception. People listen to them because they claim to be nationalist and because a sincere nationalist feeling not infrequently breaks through the false Loyalist reasoning.'

In the person of Surendranath Banerjee, Bengal possessed the quintessential moderate politician engaged in double talk; it was from his coterie that Bipin sought to break away so he could put his oratorical talents at the service of a new national cause. Supported by Aurobindo, he and his young companions—Surendranath Haldar, Chittaranjan Das and Hemendra Prasad Ghose—would soon form the nucleus of the Bengali Nationalist Party, which openly challenged the moderate ascendancy. Aurobindo and Bipin thus began a long political collaboration and a mutual friendship and admiration that would never wane.

Contrary to all expectations, under Aurobindo's influence, the elegant residence at Wellington Square, with its English furniture and polished parquet floor, hosted the first debates of the New Party members, gradually becoming the unofficial headquarters of the nationalist opposition.

By the end of 1905, besides their interest in a new educational system, Bengali politicians were concerned with the forthcoming session of Congress due to convene in Benares under the chairmanship of a Maharashtrian moderate, G.K. Gokhale. The climate of anti-partition feelings and the gains of the Swadeshi campaign posed the gravest challenge. It was the first time in 20 years that Congress faced such a dilemma. As the deliberations got underway, opinions diverged widely between Moderates and 'Extremists' (i.e., Nationalists) on how to react to the boycott of British goods. Nationalists from Punjab and Maharashtra (including Tilak) supported the Bengali delegates in their call for extending the boycott to the entire country.

Gokhale reluctantly endorsed a resolution in favour of the boycott on the express condition that the Nationalists refrain from blocking a resolution to welcome the Prince of Wales on his visit to India. (This extraordinary piece of bargaining exemplifies the sense of unreality affecting the Indian political class of the time.)

In early 1906, Aurobindo returned to Baroda to finish his term and await the return of the English principal he had replaced. He planned to request a leave of absence with the secret thought of a definitive furlough.

In late January, while waiting for the authorisation to leave, he wrote a tragedy in verse, *Rodogune*, based on the play of the same name by Corneille. On 28 February, he posed among his students for a farewell photograph. It was probably the last time he would wear a three-piece suit. To a friend who asked why he looked so placid and serene, he replied: 'My prayer is answered, and I will be leaving Baroda very soon.'

1906: *Bande Mataram*

Yugantar, a Singular Newspaper

From one end of Bengal to the other, public opinion was inflamed by the boycott and Swadeshi. The great body of India had roused from its slumber.

Aurobindo was 33. In his calm, controlled manner, he intended to participate in this opportunity to shake off British rule. Although he did not exclude any course of action, even military force, to free his country, his arguments predicated on the right of all peoples to self-determination.

He found the young especially responsive to his words and spent long hours among them, expounding upon Swadeshi's political significance. His brother Barin particularly embodied the spirit of the youths involved in Bengal's rebellion. He concurred with Aurobindo on the need to uphold one's political position with a consistent will to action and felt that the use of unequivocal force was justified against the invaders.

He suggested the creation of a protest newspaper, 'which was to preach open revolt and the absolute denial of British rule'. As a result, the *Yugantar* (New Era) was born in mid-March. Two weeks later, Aurobindo set the tone of the new publication by writing its first Bengali editorial, entitled 'Our Political Ideal':

> For a nation whose mind and body are dependent on others, railways, telegraph, electricity, municipalities, universities, and National Congress—all the discoveries of science and all things belonging to Western political life—are only toys. It is only what is obtained by one's own exertion which is a right; the gift of others does not constitute a

> right. What Ripon [a former Viceroy] has given today, Curzon will take away tomorrow; at a thousand meetings and associations, we shall cry loudly saying, 'Alas! Our toys are gone, what a great injustice!' Childishness is a main symptom of our present political life.

Further:

> We are slaves even if we get high posts; the Civilian, the Judge, the Municipal Commissioners, the Chairman of the District Board, the Syndicate of the University, the Member of the Legislative Council wear chains; all of them are playing on the stage wearing chains. But then we have become so low-minded that we do not feel ashamed to boast of those chains being made of gold or silver. Slavery has like a thick fog enveloped our entire life.

Next, he attacked the Congress, which was to introduce a measure of Indian influence in governing the country:

> Many people are proclaiming this in the name of the object of the National Congress: 'The English officials are ruling the country well.... We shall help them in the work of administration by annually informing them of the prayers of the Indians, and only by that means will British administration be faultless.' But the officials do not accept this unasked-for help, but rather set it at naught by calling all this the slave's impudence and impertinence of unripe intelligence. Every year, the Congress appears uninvited before the officials with the object of helping them, and at last comes back with a load of insult on its head.

Distributed throughout Bengal, the *Yugantar* saw its readership soar. Aurobindo assumed editorial control, while Barin, assisted by eager and prolific young writers, poured forth articles in bold and energetic language, even to the point of including 'instructions' for urban guerrilla warfare. Surprisingly, the government censors would let these articles pass unnoticed for months before realising the potential impact of their 'explosive' contents.

The Stormy Barisal Conference

Leaving Barin to deal with printing presses and foundry proofs, Aurobindo set out for Barisal to attend Congress' provincial gathering, which was to prepare that year's plenary session of Congress in Calcutta. On 12 April, escorted by his new friends Bipin Chandra Pal and Subodh Mallik, he joined grassroots militants on their way to Barisal, where, five months earlier, a confrontation on the boycott had almost turned violent.

Even before the conference began, chants of *Bande Mataram* burst forth from the thousands of people gathered to listen to their delegates. The head of the local police enjoined Surendranath Banerjee, the Bengali veteran of Congress' politics, to refrain from singing a song 'prohibited by law'. After consulting other provincial dignitaries, Surendranath refused to comply.

The following day, 5,000 men marched in unison, chanting the *'Bande Mataram'*. The police were ordered to break up their procession. They let the front rows of older delegates—among whom Aurobindo was marching—pass by unimpeded but struck mercilessly at the rank and file following behind. The strokes of lathis rained down upon the heads and limbs of the young volunteers who, despite the blows, continued chanting. Many were seriously injured. Frantically retracing their steps, the older delegates succeeded in stopping the bloodshed.

The next day, the right of assembly was again asserted by a 6,000-strong crowd. They listened to their delegates presenting the agenda for the forthcoming Calcutta session before dispersing a few hours later by the order of the local magistrate. Under Aurobindo's pen, the *Yugantar* approved that 'the right of public meeting was asserted in defiance of executive ukase'.

Defending this right of assembly, Aurobindo then joined Bipin Chandra Pal on an extensive tour through Bengal's heartland. From town to town, Bipin's oratorical skills roused the crowds with impassioned speeches on the boycott, Swadeshi, and passive resistance. Aurobindo was struck by the atmosphere of 'high exaltation and self-forgetfulness' in the growing throngs of people. The 'black veil of darkness' so prevalent in the previous years had now almost completely vanished.

Since he had not mastered the local dialects, Aurobindo remained in the background. When the public requested to hear him, Bipin replied:

> Try to assimilate what I am telling you. When he speaks, he will speak only fire.

Despite his discretion during this six-week tour, Aurobindo's presence was reported by the Calcutta *Bengalee*, and for the first time, his name began to appear on the lists of CID spies.

National College

On 11 March 1906, a committee of experts created the previous December assembled a solemn group of Bengali notables (teachers, lawyers and landowners) as a 'National Council of Education' whose aim was to evolve and be the custodian of a new educational system. Aurobindo had accepted to become one of the 92 founding members of the Council.

Returning to Calcutta in late May, he signed its historic Memorandum of Association, whose second paragraph specified the purpose of the Council:

> To impart and promote the imparting of education... not in opposition to, but standing apart from, the existing systems of Primary, Secondary and Collegiate education....

'Not in opposition to...' was imposed by the Council's moderate members. This slight and apparently insignificant equivocation evinced the premonitory signs of what would eventually distort the new institution into an Indianised auxiliary of British education—quite contrary to what was initially intended.

The Council validated the appointment of Aurobindo, the 'obscure schoolmaster from a far-off province of India' to head the National College of Bengal. But his authority was limited to teaching matters, while administrative decisions were handed over to a 'General Manager', a lawyer associated with the Congress and appointed to keep the new institution within the Moderate fold. This control at a minor level of decision-making illustrated the prevailing strength of the moderates and their subservience to the European model.

Aurobindo's new position entailed a substantial salary reduction from 750 to 150 rupees a month, which barely covered his personal expenses, not to mention the money he regularly sent to his family. His only luxury was Subodh Mallik's hospitality at Wellington Square. Their friendship stirred the rumour mill.

On 15 August 1906—his 34th birthday—he delivered the College's inaugural address before 150 students and 20 professors.

The College curriculum included Sanskrit studies, political science, history, Arabic, vernacular Indian languages and Western philosophy. Aurobindo combined his duties as principal with lectures in English poetry and history. He guided academic deliberations and set up the topics of examinations.

The Temple of Kali

Before taking on his responsibilities at the College, Aurobindo had to return one last time to Baroda to obtain his leave of absence from the Maharajah. Pending the official stamps on his papers, he visited Deshpande in Chandod. Together they went up the river to Ganganath, the monastery of Swami Brahmananda, who had recently passed away.

The two friends then decided to head to Karnali Village. There, on the waterfront, stood a small temple dedicated to Kali, the Mother who destroys the obstacles in spiritual life. Aurobindo climbed the steps leading to the shrine and faced a carved statue of Kali adorned with shimmering fabrics and jewellery. Once again, he felt suddenly aware of an atmosphere outside any earthly reference. The statue smiled at him. A Presence pervaded the air. He was face to face with 'Her'.

Eyes open, he had entered a Reality beyond appearances, penetrated a space vibrating with a different energy. He summarised his experience at the small temple of Kali with these words: 'After that, I came to believe in God.'

A Political Maelstrom

The political agitation of the Swadeshi campaign made confrontation inevitable between the moderates, who intended India to remain within the British fold, and the 'Extremists', for whom the season of 'petitionary politics' had lasted long enough.

Recent appointments at the head of the British hierarchy had raised hopes. But John Morley, the new Secretary of State for India, though labelled as liberal, had promptly disappointed by declaring that the Partition of Bengal was 'there to stay'. The second brain of this two-headed government, Viceroy Minto, was well-known for his connections with the British Conservative Party and even more famous for his equestrian accomplishments at the Epsom Derby. Both men planned a package of modest reforms, including local elections in Bengal to choose representatives for consultative Councils.

In the new province of East Bengal, the government registered a first setback when the appointed governor resigned. Scarcely 10 months in office, Bampfylde Fuller ('the petty tyrant', as Aurobindo nicknamed him) had to be disavowed in his decision to punish two Bengali schools involved in the boycott. His departure was a victory for the popular forces and a blow to the regime.

In the west of the country, in Maharashtra and Bombay, a coterie led by lawyers Pherozeshah Mehta and G.K. Gokhale ruled supreme over the Congress's formal apparatus, which they had succeeded in keeping under iron-fisted control despite vehement opposition from Tilak and his nationalist allies.

To the east, in Bengal, moderate opinion (still prevailing in the middle class) was incarnated by Surendranath Banerjee, the Congress veteran whose authority was now disputed by Bipin Chandra's New Party.

Facing these Anglophile monoliths, there gathered a still formless nationalist opposition, comprised of intellectuals, students and labour leaders, and backed by an immense popular aspiration which was both the issue and the unknown in the conflict.

For the present, all eyes were on Calcutta and the appointment of the president for the forthcoming Congress. As the leader of the Moderate Party in the host city, it was incumbent upon Surendranath Banerjee to find an appropriate man for the position. This time, the task was particularly arduous. The presence of a growing number of grassroots extremists, trained by boycotts and street protests, threatened to shatter the trendy Congress consensus of past years. To avoid a total debacle, it was essential to block Tilak from gaining the presidency. 'The man of action in the Presidential chair of the Congress! The Anglo-Indian envisages the idea and sees in it the very image of his doom,' needled Aurobindo.

Weeks of procrastination went by. The controversy spread to all the moderate-leaning English newspapers. From Bombay, the Mehta-Gokhale clan threatened to change the Congress's venue if Calcutta could not find a president.

That was when Bipin had an inspirational flash of brilliance. He decided to set up an English-speaking opposition newspaper.

Hitherto, the nationalist opposition had been voiced only in local languages (such as Barin's Bengali *Yugantar*); in English, however, it would gain a country-wide audience. On 5 August 1906, Bipin communicated his idea to Aurobindo, who approved it immediately and agreed to contribute to the new journal. The next day, with 500 rupees borrowed from a friend, Bipin registered the name of the new paper: *Bande Mataram*.

The ink was barely dry on the first issue when Bipin departed Calcutta for another extensive political tour through East Bengal. Overnight, Aurobindo thus found himself responsible for publishing a national newspaper and contributing his voice to his country's struggle for freedom.

The *Bande Mataram*

After his work at the College, Aurobindo's second life started between the cramped printing house, which the *Bande Mataram* shared with another nationalist Bengali paper, and Subodh Mallik's residence, where he wrote his articles. In his first editorials, referring to the veritable earthquake triggered by the dismemberment of Bengal, Aurobindo plunged straight into the waters of radical politics:

> The issue has been fairly put between the Indian people and the alien bureaucracy. 'Destroy or thou shalt be destroyed,' and the issue will have to be resolved, not 'it may be a century hence,' but now, in the next two or three decades.

In fluent language and masterly style (unassailable by the censors but without complaisance), his articles announced the advent of a new Indian political consciousness. They prophesied the afflictions endured by India until her independence in 1947, the debacle—decades in advance—of British hegemony, and the Golgotha through which India would regain her soul.

> The true policy of the Congress movement should have been from the beginning to gather together under its flag all the elements of strength that exist in this huge country. The Brahmin Pandit and the Mahomedan Maulavi, the caste organisation and the trade union, the labourer and the artisan, the coolie at his work and the peasant in his field, none of these should have been left out of the sphere of our activities.

He slammed the moderate leaders and their supposed sense of diplomacy.

> The diplomacy of grown-up children! The diplomacy of the ostrich hiding its head in the sand?

His biting irony denounced a fool's game:

> The huge price India has to pay England for the inestimable privilege of being ruled by Englishmen is a small thing compared with the murderous drain by which we purchase the more exquisite privilege of being exploited by British capital.

He infused Indians with faith in themselves. 'We need faith above all things, faith in ourselves, faith in the nation, faith in India's destiny.'

He also exhorted his countrymen to prepare to fight:

> Under certain circumstances a civil struggle becomes in reality a battle and the morality of war is different from the morality of peace. To shrink from bloodshed and violence under such circumstances is a weakness deserving as severe a rebuke as Sri Krishna addressed to Arjuna when he shrank from the colossal civil slaughter on the field of Kurukshetra.

Aurobindo's articles would soon reach far beyond Bengal. The *Bande Mataram* was the only newspaper that exposed the contradictions of colonial hegemony in the light of a resurgent, modern, democratic Nationalism, the only voice to convey India's subjugation with both scrupulous realism and absolute faith in an emancipated and glorious future of an eternal India.

> The new Nationalism is a creed, but it is more than a creed; it is a method, but more than a method. The new Nationalism is an attempt at a spiritual transformation of the 19th-century Indian.

The *Bande Mataram's* spectacular success soon inflamed a barrage of hostile reactions from conventional Anglo-Indian newspapers, to which Aurobindo sent his sarcastic arrows:

> If there is one pleasing feature of the present situation, it is the remarkable unanimity with which the Anglo-Indian Press has greeted our appearance in the field with a shriek of denunciation and called on Heaven and Earth and the government and the Moderates to league together and crush us out of existence. *Statesman* and *Englishman*, *Times* and *Pioneer*, all their discordant notes meet in one concord on this grand swelling theme. The 'moderate' papers of all shades, pro-government or advocates of association with government or advocates of association-cum-opposition, have all risen to the call. The *Hindu Patriot* rejoices at our lack of influence, the *Mirror* threatens us with the prison and the scaffold, the *Bengalee mutters* about upstart journals and warns people against the morass which is the inevitable goal, in its opinion, of a forward policy. Well, well, well! Here is an extraordinary and most inexplicable clamour about an upstart journal and a party without influence or following in the country.

Two young writers, Hemendra Prasad Ghose and Shyamsundar Chakraverty, volunteered to assist Aurobindo in running and editing the newspaper. But despite Subodh's generous support, finances remained precarious.

In November, the newspaper moved to its own premises at 2/1 Creek Row, appearing in a new edition with a revamped format.

All the writers, including Bipin Chandra and Aurobindo, submitted their articles anonymously and with no remuneration. The daily dissemination of the *Bande Mataram* continued to be somewhat of a miracle.

1906–1907: Outbreak of Hostilities

Swaraj!

With the session of the Calcutta conference now scarcely a few weeks away, the moderate Congress majority was still bent against Tilak's presidency. To break the political deadlock, a moderate chieftain conceived of the brilliant idea of importing a veteran Indian politician from England, Dadabhai Naoroji.

A former professor of Mathematics and the first Indian to sit in the British Parliament, Naoroji was the author of a noted economics essay showing a correlation between India's impoverished condition and the British management of the economy. For the moderates in Congress, Naoroji was the perfect choice for the presidential seat. Tilak and his supporters were 'faced with an accomplished fact'. The suspense in Calcutta's circles reached dizzying heights.

Despite this seminal event, Aurobindo's personal participation was thrown in jeopardy as he fell ill. After several months of practising pranayama '....with no other result than an increased health and energy, some psycho-physical phenomena, a great outflow of poetic creation, a limited power of subtle sight mostly with the waking eye, I had a complete arrest and was at a loss'. The yogic progression had stopped, leaving him with the weight of the ordinary consciousness.

This first eclipse in the yoga was compounded by a flu epidemic that broke out in Calcutta when the region was hit by torrential storms. Lacking the protective energy field of the pranayama, Aurobindo was contaminated and had to take to his bed. Mrinalini, who had joined him in Calcutta, nursed him as he hovered for several days between life and death. When the fever finally subsided, he left for Deoghar to recover and recharge himself.

However, there was no question of missing the Congress session opening two weeks later. During his absence, the opposite camps clashed over the agenda of the meeting. Since the moderates' ploy had imposed Naoroji ('the man of the past') as the Congress president, it was imperative that the Nationalists, led by Tilak and Bipin Chandra, imposed their own agenda: boycott, Swadeshi, national education and political autonomy. The Moderates agreed to a boycott and Swadeshi, watered down and limited to Bengal, but did not want to hear about autonomy. Three days before the opening, the Nationalists gathered huge crowds in the centre of Calcutta and threatened to demand drastic amendments in the plenary session if they could not obtain an acceptable agenda.

That was the situation when Aurobindo returned from Deoghar. In political circles, it was by now an open secret that the principal of the National College was also the brilliant editor of the *Bande Mataram*. His friends swarmed around him, seeking his counsel and listening to his words.

No one but R.C. Majumdar, the 'dean' of Indian historians, could better appraise the presence of Aurobindo at the Calcutta Congress: 'The Extremist Party, now with an all-India outlook, had an accession of immense strength when it was joined by Aurobindo Ghose, who proved to be a host in himself,' wrote the historian in *Struggle for Freedom*, his encompassing history of the Indian people. 'Indeed the entry of this new personality in the Congress arena may be regarded as a major event of the year in Indian politics.... But far more valuable to the Extremist Party than even his speeches was his own striking personality. Fired with religious fervour, he preached Nationalism as a religion, and he, the prophet of this new religion, infused, by his precepts and example, courage and strength into everyone who came in touch with him.'

On 26 December 1906, the 22nd Indian National Congress opened with its customary pomp and a dull, conventional presidential address. All the big names of Indian politics (Mehta, Gokhale, Tilak, Banerjee) convened in the 'Subjects Committee' to discuss the terms of the resolutions to be voted by the full assembly. It was the first time Aurobindo took part in these secret talks. As a consummate tactician, Tilak managed to hammer out a compromise on the boycott and Swadeshi, which, to the dismay of the Moderates, was endorsed by the general assembly. 'You would not and could not have treated me like this in Bombay,' Mehta hissed in Tilak's ear.

However, it was Dadabhai Naoroji's closing speech that carried the day. Transported with joy by the agreement between Nationalists and Moderates, to everyone's surprise, the president asserted that the Congress goal was now to secure 'Swaraj' (by which he meant a form of colonial autonomy). The word Swaraj resounded like a thunderbolt. For the first time, the Congress platform dared to mention autonomy in India. The next day, in the *Bande Mataram*, Aurobindo wrote:

> Dadabhai Naoroji was made president in order to dish the Extremists; yet it was this Moderate president who gave us the cry of Swaraj which the Extremists have made their own and which is stirring the blood of the nation to great actions and great ideals.

In Aurobindo's articles, in the speeches of his friends and in the heart of an entire people, Swaraj would soon become synonymous, not only with autonomy but with independence.

Foundation of the Muslim League

Three months prior to the Congress session in Calcutta, on 1 October 1906, Viceroy Minto had discreetly opened his official residence at Simla to a delegation of Muslim leaders headed by Aga Khan. The meeting, unreported at the time, was to put in place a strategy that has long borne the English signature of 'divide and conquer'. To this end, Colonel Dunlop Smith, Lord Minto's private secretary, had thoroughly prepared the meeting and composed the draught of an address to be read to the Viceroy by the Muslim delegates since he 'knew the art of drawing up such petitions in good language'. The Muslim delegates would express their 'worries' that the elections resulting from the forthcoming reforms in the territories would not allow the Muslim minority to be adequately represented in the provincial legislatures; therefore, they ought to request the application of a quota system based on religion, which alone would guarantee their fair share of power.

Everything had gone as planned. Responding to the 'worries' of the 70-odd Muslim delegates present, Minto had read his own prepared statement, also carefully crafted:

> You justly claim that your position should be estimated, not merely on your numerical strength but in respect to the political importance of your community and the services it has rendered to the Empire. I am entirely in accord with you.... Like you, I am firmly convinced that any electoral representation in India would be doomed to mischievous failure which aimed at granting a personal enfranchisement, regardless of the belief and traditions of the communities composing the population of this continent.

From the Viceroy's mouth, the long dialectical career of the supranational status of Islam had begun, and it is still alive today. Historians agree that Minto's address stands as a highlight of modern sectarian politics in India.

That evening, Lady Minto copied excerpts of a letter she had just received from a government aide in her diary:

> I must send your Excellency a line to say that a very, very big thing has happened today. A work of statesmanship that will affect India and

> Indian history for many a long year. It is nothing less than the pulling back of 60 million people (the Muslim population) from joining the rank of the seditious opposition.

Upon receiving the day's report, Secretary Morley himself expressed his enthusiasm to the Viceroy:

> All that you tell me of your Mohammedans is full of interest, and I only regret that I could not have moved unseen at your garden party.

Such is the way in which these senior civil servants airily fomented discord between communities that time had begun to bind together by summoning the grievous past of Muslim invasions and bloody strife on Indian soil.

Two days after the end of the Calcutta Congress, on 30 December 1906, in the sumptuous Dhaka residence of Nawab Salimullah (the very same individual to whom Lord Curzon had lent £100,000 of public money), the Muslim League was born—an organisation whose stated objective was to counterbalance the influence of the Indian National Congress, considered too Hindu.

Over the next 40 years, the Muslim League would develop into the principal political platform for claiming separate Muslim treatment in India; it would be Muhammad Ali Jinnah's main political arm to launch his movement of secession from India and form a new nation, Pakistan, in 1947.

Doctrine of Passive Resistance

Aurobindo's fever lingered. Handing over the *Bande Mataram* to the care of his colleagues, he once again left Calcutta with Mrinalini.

In the bracing air of Deoghar, he immediately set to writing. Within a week, he composed *Prince of Edur*, a romantic drama based on the exploits of an 8th-century Rajput warrior whose motto, 'Dare greatly and thou shalt be great,' would not have been out of place on the *Bande Mataram* frontispiece. He felt better.

Then he wrote a new essay for the *Bande Mataram*, 'The Doctrine of Passive Resistance'. It is a sweeping indictment of the Indian political leaders, who had yet to realise that the old dialectic of entreaty had become obsolete. Perhaps, worst of all, 'their want of courage and faith in the nation, their rooted distrust of the national character, disbelief in Indian patriotism and blindness to the possibility of true political strength and virtue in the people, precluded them from discovering the rough and narrow way to salvation'.

Aurobindo's assessment of their 'accomplishments' was blunt: a half-century of 'political agitation' had been wasted on trivial conquests. All they had obtained turned out to be 'palliatives which could not even be counted upon to palliate'. Blinded by the belief in English invincibility and in India's abject deficiency, they had not understood that London had bought their cooperation at the price of minor concessions, thus keeping the country under the yoke of colonisation at a minimal cost. The only strategy for India was to dare to gain freedom and independence, insisted Aurobindo.

> Political freedom is the life-breath of a nation; to attempt social reform, educational reform, industrial expansion, the moral improvement of the race without aiming first and foremost at political freedom, is the very height of ignorance and futility.

Contrary to Congress' 'begging policy', the programme of the New Party incited a cathartic awakening and inspired people to claim their sovereignty by urging a passive resistance (or *defensive resistance*), whose goal was to circumvent the British administration by refusing to cooperate and by boycotting foreign goods. However, Aurobindo never lost sight of the fact that, in the face of violence, passive resistance could be stained with blood. That is why he warned:

> To submit to illegal or violent methods of coercion, to accept outrage and hooliganism as part of the legal procedure of the country is to be guilty of cowardice, and, by dwarfing national manhood, to sin against the divinity within ourselves and the divinity in our motherland. The moment coercion of this kind is attempted, passive resistance ceases and active resistance becomes a duty.

This position underscores the major difference with what would be known later as Gandhi's 'passive resistance'. About the time when Aurobindo outlined these principles of passive resistance as part of a national struggle for emancipation, Gandhi was preparing to confront the discriminatory laws of the white South African regime. From the outset, he subscribed to the spiritual principle of total *ahimsa*, which excluded all violence against white supremacy. Some 10 years later, when he applied this rule of total non-violence in India, Gandhi was catapulted to worldwide fame. In contrast, Aurobindo continued to assert that the rule of absolute non-violence was incompatible with the struggle for national liberation.

Aurobindo's essay on passive resistance appeared in the *Bande Mataram* in seven instalments spread over a two-week period. In it, he drew the forms of India's revival, detailing the methods and objectives of the nationalist programme, examining potential obstacles and analysing the objections and concerns that the fight for independence would not fail to arouse among his countrymen.

Communal Violence

In April 1907, critical developments called Aurobindo back to Calcutta. The British had succeeded in weakening the disobedient Hindu majority, and the Muslim League had formally approved the Partition of Bengal. It was the beginning of the political fracture between India's two major communities in modern times.

Communal clashes erupted in East Bengal. In March, an anti-partition rally in Comilla was attacked by a Muslim mob incited by Nawab Salimullah. The police turned a deaf ear to the Hindus' calls for help. The fighting lasted three days before the authorities intervened to restore peace. In the *Bande Mataram*, Aurobindo denounced it as a set-up: to destroy the spirit of the Swadeshi, the government had bribed gangs of Muslims to attack Hindu militants in local areas.

He read in the British exploitation of Muslim fanaticism the incapacity to face the situation by political means. Alluding to the terrifying past of Muslim invasions, massacres, plundering and destruction—the suffering inflicted on India for centuries—he pointed to the grave danger of fighting 'poison with poison': 'With panic-stricken men the fear of the lesser danger is easily swallowed in the terror of the greater.'

Yet he never stigmatised the Muslim community. The future Indian nation that he evoked in the *Bande Mataram* columns was to be a paradigm of unity and integration:

> The new (Nationalism) overleaps every barrier; it calls to the clerk at his counter, the trader in his shop, the peasant at his plough; it summons the Brahmin from his temple and takes the hand (of) the Chandala (outcast) in his degradation; it seeks out the student in his College, the schoolboy at his books, it touches the very child in its mother's arms and the secluded zenana (harem) has thrilled to its voice; its eye searches the jungle for the Santal (indigenous tribes) and travels the hills for the wild tribes of the mountains. It cares nothing for age or sex or caste or wealth or education or respectability; it mocks at the talk of a stake in the country; it spurns aside the demand for a property qualification or a certificate of literacy. It speaks to the illiterate or the man in the street in such rude vigorous language as he best understands, to youth and the enthusiast in accents of poetry, in language of fire, to the thinker in the terms of

> philosophy and logic, to the Hindu it repeats the name of Kali, to the Mahomedan it spurs to action for the glory of Islam. It cries to all to come forth, to help in God's work and remake a nation, each with what his creed or his culture, his strength, his manhood or his genius can give to the new nationality. The only qualification it asks for is a body made in the womb of an Indian mother, a heart that can feel for India, a brain that can think and plan for her greatness, a tongue that can adore her name or hands that can fight in her quarrel.

At Subodh Mallik's house, where he wrote his columns, Aurobindo continued to live a simple and frugal life. Visitors could sometimes catch a glimpse of him writing on the back of an envelope while a *Bande Mataram* colleague waited nearby to finalise the next day's edition. In the evening, he might join the conversation with guests while keeping an eye on the papers near him. Careless of his appearance, dress, money and food, he spoke little and often appeared distant. Neither his slim figure nor discreet presence impressed until one met his eyes: 'wonderful, indescribable eyes', remembered a visitor. Abinash, who had left Barin's *Yugantar* to assist Aurobindo, recalled:

> He was always meditating deeply about something. I found him always sitting in the same posture with a pen in his hand, deeply immersed in thought. When he looked at one, he seemed not to view one, as if mentally he was soaring far, far away.

A Radical Brother

While the *Bande Mataram* grew in popularity under Aurobindo's editorship, Barin had pursued his own path of political radicalism. Day after day, the *Yugantar* inflamed Bengal with articles bordering on sedition. The paper's success continued unabated. On the other hand, neither the collapse of the Calcutta Samiti nor his failure to find a temple in the jungle weakened Barin's determination to launch a community of warrior monks.

Several months earlier, he had planned to assassinate Bampfylde Fuller, the first governor of East Bengal, who resided in the capital Dhaka. Together with a companion, Barin had followed the governor's trail throughout the province, looking for an opportunity to liquidate him. Informed that the governor's train would stop by a railway junction north of Calcutta, the two conspirators had plotted to climb aboard and eliminate their man. Regrettably for them, however, the train never arrived. Disappointed, they returned to Calcutta, where Aurobindo advised them to go home.

Dejected but not defeated, Barin then returned to his idea of the warrior monks. At Maniktala, on the northern outskirts of Calcutta, Dr Ghose's sons had inherited a few acres of overgrown land surrounding a dilapidated house, the Maniktala Garden. Even though the site did not have the prestige of the Narmada river, it was close to the city and yet distant enough to be discreet. That is where Barin decided to install his 'Ashram'. Designed as a centre for spiritual practice and study, he would extend it into a bomb-making and training facility for revolutionary recruits.

In early 1907, alternating with his journalistic activities at the *Yugantar*, Barin installed himself in the Garden along with with a few volunteers. The discipline was strict. Beginning at four in the morning, the day included meditation and physical exercise. Upendranath lectured on the Upanishads and political science, Barin expounded on the Bhagavad Gita and the Russo-Japanese War, and Ullaskar drilled the recruits in the proper use of explosives.

1907: Repression

The Voice of the People

The voice of the *Bande Mataram* became the voice of the people. 'No paper that we know of has ever evoked such a passionate personal enthusiasm as the *Bande Mataram* did during its short tenure of life,' recalled a college professor. 'The *Bande Mataram* gave vent to what was boiling in people's hearts. It said things that others did not, could not or dared not articulate… somehow it touched the heart of people lulled into slavery for so long,' observed another witness of the time. For Bipin, 'Every morning, not only Calcutta, but the educated section of almost all parts of India looked forward to its strong statements on the burning issues of the day.' In their memoirs, some of Gandhi's followers would acknowledge their debt to the *Bande Mataram's* scathing editorials. The paper's impact became known to both Gandhi in South Africa and Nehru in England. In Europe, it contributed to the radicalisation of part of the Indian community, which embraced nationalist aims.

The *Bande Mataram* was also read by the British. Having gone through 'The Doctrine of Passive Resistance', the Director of CID, Calcutta, deemed the articles 'very well written and the tone wonderfully restrained for Bengali lucubrations'. He concluded that the movement 'should be watched for it might develop into dangerous proportions under favourable conditions'. Every week, the British press, including the venerable *Times*, reproduced excerpts from the *Bande Mataram* in its columns. Aurobindo invariably put forward that 'even if an alien rule were benevolent and beneficent, that could not be a substitute for a free and healthy national life'.

When the *Times* professed that 'the Indian Nationalist Movement is a pure product of racial hatred' and that 'to foment hatred is the only method of these Indian agitators and the sole object of their speeches and their writings' the retort of the *Bande Mataram* was lightning-swift:

> Our motives and our objects are at least as lofty and noble as those of Mazzini or of Garibaldi whose centenary the *Times* was hymning with such fervour a few days ago.... That the struggle to realise our ideal must bring with it temporary strife, misunderstanding, hostility, disturbance, that in short, it is bound to be a struggle and not the billing and cooing of political doves, we have never attempted to deny.... If England chooses to feel aggrieved by our nation-building, and obstruct it by unjust, violent or despotic means, it is she who is the aggressor and guilty of exciting hatred and ill-feeling.

Aurobindo primarily intended his articles for the Indian middle class, for 'everything depends on the success or failure of the middle class in getting the people to follow it for a common salvation'. Aware of the fears caused by the hysterical propaganda, he strove to offer reassurances:

> [This movement] is not a negative current of destruction, but a positive, constructive impulse towards the making of modern India. It is not a cry of revolt and despair, but a gospel of national faith and hope. Its true description is not Extremism, but Democratic Nationalism.

The middle class needed to dispel its illusions about the approach to independence. Its first illusion was to expect India's resurgence to result miraculously and painlessly from British democratic values.

> For a subject people, there is no royal road to emancipation. They must wade to it through struggle, sacrifice, slaughter, if necessary. History suggests no short-cut.

A second illusion stemmed from the belief that ethical and religious observances might bring about the country's renaissance and deliver independence by dint of earnest moral practices. This idea (which would reach its height under Gandhi) was particularly attractive to a gentle and peaceful people, predisposed to religious fervour, but it was yet another chimera, and Aurobindo insisted that....

> .... Politics is the work of the Kshatriya [warrior] and it is the virtues of the Kshatriya we must develop if we are to be morally fit for freedom.

A third illusion was to expect freedom to derive from economic prosperity. For Aurobindo, it was neither by the virtues and methods of the priest nor 'by the virtues and methods of the Vaishya (merchant) that we shall finally win our independence'.

Against the Swadeshi

New communal clashes had broken out in East Bengal. At Mymensingh, Dewangunj and Jamalpur, the same scenario repeated itself: a Swadeshi Hindu rally was attacked by a Muslim mob incited by an external leader. Although the aggression was clearly premeditated, the authorities did nothing to prevent it and even less to protect the Hindu activists from the robbery and violence that ensued. Within a few weeks, several villages were looted, temples desecrated, and women raped. Many serious injuries were reported. A number of men were brutally murdered. Once order had been partially restored, it was the turn of the courts to step in: Swadeshi activists were usually found guilty of inciting violence, while Muslim cut-throats were released. In this eastern region of Bengal, the government strategy thus worked flawlessly. While the Partition had been felt as an affront by Hindus and Muslims alike, the two communities were now divided by bitterness and anger. Still, Aurobindo refused to be fooled:

> There is no doubt considerable resentment against men like Nawab Salimullah for fomenting the disturbances; but there is no deep-seated resentment against the low-class Mahomedans who are merely the tools of men who themselves keep safely under cover. The fight is not a fight between Hindus and Mahomedans but between the bureaucrats and Swadeshists.

In the rest of the country, Swadeshi agitation had begun to spread to other provinces. In plague-prone Punjab, farmers also protested against the new water rates, and riots broke out in Lahore and Rawalpindi. Sikh troops were rumoured to want to defect. A panicked provincial governor requested and obtained deportation orders for Ajit Singh, the peasant leader, and Lala Lajpat Rai, a nationalist member of Congress. Both were imprisoned on 9 May and deported to Burma without trial. During the night, Aurobindo was awakened by a telegram informing him of their arrest. He immediately took up his pen:

> Lala Lajpat Rai has been deported out of British India. The fact is its own comment.... The bureaucracy has thrown down the gauntlet. We take it up. Men of the Punjab! Race of the lion! Show these men who would stamp you into the dust that for one Lajpat they have taken away, a hundred Lajpats will arise in his place. Let them hear a hundred times louder your war-cry – *Jai Hindusthan!* (Victory to India)

The time of repression had come. Aurobindo even deemed it logical that the government should react strongly against the Nationalists: it was proof that the threat was serious, that the Swadeshi protest had reached its goal. More than ever, his own role was to expound the government's strategy so everyone knew what to expect.

The authorities had resolved to crack down on the Swadeshi campaign. By unleashing mobs of Muslim thugs on Hindu militants in Bengal, they had managed to quell dissent in several districts. However, Aurobindo anticipated that the long-term strategy against Swadeshi would be to attack its means of propagation: the political platform, the young and the press.

Bipin Chandra, who had undertaken an extensive speaking tour in the southern provinces of Madras, Orissa and Andhra Pradesh, narrowly escaped Lala Lajpat Rai's fate. From London, Secretary Morley himself had to veto repeated appeals for Bipin's deportation from the Governor of Madras, panicking at the sight of the huge crowds eager to hear the charismatic speaker.

The government strategists also targeted the young. By issuing the Risley Circular, which muzzled political contestation in the educational system, the British showed they had grasped the importance of the issue: high school students were forbidden to attend political rallies, older students were prohibited from assembling and their teachers banned from discussing patriotism in classrooms.

Undaunted, Aurobindo continued to chronicle the government's repression. When a new decree against public gatherings was issued to add to the government's coercive arsenal, he asked:

> What will be our next course? The question is whether we shall persist in carrying on our movement rigidly within the pale of the law... or follow the example of the Irish by passive resistance to the law itself.

Against the Press

On 7 June 1907, a notice was served upon the *Bande Mataram* that the Governor of Bengal was reviewing certain articles 'the language of which is a direct incitement to violence and breach of the peace'. The threat was implicit. However, it took more than this to impress Aurobindo: 'The question of complying or not complying with the warning does not arise. We merely note it and pass on.' Redoubling his condemnation of the government's duplicity against Hindu and Muslim communities, he held up to ridicule the 'Comic Opera Reforms' concocted by Secretary Morley. With biting humour, he urged his countrymen to rise to a spirit of fervent idealism:

> We cannot sufficiently admire the vigorous and unselfish efforts of the British government to turn all India into a nation of Extremists. We had thought that it would take us long and weary years to convert all our countrymen to the nationalist creed. Nothing of the kind. The Government of India is determined that our efforts shall not fail or take too long a time to reach fruition. It will not suffer us to preach Nationalism to the people, but in its noble haste and zeal is resolved to preserve the monopoly of the nationalist propaganda to itself.

On 1 July, police stormed the *Yugantar* premises. Enjoined to name the newspaper's editor, the young man on duty that evening brainlessly boasted that he was the head of the publication. Four days later, he was arrested, charged with sedition and imprisoned.

Panicking in his cell, he pathetically tried to retract his confession by claiming to have been abused by these 'Swadeshi agitators'. In an instant, the credibility of the entire movement threatened to collapse, especially as young Bhupendranath Dutt was none other than Vivekananda's own brother. Fortunately, Aurobindo could persuade him to summon his courage by suggesting a line of defence more in keeping with his ideals. At his trial, he refused to plead his innocence but read the statement Aurobindo had prepared for him:

> I am solely responsible for all the articles in question. I have done what I have considered in good faith to be my duty by my country. I do not wish the prosecution to be put to the trouble and expense of proving what I have no intention to deny. I do not wish to make any other statement or to take any further action in the trial.

It was the first time a political defendant challenged the competence of a British court in India. The case caused a sensation. On 24 July, Bhupendranath was sentenced to one year forced labour. He became a national hero, and the *Yugantar's* prestige soared.

On 30 July, six days after Bhupendranath's sentence, a police squad descended on the cramped offices of the *Bande Mataram*. Noting that the police inspector did not have an arrest warrant, the editor on duty refused to answer his questions. After searching the premises for several hours, the police left with their paper harvest. Inspectors would spend two weeks sifting through their catch in the hope of establishing Aurobindo's editorial responsibility. Despite the lack of hard evidence, an arrest warrant was issued against him.

On 16 August, at dinner time, Aurobindo learnt that a police officer had shown up at the *Bande Mataram* offices with an arrest warrant. In consultation with his lawyer friends, he decided to give himself up. At the police station, he was formally charged and released on bail. The next day, the Calcutta Commissioner of Police served him notice to appear before the Chief Presidency Magistrate, Judge Kingsford, on 26 August.

In Calcutta, the news of his indictment spread like wildfire. All newspapers, including those which had not spared their criticism against the *Bande Mataram*, vied with each other in testifying to Aurobindo's patriotic feelings and lack of personal ambition. The *Indian Patriot* was the most lavish in its praise:

> Mr Aurobindo Ghose is no notoriety hunter, is no demagogue who wants to become prominent by courting conviction for sedition. A man of very fine culture, his is a loveable nature; merry, sparkling with wit and humour, he is one of those men to be in whose company is a joy and behind whose exterior is a steadily glowing fire of unseen devotion to a cause.

No one expressed Bengal's emotion better than the poet Rabindranath Tagore:

> *Rabindranath, O Aurobindo, bows to thee!*
> *O friend, my country's friend, O voice incarnate, free,*
> *Of India's soul!...*
> *When I behold thy face, 'mid bondage, pain and wrong*
> *And black indignities, I hear the soul's great song....*

Before standing trial, Aurobindo resigned from the National College, delivering a short farewell address to the college students:

> In the meeting you held yesterday, I see that you expressed sympathy with me in what you call my present troubles. I don't know whether I should call them troubles at all, for the experience that I am going to undergo was long foreseen as inevitable in the discharge of the mission that I have taken up from my childhood, and I am approaching it without regret....

As the trial opened on 26 August, the prosecutor had to demonstrate the seditious nature of the *Bande Mataram* articles as well as prove that Aurobindo was, in reality, its editor-in-chief. He was in the same frustrated condition as the Calcutta *Statesman* thundering against the *Bande Mataram's* articles:

> .... too diabolically clever, crammed full of sedition between the lines, but legally unassailable because of the skill of the language.

Confronted with this challenge and to make his case credible, the prosecutor fell back upon the English reprint of two subversive pieces already published in the *Yugantar*. In the absence of physical proof, however, he found it impossible to associate Aurobindo with the articles in question.

Rather than conceding defeat, the prosecutor then called in the *Bande Mataram* founder and original editor, Bipin Chandra Pal. But Bipin refused to testify against Aurobindo. Held in contempt of court, he was convicted by summary trial and sentenced to six months in jail.

In the end, the prosecutor could only give vent to his frustration: 'I do not care whether Aurobindo is the editor or not. I submit that he is the newspaper itself!'

For reprinting the two *Yugantar* articles, the *Bande Mataram* was condemned in the person of its printer, a frontman who had knowingly accepted this role. Judge Kingsford refuted any seditious character in the general tone of the newspaper. In acquitting Aurobindo, he noted that this is 'a man of exceptionally good attainments who had differentiated himself from the ordinary staff by refusing to take any fixed salary for his labour'.

The news of Aurobindo's acquittal was celebrated throughout the country. Rabindranath Tagore was one of the first to congratulate him, adding in jest, 'What! How you have deceived me!' Smiling, Aurobindo replied: 'Not for long.'

1907–1908: The Breakup

The Silent Man

The *Bande Mataram* trial propelled Aurobindo to centre stage.

> I was never ardent about fame... it was the confounded British government that spoiled my game by prosecuting me and forcing me to be publicly known as a 'leader'.

In the absence of Bipin Chandra, who was serving his sentence ('the maximum penalty permitted by the law for the crime of possessing a conscience'), Aurobindo became the *de facto* leader of the Nationalists in Bengal. He now had to prepare his camp for the forthcoming session of Congress, where the Moderates, who had lost ground in Calcutta, would seek to regain the advantage.

This time, on paper at least, the nationalist side had the upper hand. Tilak had every chance of being elected president. His party held the majority in Nagpur, where this next Congress was to convene. Sensing danger, the Nagpur Moderates called their Bombay supreme leaders to the rescue. Pherozeshah Mehta (head of the Congress in Bombay) summoned the Central Executive Committee in the presence of the British Commissioner of Police and decided there and then to move the Congress from Nagpur to Surat, where the moderates still held a majority. In the *Bande Mataram*, Aurobindo protested vehemently:

> If you will not allow us a place in the assembly you call National, we will make one for ourselves out of it and around it, until one day you will find

> us knocking at your doors with the nation at our back and in the name of an authority even you will not dare to deny.

At the beginning of December, as a preview of what was to follow, Bengali Nationalists and Moderates assembled at Midnapore (East Bengal) to map out the Surat Congress. But after electing a president of their choice, the Moderates refused to table the issue of Swaraj (autonomy) despite the petition of the young Nationalists. The lathis came out of hiding, and the assembly was thrown into chaos. As the president turned to Aurobindo and begged him to restore calm, he remained stolid. The Moderates were forced to cancel the debate and move to another venue.

It was unprecedented: the Moderate machine had lost its ability to keep control over ebullient youths who proclaimed their existence and their rejection of politics as usual. The modest provincial conference of Midnapore marked a turning point. 'The nationalist organisation is now an accomplished fact.... Midnapore has taken the initiative in giving nationalism an organised shape and form,' predicted Aurobindo in the *Bande Mataram*.

In Calcutta, the name of the man who had emerged victorious from a confrontation with British justice was on everyone's lips. People had divined that Aurobindo was the mastermind behind the push for freeing the country from the foreign yoke. Visitors lined up at Subodh Mallik's house to see him. On 15 December, he spoke in public and outlined the nationalist agenda.

The *Manchester Guardian* requested an interview. The journalist described Aurobindo as: 'Grave with intensity, careless of fate or opinion, and one of the most silent men I have ever known. He was of the stuff that dreamers are made of, but dreamers who will act out their dreams, indifferent to the means.'

Before travelling to Surat, where a decisive confrontation laid before him, Aurobindo confided to Mrinalini:

> At present I have not got a moment to spare; the burden of writing is on me, the burden of works regarding the Congress is on me, and also that of settling the affairs of *Bande Mataram*. I can hardly cope with the work. Besides I have my own work (yoga) to do which I cannot neglect … the pressure from all sides is enough to drive one mad.

The Surat Congress: The Breakup

On the morning of 21 December 1907, a special train packed with Bengali militants set out for Surat. On board were Aurobindo and his brother Barin, the complete staff of the *Bande Mataram* and an army of young nationalist volunteers.

The train took longer than expected to reach its destination because of the many stops caused by crowds eager to look in the face of their new hero. At each stop, men shouting 'Bande Mataram' searched first-class cars, then second, finally to locate their man in a third-class compartment, a broad smile on his face. Occasionally, Aurobindo stepped down onto the tracks to say a few words, and invariably he was wreathed with garlands before the train left again. The secretary of the Moderate Party (who travelled first class) tried unsuccessfully to draw Aurobindo beside him. At Bombay, a large meeting had been organised, and in the human wave converging onto the square to greet Aurobindo, Barin saw 'the awakening of the whole nation from its age-long sleep and inertia into conscious life'.

Finally, on 24 December, they reached Surat. An air of festivity presided over the *pandal* (central pavilion). Swarms of servants hastened between the luxurious tents sheltering the moderate dignitaries while the Nationalists crowded into houses, dormitories and makeshift shelters in the city centre. Tilak and Aurobindo finalised their party strategy without paying too much attention to admirers streaming through the house in the hope of catching a glance of them together.

The final delegate count stood at 1,100 for the Nationalists against 1,300 for the Moderates. But rumours had circulated that the Moderates would take advantage of their narrow majority to modify the Congress constitution so as to prevent an extremist takeover in the years to come. For the young Nationalists, the Congress presidency should be conferred, if not to Tilak, then at least to Lala Lajpat Rai, who had just been released from jail in Burma. If they could not impose their presidential choice by the numbers, they had decided to break up the Congress.

Tilak was soon informed that, on Gokhale's orders and in disregard of rules, the draft resolutions on which the Congress was to vote would not be available to delegates before the plenary session. This clearly suggested that the Moderates were planning to renege on the positions conceded at the previous Congress session in Calcutta.

All nationalist attempts to enter into private discussions with the Moderates were haughtily rejected by the latter.

On the second day's afternoon, 10,000 people crowded into the pandal to inaugurate the 23rd plenary Congress session. As moderate officials ascended the rostrum to endorse the new preselected moderate president, Tilak finally received a copy of the draft resolutions. As he feared, all the Calcutta political advances had been cancelled. When Surendranath Banerjee, the Bengali moderate leader, moved to the rostrum, loud cries arose from the Nationalists' ranks. 'Remember Midnapore! Remember Nagpur!' The session was suspended.

The next day was decisive. The young Nationalists had informed Aurobindo of their intention to break up the Congress if they could not obtain a fair hearing. However, they would wait for his signal before throwing down the gauntlet.

At 1 pm, the pandal was overflowing, and Aurobindo was sitting in the front row, surrounded by a dozen young Bengalis. Tilak had sent word to the officials that he wished to address the

Congress before the inaugural speech of the designated president, Moderate Rash Behari Ghose. But as he approached the rostrum, the president, pretending to ignore him, launched into his speech. Facing the crowd, his arms broadly upon his chest, Tilak demanded to be heard and confronted the henchmen rushing up to restrain him. Aurobindo gave the signal. The young Nationalists rose as one. A red shoe with a metal tip took flight, ricocheted on a Moderate dignitary and hit Pherozeshah Mehta. The assembly was thrown into chaos. Moderate leaders fled precipitately. Aurobindo was escorted out of the compound. The session of Surat was suspended sine die. The Congress had broken up.

Aurobindo expected the breakup to free the pent-up energy and bolster the desire for independence. As for the British government, they had envisioned the breakup and were preparing for merciless repression against the Nationalists.

The next day, under police protection, the Moderate leaders improvised a custom-made 'Convention'. Henceforth, each delegate to this new version of Congress was to sign a 'credo' of allegiance to the principles of British-inspired liberalism. Aurobindo and the young Nationalists refused to sign. Tilak hesitated but eventually sided with his friends. The principle of 'direct democracy' had stamped out the Congress system with its secret conclaves and fabricated majorities.

Aurobindo had been correct in his assessment: the nationalist sentiment was gradually to prevail as the dominant political force in India—despite the repression of its militants.

The new Moderates' Convention would not endure the test of time, its membership dwindling year after year. Eight years later, in 1916, returning to his country after a long ordeal of deportation in Burma, Tilak would resuscitate the Congress into a shelter of nationalism devoted to India's complete independence. Ultimately, the Moderate Party was renamed 'Liberal' and committed to the goal of independence.

The balance of power had shifted. The Nationalist Party was now a political entity of its own. The three days in Surat, which mark such a dramatic departure in India's political emancipation, are barely mentioned in history books. Aurobindo's role is ignored, for it is only 40 years later, in a private letter, that he mentions giving the signal that provoked the breakup.

Nirvana

On 1 January 1908, in the morning, the train bringing Aurobindo and Barin back from Surat entered Baroda station.

Friends, students and many unknown well-wishers awaited Aurobindo as he stepped out of his compartment. The young men clutched the carriage transporting the two brothers and escorted them to the residence of Khaserao Jadhav.

A visitor was awaiting them: Vishnu Bhaskar Lele, a yogi whom Barin had met while searching for a master to chaperone his project of warrior monks. Lele was a simple civil servant, but his eyes glowed with the evidence of an inner life.

Aurobindo informed him about his practice of pranayama and the results he had attained until everything had stopped. Lele suggested that he should suspend all his outer activities and join him in meditation.

Aurobindo accepted, but not before reporting on the Surat events to the packed crowd of well-wishers camping on the lawns outside Khaserao's house. Then he made a courtesy call to his former employer, the Maharajah.

Finally, he joined Lele in a friend's townhouse and there, in a small room at the top, the two men sat facing each other on the floor.

> 'Sit in meditation,' he said, 'but do not think, look only at your mind; you will see thoughts coming into it; before they can enter, throw them away from you till your mind is capable of entire silence.' I had never heard

> before of thoughts coming visibly into the mind from outside, but I did not think of either questioning the truth or the possibility, I simply sat down and did it. In a moment, my mind became silent as a windless air on a high mountain summit and then I saw a thought and then another thought coming in a concrete way from outside; I flung them away before they could enter and take hold of the brain and in three days I was free.

These three days of meditation with Lele would provoke a radical change of consciousness. Ordinary reality had been abolished in what the Upanishads call the consciousness of the silent Brahman, and which Buddhism calls Nirvana. Years later, Aurobindo attempted to put words on this new sensory revelation.

> It threw me suddenly into a condition above and without thought, unstained by any mental or vital movement; there was no ego, no real world—only when one looked through the immobile senses, something perceived or bore upon its sheer silence a world of empty forms, materialized shadows without true substance. There was no One or many even, only just absolutely That, featureless, relationless, sheer, indescribable, unthinkable, absolute, yet supremely real and solely real. This was no mental realization nor something glimpsed somewhere above,—no abstraction—it was positive, the only positive reality—although not a spatial physical world, pervading, occupying or rather flooding and drowning this semblance of a physical world, leaving no room or space for any reality but itself, allowing nothing else to seem at all actual, positive or substantial.

After those three days, Aurobindo returned to his friends at Khaserao Jadhav's residence. He noticed that the silence endured effortlessly in him.

Inspired Political Appeals

Later in the month, he was invited to attend a series of political meetings and asked to address a 1,000-strong nationalist rally in Bombay. 'How am I going to speak? Not a single thought is coming to me,' he confided to Lele. Paradoxically, while he had approached Lele to liberate his inner energy for the service of his country, he had come upon this silence and the utter unreality of all human activities. 'Greet the Divine in the audience with a pranam,' advised Lele, 'and the speech will come to you from another source.'

Aurobindo stepped onto the podium and bowed to the audience, clasping his hands. A newspaper title flashed across his mind, and a voice—his own—started to speak.

His speech kept the audience in suspense for more than an hour. Words sprang from his mouth without disturbing the stillness abiding in him. 'The whole speech came down from above; not a single thought or expression was mine. It got hold of my organ of speech and expressed itself through it from beginning to end,' he would later recall. Exalting courage, disinterestedness, devotion to the Mother and confidence that a Divine Power was at work, he appealed to his compatriots to embrace nationalism as one embraced a religion.

His friends in Maharashtra did not want him to leave. After Bombay, he would speak at Nasik, Dhulia, Amravati… nine addresses in the same state of mental silence, in the same inspired vein, enthralled the crowds. Words came out slowly, distinctly, as he stood motionless, fascinating the audience with the hypnotic charm of his voice.

Before leaving Bombay, Lele had told Aurobindo: 'Surrender yourself to the Divine within and be guided by Him. If you can do that, you needn't do anything else.' Aurobindo was grateful to Lele for confirming what would become the rule of his life and the foundation of his yoga:

> To put himself entirely into the hands of the Divine within and move only as he was moved.

1908: The Bhagavad Gita

Silence

A letter from Mrinalini awaited Aurobindo as he arrived in Calcutta. She felt abandoned in Deoghar and expressed her impatience to return to a normal conjugal life. He answered her this sibylline note:

> The state of my mind has at present undergone a change; about that I would not reveal in this letter. Come here, then I will tell you what I have to say. The only thing that can be stated for the moment is that henceforward I am no longer subject to my own will.

Mrinalini and the faithful Sarojini joined him in a newly rented house at 23 Scott's Lane. It was spacious enough to accommodate, besides his wife and sister, the indispensable Abinash, who took up again his butler-cum-aide-de-camp duties with his customary dedication. Aurobindo returned to his teaching at the National College, perhaps to earn some money, and resumed his articles for the *Bande Mataram*. He devoted several hours a day to yoga, receiving occasional visitors, before returning to his silence as soon as they had departed. Abinash watched over the household, managed everyday necessities, and borrowed from the *Bande Mataram* treasurer to supplement the College's meagre pay.

Aurobindo's writing now flowed from complete silence:

> It gets done without any thought entering my mind or the silence being in the least disturbed or diminished.

One day, as one of his colleagues requested the next editorial, Aurobindo, who had not prepared anything, took up a piece of paper and began to write. 'In this silence that supports the stars,' his words opened up unexpected connections between the convulsions of politics and the hieratic immobility of 'That' which abided within him. Fifteen minutes later, he handed over the article. He had not stopped once to think, to cross out words or to revise his page.

Violence and Meditation

At the end of February, Lele arrived in Calcutta with a disciple. They stayed at Scott's Lane, and Abinash recorded in his notebook the effect of this arrival on the meals' frugality. The lunch of rice and lentils was replaced by a boiled potato or a green banana served with a handful of rice. The men observed the day of *puja* by fasting and visiting Ramakrishna's monastery at Belur Math, or they called at the temple of Kalighat to have the *darshan* of Goddess Kali. The household readily complied with this observance of sobriety. Lele asked Aurobindo if he had pursued his recommendations of following the inner voice and meditating twice a day:

> When I told him that I had given up meditation—in fact the meditation was going on all the time—he said, 'Ah, the devil has got hold of you.' He did not wait for me to explain anything to him. Since then, we began to follow our own separate ways.

It was Barin who had requested Lele's presence in Calcutta as he hoped to secure his spiritual guidance for his community at Maniktala Garden.

Owing to the recent government repression, the recruiting at the Garden had made swift progress, and the dozen or so recruits had become hardened. They were making bombs, and Barin plotted to assassinate Governor Fraser, who had replaced Governor Fuller. However, because of their clumsiness and failed detonators, he and his comrades had to make several attempts before the governor's train finally hit the charge of dynamite destined for him. On 5 December 1907, near Narayangarth in East Bengal, the blast lifted the locomotive in the air... without causing the train derailment. Unharmed, the governor stepped down onto the track to examine the damage and order an investigation.

Frustrated by this attempt, three group members—Ullaskar Dutt (former chemistry student and pyrotechnician), Hemchandra Das (just back from Europe with the latest bomb-making technology) and Prafulla—had tested a new explosive mixture with picric acid, which was lighter and more manageable than dynamite. Prafulla was accorded the honour of throwing the test bomb onto a massive rock below the hilltop they had selected. But the mixture, more unstable than expected, exploded in mid-air, gravely wounding Ullaskar and killing Prafulla on the spot.

It took no time for Lele to realise what kind of sports Barin and his friends practised. He cautioned that yoga and bomb worship were incompatible, that bloodthirsty violence was contradictory to the heart's purification sought by yoga, as it alienates man from his soul, from his spiritual destiny. However desirable India's liberation might be, it should take place peacefully, without bloodshed, Lele insisted.

The young men sneered. What! The occupying British would pack their bags of their own accord, without objection and without being impelled to do so—depart India as peaceful gentlemen? Who would swallow such a tale? The boys regarded themselves as devotees of the cult of force, worshippers of Kali, the terrible Mother with her garland of human skulls, and not as disciples of the god of love. 'If you do not abandon your project,' Lele warned them, 'you will run into a terrible catastrophe.'

Aurobindo knew what was brewing at the Maniktala Garden. Barin made frequent visits to Scott's Lane to keep his brother informed of his plans, and he even stored weapons in the house. Aurobindo tempered the most imprudent initiatives of his younger brother but did not put a stop to his activities.

In fact, in the *Bande Mataram*, he stated unequivocally:

> We should be absolutely unsparing in our attack on whatever obstructs the growth of the nation, and never be afraid to call a spade a spade.... Open attack, unsparing criticism, the severest satire, the most wounding irony, are all methods perfectly justifiable and indispensable in politics. We have strong things to say; let us say them strongly; we have stern things to do; let us do them sternly. But there is always a danger of strength degenerating into violence and sternness into ferocity, and that should be avoided so far as it is humanly possible.

The question of violence remained fundamental. The sacrifice of his life for India's liberation was a prerequisite he had long accepted, and his brother and the young recruits of the Garden had taken the same oath.

> This world of our battle and labour is a fierce dangerous destructive devouring world in which life exists precariously and the soul and body of man move among enormous perils, a world in which by every step forward, whether we will it or not, something is crushed and broken, in which every breath of life is a breath too of death.

Karmayoga

It was Krishna's teaching in the Bhagavad Gita which helped Aurobindo discover 'a higher Law by which the soul shall be free from this bondage of works and yet powerful to act and conquer in the vast liberty of its divine being'.

In the Gita, the symbolic backdrop of this realisation is the Kurukshetra battlefield, during the famous dialogue between

Krishna and his friend and disciple, Prince Arjuna. About to engage in a decisive battle for the future of the kingdom, Arjuna's self-confidence was shattered when he realised that he was required to kill the members of his clan and family. Overwhelmed, he put down his weapons and turned to Krishna, God incarnate among men, to besiege his help:

> Give me a true law, a clear rule of action, a path by which I can again confidently walk.

In time suspended on the battlefield, it is this rule of action that Krishna divulged to Arjuna:

> Abandon all laws of conduct and take refuge in Me alone; I will deliver you from all sin and evil; do not grieve.

This is the revelation of Karmayoga or yoga of Works. Through this yoga, Arjuna would then enter a consciousness liberated from the self-serving burden of the ego and become capable of following Krishna's directives.

> I am the eternal Worker within you and I ask of you works. I demand of you not a passive consent to a mechanical movement of Nature from which in yourself you are wholly separated, indifferent and aloof, but action complete and divine, done as the willing and understanding instrument of the Divine, done for God in you and others and for the good of the world.

Like Arjuna, Aurobindo surrendered his will to this inner Divine who whispered *another* way of feeling, *another* way of acting upon reality. All his activities became subject to a Will other than his own. In the state of receptive passivity of the Self, he learned to live the divine Omniscience in all circumstances.

Violence and Destruction

The Gita approaches violence and destruction in association with progress; by this singularly daring teaching, it seeks to integrate a difficult conflicting truth within the evolutionary march of humanity. Aurobindo's vision justifies it:

> We have to look courageously in the face of the reality and see that it is God and none else who has made this world in his being AND THAT SO HE HAS MADE IT. We have to see that Nature devouring her children, Time eating up the lives of creatures, Death universal and ineluctable and the violence of the Rudra forces in man and Nature are also the supreme Godhead in one of his cosmic figures. We have to see that God the bountiful and prodigal creator, God the helpful, strong and benignant preserver is also God the devourer and destroyer.... The discords of the worlds are God's discords and it is only by accepting and proceeding through them that we can arrive at the greater concords of his supreme harmony, the summits and thrilled vastnesses of his transcendent and his cosmic Ananda (felicity).

Hence, for Aurobindo, being conscious begins by refusing 'to put away the responsibility for all that seems evil or terrible on the shoulders of a semi-omnipotent Devil or to put it aside as part of Nature ... or to throw the responsibility on man and his sins, as if he had a preponderant voice in the making of this world or could create anything against the will of God'.

Is this law of violence and destruction forever part and parcel of our human evolution? Is it an inescapable constituent of life, or only an evolutionary necessity, which will disappear like the gills of the fish when they emerged from the water?

> No real peace can be till the heart of man deserves peace; the law of Vishnu cannot prevail till the debt to Rudra (the god of violence) is paid. To turn aside then and preach to a still unevolved mankind the law of love and oneness? Teachers of the law of love and oneness there must be, for by that way must come the ultimate salvation. But not till the

> Time-Spirit in man is ready, can the inner and ultimate prevail over the outer and immediate reality. Christ and Buddha have come and gone, but it is Rudra who still holds the world in the hollow of his hand.

Fatal Explosion

On 28 April 1908, Aurobindo moved his family to 48 Gray Street. The *Bande Mataram* came out in a new format. Its editor warned of impending perils:

> The times are thickening already with the shadow of a great darkness. The destruction of the Congress, begun at Surat, is the prelude for the outburst of the storm that has long been brewing. Great issues were involved in that historic struggle at Surat of which none of the actors were aware.... Revolution, bare and grim, is preparing her battlefield.... We could have wished it otherwise, but God's will be done.

As if to support this forecast, the new 'Moderate Convention' meeting in Allahabad rejected any form of association with the Nationalists. They confirmed the Surat breakup. After a brief debate with his associates, Pherozeshah Mehta had prevailed over 'the feeble patriotism and wavering will of the Bengal Moderates'.

> The entire moderate party have agreed to betray the mandate of their country and the future of their people.... No Nationalist henceforth can consent to seek reconciliation with them or clasp the hand that has sold the country for a foreign hire.... The day of compromises is past.

At the Maniktala Garden, despite their pyrotechnic failures, Barin and his group continued to hope that their fortune would turn. Since Governor Fraser was now on his guard, a new target had been found in the person of Judge Kingsford. His decision to acquit Aurobindo appeared to be an exception in a magistracy marked by clear-cut support for the government's repressive strategy. This judge had sentenced nationalist journalists to heavy prison terms and ordered the public flogging of a young Bengali man guilty of disrupting his courtroom by shouting *Bande Mataram*. To kill him, the pyro-technicians of the Garden had hidden a small bomb in a thick legal volume that one of them, disguised as a deliveryman, came to hand over to his servant. The judge, undoubtedly overworked, never found the time to open his 'present'. That was fortunate, for the charge of picric acid would have left him no chance.

For some time now, Barin had been preoccupied with the furtive presences lurking around the Garden and near his brother's house in Calcutta. The group had been found out. Their many attempts against Governor Fraser had allowed the CID to identify them. The government knew of the Maniktala Garden, Barin was followed everywhere, and Aurobindo's house was watched day and night. The Calcutta chief of police had been ordered not to intervene: the suspects had to be caught red-handed.

Fearing for Judge Kingsford's life, the government had transferred him 400 miles north of Calcutta and assigned four policemen to keep watch over him. In Muzaffarpur, the judge had resumed his activities at the district court and reorganised his library—still without opening his 'present'. Barin then decided to take action. At the end of April, he sent two of his men to reconnoitre Muzaffarpur.

On 29 April, carrying a bomb loaded with dynamite, Khudiram Bose and Prafulla Chaki hid outside the clubhouse where Judge Kingsford and his wife played bridge with the wife and daughter of a local barrister.

When the game was over, the porter called the two coaches in front of the club entrance. The two ladies got into the first coach, which started off and passed in front of the thicket where the two men were hiding. Khudiram ran up and threw his bomb through the open window. It exploded instantly, mortally wounding the two passengers.

In the confusion that ensued, the two assassins fled separately. Khudiram walked all night to the nearest train station. Spotted in the early morning by two gendarmes, he was escorted back to Muzaffarpur, where he confessed to being the bomb thrower. Prafulla was arrested the next day on a train to Calcutta. He pulled out a revolver and fired at the policemen, then turned his arm and shot himself in the head.

Two days later, on 1 May 1908, Aurobindo learnt in a daily newspaper that Police Chief Halliday knew the identity of the perpetrators of the failed assassination against Judge Kingsford. As a precaution, he instructed Barin to remove the weapons from Maniktala Garden and to burn compromising papers. Barin concealed his weapons and explosives with regret, then burned a few papers before falling soundly asleep.

1908–1909: Alipore

Prison

At the beginning of May 1908, before dawn, Aurobindo was jolted from his sleep by the screams of Sarojini rushing into his bedroom. She was pursued by a man with a handgun. The house of Gray Street swarmed with policemen, 35 in all, including several British officers. While a very shocked Mrinalini retreated with her sister-in-law, Aurobindo confronted the police officer wielding a search warrant.

Seven other police squads stormed the homes of Aurobindo's and Barin's close friends and relations in Calcutta. Explosives were discovered at relatives of Ullaskar's (the group's pyro technician), and a manual for bomb-making was found at Hemchandra Das's.

At Maniktala Garden, Barin, romantically assuming that he could protect his comrades and his elder brother by claiming to be the solely responsible leader for the group's activities, led the police to the cache of arms and explosives.

Handcuffed and with a rope around his waist, Aurobindo was taken to police headquarters, where Abinash and the *Bande Mataram* staff were already in custody. The police harvest on this first day was bountiful: 33 suspects apprehended, thousands of documents and many weapons seized.

Aurobindo had often envisioned this situation, but the brutality of the arrest disconcerted him:

> When I was arrested and hurried to the Lal Bazar Hajat (police headquarters), I was shaken in faith for a while, for I could not look into

> the heart of His intention. Therefore I faltered for a moment and cried out in my heart to Him, 'What is this that has happened to me?'

After three days of questioning, he was indicted. Suspected to be the real leader of the terrorist group, he was transferred to Alipore Jail, the vast, notorious penitentiary south of Calcutta, and kept in solitary confinement. The seriousness of the charges against him had precluded any possibility of bail.

A 50-square-foot cell, a metal gate with bars overlooking a tiny courtyard encircled by high walls, no window, two coarse blankets, a small bowl with which to drink, eat, wash and two baskets coated with bitumen as toilet facilities, constituted his new world. His days were now punctuated by morning ablutions in the courtyard, three meals of *lafsi* (rice gruel) and a changing of the guard, to whom he had to answer to confirm his presence.

Lessons of God

Alone in his small cell, Aurobindo experienced the endless hours of solitary confinement:

> In this solitary prison, not having anything else to do, I tried to meditate for a longer period. But for those unaccustomed, it is not easy to control and steady the mind pulled in a thousand directions. Somehow I was able to concentrate for an hour and a half or two, later the mind rebelled while the body too was fatigued. At first, the mind was full of thoughts of many kinds. Afterwards, devoid of human conversation and an insufferable listlessness due to the absence of any subject of thought, the mind gradually grew devoid of the capacity to think.

Time hung heavily. Even the power of transcendence of Nirvana could do nothing to alleviate the despotism of this materially stupid brain activity. There was a condition when it seemed a

1,000 confused ideas were hovering around the doors of the mind but with gates closed; one or two that were able to get through were frightened by the silence of these mental states and quietly ran away. In this dull uncertain state, he suffered intense mental agony. But one afternoon....

> .... as I was thinking, streams of thoughts began to flow endlessly and then suddenly grew so uncontrolled and incoherent that I felt that the mind's regulating power was about to end. Afterwards, when I came back to myself, I could recollect that though the power of mental control had ceased, the intelligence was not self-lost or did not deviate for a moment, but it was as if watching this marvellous phenomenon quietly. But at the time, shaking with the terror of being overcome by insanity, I had not been able to notice that.

This latter realisation had objectified his experience: his real self was not going mad at all but simply enjoying the phenomenon that was happening to him.

> Then I called upon God with eagerness and intensity and prayed to him to prevent my loss of intelligence. That very moment, there spread over my being such a gentle and cooling breeze, the heated brain became relaxed, smooth and supremely blissful such as in all my life I had never known before. Just as a child sleeps, secure and fearless, on the lap of his mother, so I remained on the lap of the World-Mother. From that day, all my troubles of prison life were over.

It was the first 'lesson' he received from God.

> Afterwards, on many occasions during the period of detention, there arose signs of anxiety, moments of mental unease due to the lack of activity, bodily trouble or perturbations in the lean periods of yogic life, but that day, in a single moment God had given my inner being such a strength that these sorrows as they came and went did not leave any

> trace or touch on the mind. Relishing strength and delight in the sorrow itself, the mind was able to reject these subjective sufferings.

Henceforth, Aurobindo understood that his yoga practices would not be accomplished through personal effort and that a spirit of reverence and complete self-surrender were the paths to attaining perfection in yoga. He was to accept and utilise whatever realisation the Lord would give out of His benignity.

What he called 'his' yoga would then become contingent upon the giving up of all human frailties to the Divine. To abdicate the workings of ordinary nature so that the Divine use them and convert them as He pleased—such was the endeavour Aurobindo would pursue in all fields of existence: mental, vital and physical. He aimed at renouncing the ego. The reversal of consciousness he had just experienced in the most obscure and constricted mental consciousness laid the foundation of all the transformations to come. It was the cardinal event of his yoga.

Krishna

Ten days after his incarceration, Aurobindo was allowed to write to his family to request some personal effects and his books— most importantly, the Gita and the Upanishads. Thanks to the intervention of the prison doctor, he was also permitted two daily walks in the courtyard beyond his door.

> Travelling to and fro, I would recite the deeply moving, immortal, powerful mantras of the Upanishads, or, watching the movements and activities of the prisoners, I tried to realise the basic truths of the immanent Godhead, God in every form. In the trees, the houses, the walls, in men, animals, birds, metals, the earth, with the help of the mantra: *All this is the Brahman*, I would try to fix or impose that realisation on all of these. As I went on doing like this, sometimes the prison ceased to appear to be a prison at all. The high wall, those iron bars, the white

> wall, the green-leaved tree shining in sunlight—it seemed as if these commonplace objects were not unconscious at all, but that they were vibrating with a universal consciousness, they loved me and wished to embrace me, or so I felt. Once in a while, it seemed as if Krishna Himself was standing under the tree, playing upon his Flute of Delight and, with his sheer charm, drawing my very soul out. The manifestation of these emotions overpowered my whole body and mind, a pure and wide peace reigned everywhere. The hard cover of my life opened up and a spring of love for all creatures gushed from within.

In his minuscule Indian jail cell, Aurobindo was beginning the yoga of Love or Bhakti Yoga, the third revelation of the Gita (after the yoga of Knowledge and the yoga of Works).

The Trial

On 18 May 1908, Aurobindo and more than two dozen co-defendants were transferred under escort to the Alipore courthouse. Barely out of the prison compound, the prisoners in the police van erupted in singing, joking and laughing; this joyous mood of the young rebels never abated during the long ordeal of the trial.

As they arrived at the tribunal, the contrast between the rigidity of the guards and mounted police, and the jovial carelessness of the youths walking barefoot, was striking. The reporter of the *Empire* could not hide his surprise: 'Not a soul of this gang seems to have the slightest concern!' he exclaimed in his article.

Suspected of 'rebellion to overthrow the government' and 'armed conspiracy against the King', the prisoners were taken to the courthouse every morning and returned to jail every evening after protracted hearings, which more often than not turned into agitated and abusive shouting matches between the judge, prosecutor, attorneys and witnesses.

This preliminary phase of the prosecution would last five months. It was supervised by Leonard Birley, a young and ambitious magistrate. The Crown was represented by prosecutor Norton, a veteran lawyer from Madras, who was assisted by a group of investigators. In order to charge each defendant, the prosecution had to sift through hundreds of testimonies, interview dozens of witnesses, and examine and sort through thousands of court exhibits.

Before resorting to such a costly process in human and material resources, the authorities had toyed with a simpler alternative for getting rid of Aurobindo: deportation. Andrew Fraser, the Governor of Bengal, had long pleaded the case for his banishment to Viceroy Minto:

> The man is able, cunning, fanatical. He is the leader. He has been in the forefront of all, advising seditious writing and authorising murder. But he has kept himself, like a careful and valued General, out of sight of the 'enemy'. We cannot get evidence against him, such as would secure his conviction in a court. But we have been fortunate enough to get papers which show his connection with the conspiracy, quite sufficient to convince the reasonable mind and justify deportation.

However, Minto had to take into account the impact that such a decision would have in Britain, especially after the criticism caused by the recent deportation of Lajpat Rai, the Punjabi nationalist leader. So Minto decided to dismiss his subordinate's pleas and trust his magistrates and his police to take down Aurobindo.

It was with an ironical distance that Aurobindo would later recount the legal proceedings:

> The nature of the case was a little strange. Magistrate, counsel, witnesses, evidence, exhibits, accused, all appeared a little *outré*. Watching, day after day, the endless stream of witnesses and exhibits, the Norton's unvaried dramatic performance, the boyish frivolity and

> light-heartedness of the youthful magistrate, looking at the amazing spectacle I often thought that instead of sitting in a British court of justice, we were inside a stage of some world of fiction.

Norton's endless harangues brought out his mockery:

> It was hard to admire his depth of legal acumen—which was as rare as winter in summer. But in the ceaseless flow of words, and through verbal quips, in the strange ability to transmute inconsequential witness into something serious, in the boldness of making groundless statements or statements with little ground, in riding roughshod over witnesses and junior barristers and in the charming ability to turn white into black, to see his incomparable genius in action was but to admire him.... He could create such a wonderful plot by his self-created and abundant suggestion, inference and hypothesis that the great poets and writers of fiction like Shakespeare and Defoe would have to acknowledge defeat before this grand master of the art. It gave me great happiness that Mr Norton had chosen me as the protagonist of this play.

Aurobindo was no less jocular towards the investigating Judge Birley:

> From the start, charmed by Mr Norton's learning and rhetoric, he had been completely under his spell. He would follow, so humbly, the road pointed out by Norton. Agreeing with his views, he laughed when Norton laughed, grew angry as Norton went angry. Looking at this daft childlike conduct, one sometimes felt tenderly and paternally towards him. Birley was exceedingly childlike. I could never think of him as a magistrate, it seemed as if a school student, suddenly turned teacher, was sitting at the teacher's high desk.

The proceedings would have been utterly boring had they not liven up by the heckling of the young defendants, their cajoling, outbursts and jokes—all of which ultimately pushed the judge to the edge: he threatened to chain them or, even worse, to suppress their meals. The young men then brought books and began reading Bankim Chatterjee's novels, the Gita.... The judge banned the books.

However, neither the power of the administrative juggernaut, nor the chains, nor the armed men guarding them, hindered the mood of the young men. What will remain in Indian memory will not be so much the solemn dramaturgy of the Alipore Bomb Trial as the happy faces of these young people. Aurobindo wrote:

> Looking at these lads, one felt as if the liberal, daring, puissant men of an earlier age with a different training had come back to India. That fearless and innocent look in their eyes, the words breathing power, their carefree delighted laughter, even in the midst of great danger, the undaunted courage, cheerfulness of mind, absence of despair or grief, all this was a symptom not of the inert Indians of those days, but of a new age, a new race and a new activity. If these were murderers, then one must say that the bloody shadow of killing had not fallen across their nature, in which there was nothing at all of cruelty, recklessness or bestiality. Without worrying in the least about the future or the outcome of the trial, they spent their days in prison with boyish fun, laughter, games, reading and in discussions. Quite early they had made friends with everyone, with officers, the sentries, convicts, European sergeants, detectives, court officials and without distinguishing between friends and enemies, high and low, had started to tell stories and jokes.

Their joyful vitality ultimately mollified the guards' suspicions. Body searches were routinely skipped; it was almost as guests in a summer camp that the prisoners were returned to their cells every evening. The prison visiting room became the scene of amiable encounters with friends and family, who brought fruit and sundry presents, among which were concealed weapons.

Silence and Yoga

Aurobindo's incarceration became somewhat more merciful. The authorities began showing small acts of kindness towards him. The prison deputy director and the chief medical officer stopped by almost daily 'for a little chat'. Every other day, the doctor had a milk ration sent from the infirmary to replace the animal grub served as a meal.

This current of sympathy towards a silent detainee requesting neither help nor favour was not due solely to his notoriety but, as he later explained in a letter to a disciple, to 'an instance in which the perception of the Divine in all, accompanied by an intense experience of universal love or a wide experience of an inner harmony had an extraordinary effect in making all around kind and helpful, even the most coarse and hard and cruel'.

Alipore turned out also to be an opportunity to feel a common bond with the poorest classes, this deep India, this Motherland for whom Aurobindo had dedicated his life:

> I had felt really happy that no discrimination had been made between the common uneducated masses and myself; moreover, this arrangement added fuel to the flame of my adoration of the Mother. I took it as a marvellous means and favourable condition for learning yoga and rising above conflicts. I was one of the extremists, in whose view democracy and equality between the rich and the poor formed a chief ingredient of nationalism.... During my stay in the Alipore Jail, I ate, lived, went through the same hardship and enjoyed the same privileges with the other convicts, my fellow nationals, the peasants, ironmonger, potter, the doms and the bagdis, and I could learn that the Lord who dwells in every body, this socialism and unity, this nationwide brotherhood had put its stamp on my life's dedication.

One of the boys, Naren Goswami, was particularly forward with Aurobindo, always seeking opportunities to talk to him and peppering him with questions. The curiosity of this tall, voluble fellow soon aroused suspicion. His comrades grilled him. Finally, he confessed that he had agreed to become a police informer in exchange for his release. He swore, however, that he merely intended to deceive the police by providing false information, which would ultimately confuse the prosecution and bankrupt the trial.

It soon transpired that his father, a well-to-do landowner, had also collaborated with the police to help in the release of his son. The principal issue was whether or not Goswami would corroborate Norton's thesis about Aurobindo's explicit role as the head of the conspiracy.

In mid-June, hearings were suspended while the prisoners were transferred to a large common cell. All were ecstatic at being reunited, singing and laughing long into the night. Aurobindo isolated himself as best he could. Withdrawn in a corner of the vast hall, he tried to preserve his poise, lest the company of others would affect the inner state of detachment and peace he had attained.

> I did not understand that for the fullness of my spiritual experience it was necessary to evoke opposite emotions, hence the Inner Guide suddenly deprived me of my dear solitude, and flung me into the stream of violent outward activity.

In the daytime, he worked on his Bengali or taught his companions about the concepts of British justice, coached them to reflect on morality and immorality in politics, and on anarchism and imperialism.... Sometimes, he even enjoyed impersonating Prosecutor Norton while Ullaskar (the pyrotechnician) imitated Judge Birley.

Outside of these lively exchanges, he remained in concentrated silence, which imposed a distance and respect, while the striking fixity of his black eyes seemed to contemplate a far-off world.

> 'When he smiles,' one of the young men commented, 'there is no muscle contraction like with us; the smile is in the eyes.'

They also noticed his shiny black hair, as if lustred in oil, while theirs dried up in the parched air of the prison. One of them gathered his courage:

> Do the guards give you oil in secret?

Aurobindo smiled:

> The practice of yoga has caused some bodily changes. My hair uses the fat directly from my body.

After his morning ablutions, Aurobindo maintained a headstand (*Salamba Sirsasana*) for several hours. One day, while in this posture, the Governor of Bengal made an unannounced visit. Receiving no reaction to his presence, he watched awhile and finally, after half an hour, left the room without uttering a word.

Sometimes, it seemed to the boys that Aurobindo's body was an independent, detachable object while he himself was 'elsewhere'. They remembered the particular occasion when, in an act of provocation, a huge Scottish Highlander had grabbed Aurobindo, thrown him across his shoulders and twirled him about with affected hilarity. Aurobindo had remained inert, without a trace of emotion or irritation—as if he were not the twirling body. The giant had then quickly stopped and rested him on the ground without a word.

Executions

The court hearings resumed after a one-week suspension. Norton triumphantly announced that Naren Goswami had agreed to become a prosecution witness in exchange for his pardon. His deposition would last until the first week of July. He narrated at length his enlistment in the secret society in 1906, his meeting with its leaders, Aurobindo and Jatin Banerjee, and the revolutionary activities in which he had taken part. He identified Aurobindo by pointing to him in the courtroom. He also disclosed the names of other hitherto unsuspected members of the conspiracy, who were immediately apprehended by the police.

As a man of action, Barin refused to accept that his destiny be determined by a police informer. Escape seemed to be the only answer to Goswami's betrayal. Some guns had been secured during the prison visits, and Barin had devised a plan of escape, even contemplating taking to the hills to raise an army and continue the fight. His enthusiasm had converted some of his comrades to his programme, but before implementing it, he had to inform his brother. Aurobindo listened quietly and replied that, for his part, he intended to face the trial.

On 13 August, the defendants were called up one by one to the bar to make a personal statement. Aurobindo abstained from any declaration. Most detainees did the same. The next day, following the customary procedure, two defence lawyers requested to cross-examine Naren Goswami, Norton's star witness. Pressed by the government to complete his hearings, which had already dragged on too long, the judge rejected their request. On 15 August, the lawyers tried again. Again, Birley refused to grant their request.

On this particular 15 August, Aurobindo celebrated his 36th birthday. All the inmates wore broad smiles on their faces. To the correspondent of the *Empire*, who did not conceal his astonishment at the defendants' joyous mood, one of them pointed to Aurobindo, whose face, 'hitherto grave and prepossessed, had been metamorphosed into one of sprightliness and sunniness'. To the intrigued reporter, Aurobindo explained that since 1906, his birthday had always coincided with important phases of India's march to Independence: from the inauguration of the National College to the trial of the *Bande Mataram*, and today, through these ongoing legal proceedings, the propagation of a revolutionary movement. 'You can add to those coincidences the fact that I shall very probably be coming back from the Andamans on my birthday next year,' he concluded with a facetious smile.

Finally, on 19 August, 31 defendants were formally charged with 'acts of war against the King'. On the basis of Goswami's testimony, Aurobindo was suspected of being one of the instigators of the conspiracy. It made him liable to lifetime deportation.

Pending the actual trial, the defendants were to be held in detention until the second batch of defendants (recently arrested on the basis of Goswami's denunciations) passed through Birley's court. All were returned to their cells, except for Goswami, who was transferred to the European Quarter to protect him from reprisals.

Unbeknownst to Aurobindo, the most determined of his companions had devised a plan to eliminate Goswami. They believed it had become vital to silence him, for he was rumoured to prepare a new denunciation of nationalist sympathisers. Satyen Bose, one of Aurobindo's relatives known for his experience with guns, would attract the traitor by offering to turn himself into a prosecution witness. On the morning of 31 August, Goswami agreed to leave the protection of the European Quarter to go to the prison hospital, where Satyen Bose, flanked by Kanailal Dutt, awaited him. The two prisoners were armed with revolvers. After a scuffle and a wild chase on the prison grounds, Goswami was shot and killed.

Pandemonium erupted at Alipore. Following a meticulous body search, all the prisoners were transferred to individual cells with nothing but the clothes on their backs. A squad of armed Highlanders was requisitioned to stand guard day and night with shoot-on-sight orders. Visits and articles from outside were prohibited, as were books and personal exchanges among prisoners.

Satyen Bose and Kanailal Dutt were deferred to a special Court of Justice. Before the judge, Kanailal, who had fired the deadly shot, acknowledged his role, invoking Goswami's betrayal to justify the execution. He was sentenced to hang and did not appeal the verdict. Satyen, initially exonerated by a mixed jury, was also sentenced to the gallows after the public prosecutor obtained the review of his trial before a higher court.

In October, Kanailal's execution aroused immense emotion in Bengal. Even the *Times* of London reported the slow procession of his remains through the streets of Calcutta, strewn with rice and coins. To prevent the risk of a popular uprising, Satyen Bose's remains were discreetly incinerated in the prison compound, and his ashes were scattered in secrecy.

One of the youngest members of Barin's group, Nolini Kanta Gupta (who later became one of Aurobindo's closest disciples and the Ashram's secretary), did later acknowledge that Kanailal and Satyen had shot Goswami to save Aurobindo.

Explorations

Aurobindo was undoubtedly the only prisoner in Alipore not to deplore the new drastic regime imposed after Goswami's assassination. A new period of solitude began.

> What happened to me during that period I am not impelled to say, but only this that day after day, He showed me His wonders.

Many years later, however, he was content to illustrate his discoveries of so-called miraculous powers with a few examples:

> I had a questioning mind: 'Are such siddhis as *utthapana* (powers of levitation) possible?' I then suddenly found myself raised up in such a

> way that I could not have done it myself with muscular exertion. Only one part of the body was slightly in contact with the ground and the rest was raised up against the wall. I could not have held my body like that normally even if I had wanted to.

Called *utthapana*, these powers of levitation, cultivated by the fakirs of legend, aimed at circumventing the dominance of physical forces such as gravity. Aurobindo practised keeping his arms in the air without muscular contraction. He succeeded so well that he fell asleep in this position—until he was suddenly awakened by the screams of the guard who thought him dead. Although he had no intention of becoming a fakir, he was determined to investigate the body's unusual abilities. He experimented with the powers of *anima* (subtlety), which awakens the body's internal dynamism and liberates it from the limitations of gross materiality, such as stiffness, strain and fatigue. He practised sleeping 1 day out of 3, then decided to fast for 10 days, 'just to see'.

On another day, the experiment involved the bites of red ants. Why should the body feel these bites as painful? He tried to reverse the current of pain and verified that 'pain and pleasure are a convention of our senses':

> We can gain release from pain in two ways. One is, we learn to bear it; and the other we find something in us which does not suffer. When we have got the separation, we can learn how to transform it into Ananda (bliss).

Within the 50 square feet of his cell, Aurobindo broadened his mental horizon beyond Cartesian logic. He probed invisible worlds. Without losing his critical sense, he beheld visions of which the most fruitful and important was his encounter with Vivekananda's spirit. For two whole weeks, the great Vedantist (who had died six years earlier) manifested himself to him in his meditation, imparting an intimate knowledge of unsuspected higher planes of consciousness, which he called the 'Supermind'.

He would sum up his incarceration at Alipore thus:

> I have spoken of a year's imprisonment. It would have been more appropriate to speak of a year living in a forest, in an ashram, hermitage.... The only result of the wrath of the British government was that I found God.

The conquest of the Life Divine began.

Judgement

On 19 October 1908, reporters jostled each other at the doors of the Alipore courthouse. Armed Highlanders cordoned off the van from which the defendants were extracted one by one before being shoved into the courtroom. The conspirators of Maniktala Garden were about to stand trial.

Aurobindo had not left his cell in six weeks. Rumours about him had abounded. The endless hours of meditation, the lack of sleep, the insufficient nourishment and the strange postures of his body had caused his friends to feel anxious. Although pale and thin, Aurobindo climbed down from the van and took a few steps outside. His dhoti clasped around the waist in the manner of a common man, a shawl thrown lightly over his shoulder, 'his face wore a look of serenity'.

As the packed courtroom audience rose to greet the presiding judge, Aurobindo immediately recognised the judge who had been appointed to rule on the fate of the group of revolutionaries. Charles Porten Beachcroft had been a fellow student in the Indian Civil Service. They had often met, especially in Greek classes, where Beachcroft had come in second behind Aurobindo, and during Bengali tests, where Beachcroft had got the higher marks. They had then lost sight of each other, the judge climbing the ranks of the magistracy while Aurobindo had become the main figure of nationalist opposition in Bengal.

All the same, this new phase of the trial was to be nothing more than a fastidious repetition of the previous exercise with Judge Birley. The same witnesses repeated the same statements, the same 1,500 documents and the same pieces of evidence were again examined under a microscope. This time, however, Norton was hampered by the defence lawyers who cut short his most fantastic flights of imagination and compelled him to minimum legal arguments.

No fewer than 15 lawyers stood to represent the defendants. They were paid from the defence fund set up to cover Aurobindo's legal expenses. His uncle, Krishna Kumar, had launched a national fund-raising campaign through his newspaper, the *Sanjivani*. The appeal, written and signed by Sarojini, was then relayed by other newspapers, which ended up collecting several thousand rupees from Indian and foreign donors. The government was immediately put on alert and proceeded to search *Sanjivani's* premises for the names of nationalist partisans, but the expectation of a miraculous catch fell flat when the police realised that the kitty was made up of modest donations from thousands of anonymous Bengalis.

Shared among 35 defendants, the defence fund was still not large enough to pay the legal ace representing Aurobindo. This man soon withdrew for insufficient funds. A shattered Krishna Kumar then turned to Chittaranjan Das, a less experienced lawyer and supporter of the Nationalist Party, who agreed to take on the case. The trial, which would last another six months, now began in earnest.

The crime of 'conspiracy and acts of war against the King' carried the death penalty. All the defendants pleaded 'not guilty'. Although Norton had no difficulty in connecting the Garden's youths to acts of violence, the task of implicating Aurobindo was far more challenging. Norton was unrelenting. The trial turned into a one-man hunt.

The prosecution relied on two small notes to associate Aurobindo with the group's violent activities. One of those (scribbled by Barin) used the word 'sweets' as a plausible code reference to bombs. The other 'written proofs', exhumed by overzealous policemen, were brushed aside by Charles Porten Beachcroft, a man who knew his job and prided himself on a keen sense of British justice. In the same spirit, he ruled that Birley had acted improperly in refusing Goswami's cross-examination. He proclaimed that Goswami's testimony was inadmissible in court.

However, Norton did not admit defeat easily. He dragged the proceedings on until the following March. Brandishing documents and court exhibits, recalling every witness who had already testified, he obstinately tried to convince Beachcroft of Aurobindo's responsibility.

Aurobindo refuted Norton's arguments one after the other. He had welcomed with relief the arrival of his friend Chittaranjan Das in the defence team and slipped notes to him on the best way to respond to the prosecutor until an inner voice ordered him to rely exclusively on his lawyer:

> This is the man who will save you from the snares put around your feet. Put aside those papers. It is not you who will instruct him. I will instruct him.

The High Court of History

An ominous rumble stirred through Bengal. The Alipore Trial and the harshness of government repression unleashed a cycle of mounting violence. Governor Fraser escaped an umpteenth attempt on his life; the policeman who had arrested Prafulla Chaki after the failed attack on Judge Kingsford was shot dead in Calcutta; a police spy involved in another case was found decapitated. Presuming to defeat the rising popular outrage, the Government of Bengal resorted to deportation: nine nationalist leaders, including Aurobindo's uncle, his friend Subodh Mallik and several other collaborators of the *Bande Mataram* were deported to Burma without trial. The Secretary of the Interior later admitted:

> We would have deported him too (Aurobindo) if he had not already been in prison.

The prisoners' treatment became more severe. They were now chained to each other in the courtroom and locked in a kind of wire-mesh cage. The British press was moved by these measures. The Secretary of the Interior justified them by the climate of tension spreading through the country, which demanded extra precautions against terrorists. Undaunted, Norton pursued his mission, a loaded pistol close at hand on his table. When, in February, a gunman entered the courthouse and killed the prosecutor of an adjacent trial, a shaken Beachcroft adjourned the session for the day.

In March, after an examination of all the court exhibits, Norton finally presented his concluding arguments. It lasted for yet another two weeks. Then it was the turn of the defence lawyers to deliver their conclusions. They implicitly denied the existence of any organised 'conspiracy' against the Crown, arguing that Aurobindo's articles were uniquely freedom calls for his country and for his people. Chittaranjan Das read a statement by Aurobindo:

> If it is suggested that I preached the ideal of freedom to my country, which Is against the law, I plead guilty to the charge. If that is the law here, I admit having done it and I request you to condemn me. It is for that that I have given up all the prospects of my life. It is for that that I came to Calcutta to live for it and to labour for it. It has been the one thought of my waking hours, the dream of my sleep. If that is my charge

> you can chain me, imprison me, but you will never get out of me a denial of that charge.

Chittaranjan Das then proceeded to demonstrate that most of the documents presented by the prosecutor were forged and that the testimonies of the police informers were lies. He concluded his pleading with these words:

> My appeal to you, therefore, is that a man like this who is being charged with the offences imputed to him stands not only before the bar in this Court but stands before the bar of the High Court of History and my appeal to you is this: That long after this controversy is hushed in silence, long after this turmoil, this agitation ceases, long after he is dead and gone, he will be looked upon as the poet of patriotism, as the prophet of Nationalism and the lover of humanity. Long after he is dead and gone his words will be echoed and re-echoed not only in India but across distant seas and lands.

On 5 May 1909, the very day one year ago Aurobindo entered prison, Beachcroft read out his judgment. Police reinforcements were mobilised to cordon off the neighbourhood and guard the roads.

The judgment upheld the ruling of a conspiracy against the British Crown and inflicted upon each defendant a punishment commensurate with the degree of his involvement. Fifty of its 300 pages were devoted to Aurobindo alone, 'whom more than any other the prosecution is anxious to have convicted and but for his presence in the dock there is no doubt that the case would have been finished long ago'. After an in-depth analysis of Aurobindo's public and private writings, Beachcroft concluded that the evidence 'falls short of such proof as would justify me in finding him guilty of so serious a charge as a member of the conspiracy'. The judge did not perceive in his writing any incitement to violence, only the promotion of ideas of freedom and the regeneration of his country. The handwritten note on the 'candies' (the sole contentious point) was not held against Aurobindo. Indeed, would Barin have used the words 'My dear brother' to write to Aurobindo when all Bengali men address their elder brothers as '*Sejda*'? Furthermore, written in Surat when the two brothers were attending the Congress session, the letter would have had to follow Aurobindo throughout all his moves and travels, finally to be found by the police five months later in a house in Calcutta where he had just moved. Beachcroft refused to buy Norton's fabrication.

Barin and Ullaskar Dutt were condemned to the gallows. Ten men directly involved in acts of violence were sentenced to life deportation in the Andaman Islands. Eight men were condemned to lesser terms of imprisonment. Aurobindo and all the remaining were acquitted and released straight away.

1909–1910: The Karmayogin

Slackening of the Nationalist Movement

Whether aggrieved or elated, all observers were unanimously surprised by Aurobindo's acquittal.

If the revolt against the British government could be called a conspiracy, then Aurobindo was not only one of its main figures but a leading driving force. It was Aurobindo's passion that had inspired the young revolutionaries; it was his rousing *Bande Mataram* chronicles that had sustained the nationalist fervour in Bengal. The British officials who had pleaded for his deportation had understood this and were furious that he had slipped through their net.

Upon his release from the Alipore penitentiary, Aurobindo received a standing ovation from the Calcutta lawyers gathered to celebrate his acquittal. The British archives testify to the growing flurry of dispatches concerning the man whom the Governor of Bengal now called 'the most dangerous man with whom we had to deal'. Communications between Ministers and Secretaries of State reflected their alarm. How to curb the activities of this man? The likelihood of his deportation returned to their agenda. He needed to be watched until a favourable pretext to catch him arose—for example, while he delivered a subversive speech.

Spies were assigned to follow his every move. His travels outside Calcutta were monitored, his public appearances preceded by instructions to the local authorities to break up audiences coming to hear him. The post office near his home was infiltrated by a team of CID agents charged with opening and copying every letter he sent or received.

Mrinalini could not be subjected to the tensions of this besieged life; her nerves would not have withstood another police raid. Although she had found solace and protection with her family during Aurobindo's imprisonment, she lived these events as a veritable nightmare. An old friend of her father in Calcutta offered her accommodation while Aurobindo moved to his uncle's house, where his Aunt Lilavati, very distressed by her husband's incarceration, accepted the relief of his presence.

There, at 6 College Square, in an upstairs room converted into an office, he spent his first month of freedom, receiving strings of visitors eager to see and touch the man who had narrowly escaped the gallows. All were stunned by the smile in his eyes. Rabindranath Tagore himself was mesmerised by the man who had returned from prison looking younger than when he went in.

For the anonymous contributors to his defence fund, Aurobindo published a message of gratitude:

> .... If it is the love of my country which led me into danger, it is also the love of my countrymen which has brought me safe through it.

This month of rest confirmed what he had felt in prison: the slackening of the Nationalist Movement. The government's repressive apparatus had been enhanced with new legislation enabling a single magistrate to outlaw a newspaper. As a consequence, both *Yugantar* and *Bande Mataram* closed down, and many samitis were driven underground.

The movement had also lost most of its leaders—above all, Tilak. After the attempt on Justice Kingsford's life, Tilak had been prosecuted for an article rejecting the responsibility of terrorism on 'the exasperation produced by the autocratic exercise of power by the unrestrained and powerful white official class'. He was sentenced to six years of banishment to Burma for sedition. A letter from Secretary Morley to Viceroy Minto shed light on the sham of his trial: 'It is certain that they will obtain his (Tilak's) condemnation, for the jury has obviously been made to measure; it is certainly not the Goddess of Chance who produced this astonishing result of seven Europeans, two Parsees and no Hindu.'

Nine other nationalist leaders (including Aurobindo's uncle and his friend Subodh Mallik) were in jail. Lastly, his two close companions in arms, Bipin Chandra and Lajpat Rai, had voluntarily exiled themselves, probably to escape Tilak's fate.

Repression rarefied the crowds and cooled the enthusiasm of the Swadeshi boycott. The Indian population again fell prey to discouragement and apathy. To further their advantage, Secretary Morley and Viceroy Minto concocted a new set of 'popular' reforms designed to distribute a few crumbs of advisory power to the same unchanging Indian notables.

What remained of the Congress after the Surat explosion was merely a rubber-stamp assembly for English policy, tightly controlled by the Bombay Mehta-Gokhale clique. At its December 1908 Madras session, the Congress president had even declared:

> When in the fullness of time the people have outgrown the present system of administration, they might hope for the extension to India of the colonial form of self-government, though this ideal can only be realized in the distant future.

Emboldened by the nationalist collapse, Gokhale had further added:

> Only madmen outside an insane asylum could hold the idea of India's independence as an ultimate goal. It is an insane idea, a criminal idea.

Pax Britannica triumphed.

Uttarpara Speech

In the month since coming out of jail, Aurobindo had encountered mostly lost and bewildered people.

> When I went to jail, he said, the whole country was alive with the cry of *Bande Mataram*, alive with the hope of a nation, the hope of millions of men who had newly risen out of degradation.

A hush had fallen on the country. 'What shall we do next? What is there that we can do?' people asked.

Aurobindo would attempt to revive the spirit of dissent. On 30 May 1909, he agreed to deliver a public speech at the cultural association of Uttarpara, north of Calcutta.

He confided unhesitatingly in the audience. He spoke of his initial distress in prison, his questions, the oppression of solitude, and the assault of anarchic thoughts flooding his brain. He then disclosed his prayer and the response that ensued—his liberation—Krishna's presence, the doubts and uncertainties swept aside, the 'proof' of the divine reality.

Six hundred people held their breath.

As he related his story, the experience in his solitary cell was analogous to the ordeal sustained by the country as a whole. As he had to endure the barrenness of silence in prison, 'it is the same power which has sent down that silence… so that the nation might draw back for a moment and look into itself and know His will'. For him, as for the country, it was now essential to connect daily life with spiritual reality, what he called 'the two ends of existence'—Matter and Spirit—so they harmonise within the same order of existence. Then India would rise again and regain her freedom for the service of the world.

The next day, his entire speech was reproduced in the Calcutta Press.

The *Karmayogin*

Taking advantage of his notoriety, he now combined the dynamism of his writing with his presence at public meetings, travelling from towns to villages to address appreciative audiences. The *Bande Mataram*, having foundered in the morass of the recent press laws, he launched two new weekly newspapers under his sole editorship: The *Karmayogin* (in English) and the *Dharma* (in Bengali).

The *Karmayogin* cover displayed an engraving of Krishna driving Arjuna's war chariot at the battle of Kurukshetra. Although dedicated to spirituality, literature, science and philosophy, the *Karmayogin* did not refrain from 'noticing current events only as they evidenced, helped, affected or assisted the growth of national life and the development of the soul of the nation'. With the *Karmayogin*, Aurobindo extended the theme of his Uttarpara speech:

> We believe that it is to make the yoga the ideal of human life that India rises today. It is a spiritual revolution we foresee and the material is only its shadow and reflex.

The 'spiritual revolution' he envisioned had nothing to do with temples or the fragrance of incense, but foremost with shaking the mirages of the materialistic dogma. He called out to the young:

> We say to the individual and especially to the young who are now arising to do India's work, the world's work, God's work, 'You cannot cherish these ideals, still less can you fulfil them if you subject your minds to European ideas or look at life from the material standpoint. Materially you are nothing, spiritually you are everything.... First, therefore, become Indians. Recover the patrimony of your forefathers. Recover the Aryan thought, the Aryan discipline, the Aryan character, the Aryan life. Recover the Vedanta, the Gita, the yoga. Recover them not only in intellect or sentiment but in

> your lives.… You must win back the kingdom of yourselves, the inner Swaraj, before you can win back your outer empire.'

He thought of humanity, particularly of Western materialism and the predicament which all modern European societies faced, the unbridled race towards 'progress', which never captures the meaning of life.

> We say to humanity, 'The time has come when you must take the great step and rise out of a material existence into the higher, deeper and wider life towards which humanity moves. The problems which have troubled mankind can only be solved by conquering the kingdom within, not by harnessing the forces of nature to the service of comfort and luxury, but by mastering the forces of the intellect and the spirit.'

The Two Ends of Existence

With the first issue of the *Karmayogin* barely in print, Aurobindo left Calcutta for a new tour in East Bengal. On the train to Khulna, he immersed himself in the inner world. Sometime before reaching Barisal, he distinctly heard Krishna's voice within his heart: 'I come to slay (the ego).'

When landing on the mainland at Barisal, he was taken to the temple of Kali, where he again felt the Presence in the image of the divinity. During nearly a week of encounters, speeches and meetings with town audiences and political activists, he continued to record the movements of his inner life. He now seemed capable of going effortlessly from one existence to the other: depending on circumstances, he could shift his focus from the outer to the inner as simply as one crosses the threshold between two separate rooms.

In his first speech at Jhalakati, evoking the drama of a local young man who had been deported for his political opinions, Aurobindo confronted head-on the atmosphere of profound discouragement in the audience. He exhorted his compatriots to remember *who* they were, to reconnect with the ancestral source of their strength:

> We are a people ancient as our hills and rivers and we have behind us a history of manifold greatness, not surpassed by any other race.... We are a people to whom suffering is welcome and who have a spiritual strength within them, greater than any physical force. We are a people in whom God has chosen to manifest Himself more than any other at many great moments of our history. It is because God has chosen to manifest Himself and has entered into the hearts of His people that we are rising again as a nation.

As he did at Uttarpara, he urged his audience to dwell on the spiritual dimension of the ordeals India was enduring:

> I saw the striding of the storm-blast and the rush of the rain and as I saw it an idea came to me. What is this storm that is so mighty and sweeps with such fury upon us? And I said in my heart, 'It is God who rides abroad on the wings of the hurricane, it is the might and force of the Lord that manifested itself and His almighty hands that seized and shook the roof so violently over our heads today...' Repression is nothing but the hammer of God that is beating us into shape so that we may be moulded into a mighty nation and an instrument for His work in the world. We are iron upon His anvil and the blows are showering upon us not to destroy but to re-create.

In a single month, he delivered six speeches in the same vein before returning to Calcutta for a final address at College Square. His smiling ease, the mix of casual humour and flame in his unrehearsed words subjugated the crowds. He alone could evoke India's destiny with this simplicity and credibility while dispelling fears and summoning the energy of the future. All audiences felt enlivened by his words.

Police spies continued to follow his every step, noting his every word. The organisers of his meetings were often threatened with reprisals. All branches of government, from Viceroy Minto down, were determined to silence him. The Secretary of State wrote to his colleague of the Interior:

> I would not hesitate to deport Aurobindo if he cannot be silenced in any other way. If he is allowed to go on, he will very soon have the country in a blaze again. We should certainly have deported him last December.

Minto was inclined to prosecute him:

> Aurobindo is again on the warpath. I only hope he will commit himself sufficiently for us to be able to prosecute.

A speech delivered in Calcutta in which he had stated that 'being imprisoned for a just cause was not intolerable', was scrutinised by government lawyers. They concluded that the phrase smacked of sedition, but then it had to be printed to be challenged in court. Unfortunately for them, the statement was not published in the *Karmayogin*, so the legal sleuths had to look for something else.

While intimidation and repression had worked against the leaders of the Nationalist Movement—all of whom had more or less backed down or else been removed from the political stage—Aurobindo did not bend. On the contrary, he seemed to derive energy from the force used against him. Worse, the arrows of his wit ridiculed the authorities and filled the *Karmayogin* readers with glee:

> Since the initiation of the Swadeshi movement, the army of spies and informers have grown as plentiful as insects round a bright light.... The office of the *Dharma* has recently been favoured with the loitering of watchers who spend their days gazing lovingly at the building and making affectionate and importunate enquiries as to the movements

> and habits of the editor. This open lovemaking strikes us as a little indecent; it would be better done behind a veil. And what do the authorities hope to gain by these unique researches? Do they hope to see either bombs or packets of sedition being carried into the building?... Even a bureaucracy ought to credit its political opponents with some little common sense.

'Open Letter to My Compatriots'

At the end of July 1909, Sister Nivedita, who had maintained contacts in the British administration, warned him that his deportation had been decided upon. She advised him to leave the country immediately and take refuge abroad. Instead, he chose to face up to the threat with his only weapon: his writing. On 31 July, he signed a long article in the *Karmayogin* entitled 'An Open Letter to My Compatriots'. Conceived as a political testament, this essay once again hammered away at the articles of faith of the nationalist agenda, laying the foundations for an autonomous administration that would take into account the political situation of the country.

> Our ideal of Swaraj involves no hatred of any other nation nor of the administration which is now established by law in this country.... They lie who say that this aspiration necessitates hatred and violence. Our ideal of patriotism proceeds on the basis of love and brotherhood and it looks beyond the unity of the nation and envisages the ultimate unity of mankind. But it is a unity of brothers, equals and freemen that we seek, not the unity of master and serf, of devourer and devoured....

How to build a national identity without calling into question the legality of the British administration? It was necessary, he wrote,

> .... to unite and organise ourselves in order to show our efficiency by the way in which we can develop our industries, settle our individual disputes, keep order and peace on public occasions, attend to questions

> of sanitation, help the sick and suffering, relieve the famine-stricken, work out our intellectual, technical and physical education, evolve a government of our own for our own internal affairs so far as that could be done without disobeying the law or questioning the legal authority of the bureaucratic administration, this was the policy publicly and frankly adopted by the Nationalist Party.

He prefaced his 'Open Letter' with this statement:

> Rumour is strong that a case for my deportation has been submitted to the government by the Calcutta Police and neither the tranquillity of the country nor the scrupulous legality of our procedure is a guarantee against the contingency of the all-powerful fiat of the government watchdogs silencing scruples on the part of those who advise at Simla (the Viceroy's summer residence).

He speculated that the government would not risk inflaming British opinion by resorting to extra-legal practices but would choose caution and wait for a more favourable opportunity to eliminate him. Reckoning that his new notoriety as a well-known opponent complicated the task of the authorities, Aurobindo played on his status as 'public enemy number one'. This *Karmayogin* article removed, at least for now, the threat of deportation.

Rise of Terrorism

In Calcutta, the 'Open Letter to My Compatriots' was at the centre of all political conversations.

On 7 August, in Greer Park, Bhupendranath Bose, a moderate leader, occupied the platform before a sparse audience. As *The Times* correspondent noted, 'A public speaker in England would regard such a gathering as almost an insult. The remarkable fact was, however, that dampened as the crowd was, it burst into loud cheering when Mr Aurobindo Ghose was seen standing nearby. He was unquestionably the hero of the meeting.'

The collaborationist strategy of the Moderate Party was moribund. Still, a few local leaders, such as Surendranath Banerjee, escaped disgrace by playing both sides of the fence, but other loyalists did not take such precautions. In a speech in Poona, Gokhale seethed against Nationalists ('madmen worthy of the insane asylum'), against the idea of independence ('a criminal ideal that can only lead to more repression and violence'), against the strategy of passive resistance ('a cover used by men to save their skin'). He concluded his broadside by charging nationalism with the acts of terrorism that had plagued society for months. A sensational political assassination gave new ammunition to his argument.

Less than a month before, a 26-year-old Indian, Madanlal Dhingra, had shot and killed William Curzon Wyllie, aide-de-camp to Secretary of State Morley. This assassination was perpetrated in broad daylight in London, where Dhingra was studying engineering. He justified his action with the desire to offer himself as a 'sacrificial martyr' to avenge his country. He was condemned to death and hanged on 17 August.

The Anglo-Indian press exploded with hysterical imprecations against nationalism. Yet the nationalist precept of sacrifice had nothing to do with killing Englishmen at home as an expiatory tribute! In the *Karmayogin*, Aurobindo squarely placed the assassination committed by Dhingra in the category of irrational acts:

> No man but he can say what were the real motives for his deed.... Minds imbued with these ideas (of martyrdom) are the despair of the statesman and the political thinker. They follow their bent with a remorseless firmness which defies alike the arrows of the reasoner and the terrors of a violent death.... Here his country remains behind to bear the consequences of his (Dhingra) act.

Copycat acts of terrorist violence broke out in the country. This imitative spell of Barin's methods sparked more government repression yet, thus further reducing the space for nationalist opposition. In the *Karmayogin*, Aurobindo again expressed his disapproval of acts of anarchic and disorderly violence, claiming to restore the country's freedom:

> The outbreak of terrorism compels us to restrict our circle of passive resistance lest even by the most peaceful rejection of unjust laws we should seem to be encouraging lawlessness and disorder.

On 15 August 1909, he celebrated his 37th birthday. A large group of friends and admirers came to congratulate him, and as the increasing crowd became too large for his uncle's small house, they gathered in the street beneath his balcony to express their affection, offering fruits and sweets while singing *Bande Mataram*. He thanked them with these words that were recorded by a police spy who described him as visibly touched:

> Always be patient. Never give up hope. Instability, impatience are the great problems of our nation. When you have a great purpose before you and a firm resolution in you, no difficulty, no matter how great, can divert you.

Light of the Yogi

In Bengal, the confrontation still went on to determine which side, Moderate or Nationalist, would embody the future political orientation of the province. At the beginning of September, the Hooghly Conference was the backdrop for a new crossfire between the two camps. Aurobindo, head of the Nationalists, faced the old moderate champion, Surendranath Banerjee.

As usual, the Moderates had selected the venue of the conference, Hooghly, where they controlled the Hosting Committee. As usual, too, they had covertly rewritten the resolutions voted on at previous conferences in order to mitigate their impact. But this time, they no longer held a majority. Yet Aurobindo believed that unity remained possible. He was determined to avoid an irrevocable split. He and his friends were met with a stubborn refusal to extend the boycott as a measure of economic salvation. Tumult and cacophony resulted yet again.

As the assembly visibly drifted towards chaos, Aurobindo stood up and raised a hand to demand silence. He asked the nationalist delegates to abstain from voting against the moderate resolution and to leave the hall in silence in protest. Astounded moderate delegates watched the orderly withdrawal of those impetuous youths led by a man hardly older than themselves.

In his conference report published a few days later, Aurobindo explained:

> The Nationalist Party is in practical possession of the heart and mind of Bengal. It is strongly supported in other parts of India and controls Maharashtra. It is growing in strength, energy and wisdom. It surely inherits the future. Under such circumstances, it can afford to wait.

An overt break had been avoided, leaving the future open.

Aurobindo then journeyed to Silhet, on the River Surma, for a tour of the far-flung eastern districts of Bengal, where he could measure the radical transformation which had occurred. Everywhere, he and his friends were welcomed with open arms. All shared the same aspiration for freedom and independence and, in a single voice, the conference on the Surma voted resolutions far more progressive than the Hooghly Conference. Everyone now also acknowledged Aurobindo as a yogi whose charisma stemmed from the light radiating from his being.

Returning to Calcutta in mid-September, in the small room above the family home, he received a correspondent of *India*, the nationalist weekly from South India. The reporter described the discreet figure waiting for him:

> Is this the yogi destined to liberate us by a radical transformation, to show a new way for India?

But then his eyes met Aurobindo's:

> Oh, what knowing in these eyes! What grace in them! What peace! The whole room exuded peace.

He asked Aurobindo to speak of his vision of Krishna in prison, for 'the darshan of the Supreme is a rarity in this age'. When Aurobindo responded, the combination of humility, solemnity, innocence and the light on his face dissipated the journalist's last doubts:

> Yes, I saw Krishna. I had all my visions in a waking state: they were not dreams.

Asked about the yoga he had practised during his imprisonment, Aurobindo replied:

> It was Bhakti Yoga. Leave all responsibility to the Divine. Try to realise that whatever you think, speak or do is not yours, and that it is the Divine who thinks, speaks and acts through you. Crush your ego; be without the 'I'.

On 16 October, the fourth anniversary of the Bengal Partition was drawing near, and Aurobindo was eager to celebrate it not as a day of partition but as a day of unity. In the three speeches he delivered on this occasion, he emphasised this unity, 'which cannot come into being until a perfect comradeship in aspiration, in struggle, in suffering, shall have been created throughout the length and breadth of the land: Indian fraternity based on Indian liberty and Indian equality'.

The British, however, had not given up undermining relations between Muslims and Hindus. One of the features of their new reform plan was to separate, in regional councils, Muslim representation from the rest of the population—to which Aurobindo responded that....

> .... the country, the *Swadesh*, which must be the base and fundament of our nationality, is India, a country where Mahomedan and Hindu life intermingled side by side.... Our ideal, therefore, is an Indian Nationalism, largely Hindu in its spirit and traditions, because the Hindu made the land and the people and persists, by the greatness of his past, his civilisation and his culture and his invincible virility, in holding it, but wide enough also to include the Moslem and his culture and traditions and absorb them into itself.

The partition of Bengal had aimed at diluting Hindu influence by redrawing the map of the province. If the goal was now, through an electoral plan presented as a democratic advance affirming the rights of a minority against the overwhelming Hindu majority, to extend the polarisation to the entire country, Aurobindo retorted that the plan ought to have also considered the other minorities: the Parsees, the Sikhs and the Christians, for example.

> We will not for a moment accept separate electorates or separate representation, not because we are opposed to a large Mahomedan influence in popular assemblies when they come, but because we will be no party to a distinction which recognises Hindu and Mahomedan as permanently separate political units and thus precludes the growth of a single and indivisible Indian nation.

'Under modern conditions, India can only exist as a whole,' he repeated emphatically. It followed that nationalism had to be above denominational choices and that the Indian nation had to be founded on the basis of secularism. He strongly repudiated the notion of Hindu Nationalism and called instead for Hinduism, refreshed at the source of the Vedanta, aware of its spiritual power, conscious of mankind's essential oneness, but declining to found its existence on a supremacy or a rivalry over other denominations, including Islam. It would be in failing to adhere to this golden rule of separation between civil and religious identities—especially under Gandhi's leadership—that India would suffer its greatest tragedies in the decades to come.

He tirelessly reaffirmed that faith and courage would conquer all difficulties—'faith that looks beyond all momentary obstacles and reverses and sees the goal that God has set before us, and the courage that never flinches for a moment but moves forward calmly, wisely, but strongly and irresistibly to that goal'.

Aurobindo spent most of his days working in the *Karmayogin's* office, never losing sight of his inner research.

> As for concentration and perfection of the being and the finding of the inner self, I did as much of it walking in the streets of Calcutta to my work or in dealing with men during my work as alone and in solitude.

At his uncle's, he received a visit from Ramsay MacDonald, the leader of the British Labour Party and future Prime Minister, who noted in his journal:

> I called on one whose name is on every lip as a wild extremist who toys with bombs and across whose path the shadow of the hangman falls. He sat under a printed text: 'I will go on in the strength of the Lord God'; he talked of the things which trouble the soul of man.... He was far more of a mystic than a politician. He saw India seated on a temple throne.

As a consequence of his meeting with Aurobindo, Ramsay MacDonald was one of the very few British politicians to voice his sense of the perverted waste in human resources stemming from Westminster's unbridled policies. As his intervention in Parliament on 28 April 1910 made clear:

> I feel perfectly certain that unless the India Office will insist upon its officials administering India with some generosity, some catholicity of sentiment and some serious attempt to associate with themselves men like Mr Aurobindo Ghose, the future is going to be very much darker than it is at present.

The Political Swamp

Meanwhile, Aurobindo's notoriety became increasingly intolerable to the authorities. 'I attribute the spread of seditious doctrines to him personally in a greater degree than to any other single individual in Bengal, or possibly in India,' the new Governor Baker wrote privately to the Viceroy.

That his political opponents spared no effort to muzzle him was, after all, fair game. But a stealthier antagonism raised its head: the jealousies of the political swamp. Those who had turned their devotion to India into a profession of faith, and sometimes into a gainful profession, took umbrage at his notoriety. Without losing his sense of humour, Aurobindo responded to the aspersions of Surendranath, the moderate old leader, who now called him 'an impatient idealist':

> The reproach of idealism has always been brought against those who work with their eye on the future by the politicians wise in their own estimation who look only to the present.... The advice to wait is valueless unless we know what it is that we have to wait for and why it is compulsory on us to put off the effort which might be made at present. If we can progress quickly, there must be adequate reasons given to us for preferring to progress slowly or to stand still. We have not yet heard those adequate reasons.

The cause of the gulf between Aurobindo and a certain Bengali intellectual elite was that he had left behind the intellectual perception of the world. 'He thinks himself divinely guided,' wrote a caustic Nivedita, 'but religious experience and strategy have nothing in common and should not be mixed.' Even his silence was assailed as it seemed to confirm this 'otherness'. He maintained that he was not turning his back on reality—as evidenced by his daily involvement in the public struggle—yet he was secretly reproached for being 'above' things. His lack of personal ambition was suspect.

The Noose Tightens

When all reasonable options seemed to vanish one after another, Aurobindo took a final stock of the political situation, reiterating his faith in a harmonious evolution of society:

> The perfect self-fulfilment of India and the independence which is the condition of self-fulfilment are our ultimate goal. In the meanwhile such imperfect self-development and such incomplete self-government as is possible in less favourable circumstances, must be attained as a preliminary to the more distant realisation. What we seek is to evolve self-government either through our own institutions or through those provided for us by the law of the land.

Published in the *Karmayogin* on 25 December 1909, this article, 'To My Countrymen,' which he made into a second open letter to his compatriots, marked a final appeal to reason to all Indian political classes. Like the preceding articles, however, it fell on deaf ears. The government lawyers seized upon it to flesh out new arguments to prosecute him. And inevitably, he would be charged—for the third time.

The beginning of 1910 brought in more disappointment. The National Council of Education of which Aurobindo had been a founding member in 1906, brazenly betrayed the ideals upon which it had been founded. It forbade the students to participate in the boycott celebrations in Calcutta.

Aurobindo gave vent to his indignation:

> It is only the crowning act of a policy by which they are betraying the trust reposed in them by the nation, contradicting the very object of the institution and utterly ruining a great and salutary movement.

The only good piece of news came from the Alipore Court of Appeals: two judges commuted the death sentences of Barin and Ullaskar to deportation for life. A third detainee was acquitted and released, while eight others had their prison sentences reduced. Aurobindo noted the moderation of the judges and underlined that 'death sentences for political crimes only provide martyrs to a revolutionary cause, nerve the violent to fresh acts of vengeance and terrorism'.

In fact, blind terrorism did not abate in the least. In November, Viceroy Minto narrowly escaped a bomb thrown by a stranger in Ahmedabad. A month later, members of a Maharashtra group fired at a magistrate in Nasik and killed him. At the end of January, inside the Alipore courthouse, a young Bengali shot Detective Shamsul Alam, whom Aurobindo had encountered during his arrest. From London, Paris, Berlin and New York, new revolutionary propaganda spread into the Indian emigrant community.

Since Alipore, although he had remained enduringly popular with the young, Aurobindo kept his distance from violent revolution. His visibility as the head of the Nationalist Party made his involvement impossible, but above all, the time of the *Yugantar* and terrorism was over. He felt that 'so long as young men are attached to these methods of violence, the efforts of a more orderly though not less strenuous Nationalism to organise and spread itself must be seriously hampered'.

The government turned its wrath against the Nationalist Party, holding it responsible for fostering acts of terror. Once again, Aurobindo's voice rose to denounce the executive short-sightedness:

> The disease is one that can only be dealt with by removing its roots, not by denouncing its symptoms. The Anglo-Indian papers find the root in our criticism of government action and policy and suggest the silencing of the Press as the best means of removing the root.... Our idea is that it will only drive the roots deeper: to silence Nationalism means to help Terrorism.

In February 1910, terrorist violence further intensified, and repression fell indiscriminately upon the nationalists. Aurobindo warned the government:

> A very serious crisis has been induced in Indian politics by the revival of terrorist outrages and the increasing evidence of the existence of an armed and militant revolutionary party determined to fight force by force. The effect on the government seems to have been of a character very little complimentary to British statesmanship. Faced by this menace to peace and security, the only device they can think of is to make peaceful agitation impossible.... If free speech, if free writing, if free association is made impossible under the law, it is tantamount to declaring a peaceful nationalism illegal and criminal.

In response, the government toughened the press laws. Publishers now had to deposit a bond before writing the first line—a surety that would be sequestered, along with the newspaper, at the slightest editorial misconduct. Aurobindo took note of the new regulations, which targeted above all the publications with the most modest means: one step closer towards total censorship.

It became impossible to express a contrary opinion. The Anglo-Indian press, a long-time ally of the British, did not hold back its scathing attacks against the Nationalist Party. This Aurobindo denounced:

> If the *Englishman* is tired of assassinations, we are also tired of the thankless and apparently unsuccessful task of regulating popular

> discontent and pointing out legitimate paths to national aspiration, on the one hand, and attempting to save the officials from themselves on the other.

Rumours of a new deportation project circulated within the police departments. This time it would involve removing 24 political opponents, including Aurobindo. In fact, the highest authorities of the Government of India had agreed upon a list of 52 names in addition to his own: almost all of the declared opponents of Bengal.

The End of Politics

When the appointments to the new regional councils introduced by the recent Morley-Minto reforms were made public, the worst fears were confirmed. The confessional affiliation sought by the administration had largely benefited Muslims to the detriment of Hindus. Far from easing tensions, this amplified community discord which would culminate in 1947 with the creation of the separate country of Pakistan. The Moderates, although largely discredited among the Hindu middle class, had supported the reforms and profited from the largesse of the regime.

Even in Bengal, Aurobindo recognised that the Moderates would never accept Nationalists among them. His conciliation efforts ran counter to Surendranath's demand (prompted by the Mehta-Gokhale script) for a 'creed' of good conduct prior to any nationalist participation. He finally resolved:

> 'We regret to announce to the country that there is not the least possibility of having a united Congress.' The future would belong to the Nationalists, 'and from the Moderate Party we can expect no cordial cooperation in building it. Whatever we do, we must do ourselves, in our own strength and courage.'

Taking into account the further disintegration caused by terrorism and since British leaders refused to seize upon the peaceful opportunity of a genuine national regeneration, he decided to withdraw from political action. Before doing so, he addressed the government one last time:

> The one, the only remedy for the difficulties which beset the government in India, is to cease from shutting their eyes... They are face to face with aspirations and agitations which are not only Indian but Asiatic, not only Asiatic but worldwide.

Then he addressed his compatriots to explain his decision to leave politics:

> Revolution paralyses our efforts to deal peacefully but effectively with Repression; Repression refuses to allow us to cut the ground from under the feet of Revolution. Both demand a clear field for their conflict. Let us therefore stand aside, sure that Time will work for us in the future as it has done in the past, and that, if we bear faithfully the burden of the ideal god has laid upon us, our hour may be delayed, but not denied to us for ever.

This was 1910. Aurobindo had just left public life. His appeals to resolve the contradictions of colonial hegemony by relying on a lucid nationalism were not heard.

A few years later, other Indian leaders would take up the torch and pursue the strategies he had formulated in *Bande Mataram* and *Karmayogin*, but his voice and inspiring vision would be sorely missing.

Although the notorious vices of colonialism are now buried in the mists of time, we may return for a moment to the blindness of British policymakers in India. Incapable of perceiving the elements of greatness or nobility in a civilization other than their own, the British abandoned themselves to the illusion of their racial supremacy.

That none of these men—with the notable exceptions of Judge Beachcroft and the future prime minister MacDonald—ever paid the least attention to the voice of Aurobindo, who strove ceaselessly to put forward practical solutions for an organised and peaceful transition to a free India, speaks volumes about their arrogant blindness. In his hundreds of articles, in his dozens of inspired speeches received by passionate audiences, all they sought was forensic evidence to lock him up.

The historian R.C. Majumdar would best describe his journey through Indian politics:

> Aurobindo rose like a meteor and vanished like it from the political atmosphere. But unlike the meteor, the dazzling light he shed on Indian politics did not vanish with him. The torch, which he lighted, continued to illuminate the Indian political firmament.

1910: Departure

Chandernagore

The *Karmayogin* now refrained completely from any political commentary. Its columns were filled with literature, art and yoga. Aurobindo sometimes included his own poetry or his translations of the Upanishads. He spent the days in the newspaper's office, and in the evenings a few Alipore veterans joined him to chat or improvise lectures on history or literature, as had been their habit while in prison.

One particular evening, the usual circle at the *Karmayogin* was interrupted by the arrival of an agitated young man, Ramchandra Majumdar, who warned of Aurobindo's impending arrest. He had just learned from a police officer, a member of his family, that the police were about to raid the *Karmayogin* premises. As soon as he heard the news, Aurobindo decided to leave immediately. Inside him, a voice he knew well had distinctly whispered three words: 'Go to Chandernagore.'

He left the *Karmayogin* premises with two young men, Biren and Moni, hastening through the maze of narrow alleyways leading to the Hooghly river. There they boarded a small boat with a pair of rowers.

The night was spent rowing upriver in silence. It was barely daybreak when they reached Chandernagore. The only person Aurobindo knew there was a former Alipore inmate, a respectable high school teacher whose misfortune had been to be included in one of Naren Goswami's lists. Charuchandra Roy was a sincere believer in the liberation of India but did not have the mettle to fight. Brought up in the Alipore Court, he had not fared well in prison. After his release, gained in exchange for a guarantee from the French authorities in Chandernagore, he had returned to his academic life, pledging never again to meddle in 'politics'. Biren's unexpected knock on his door filled him with dread. He declined to receive Aurobindo, suggesting that he take refuge overseas.

For several hours, incertitude hung heavy in the air. Biren, who kept watch on deck, presently spotted a man timidly approaching the boat. Feeling observed, the individual drew closer. When Biren informed him that the boat came from Calcutta, he asked: 'Would Mr Aurobindo be on board?' He was called Motilal Roy and, having heard of Aurobindo's presence had rushed to offer his services.

'Would it be possible for you to put me up?' asked Aurobindo straightaway.

Motilal would give his life if necessary! 'I came to receive you.... I will personally take care of everything.'

Aurobindo scrutinised his face and smiled. Before following his new host, Aurobindo asked Biren and Moni to return to Calcutta and inform Sister Nivedita about the unexpected turn of events and ask her to take charge of the *Karmayogin* publication.

In the room that Motilal put at his disposal, Aurobindo sat silently on the floor and withdrew within himself. When Motilal returned several hours later, he found him still sitting in the same position, staring upwards.

'He has utterly resigned himself to God,' thought the young man.

In the Steps of the Vedic Rishis

Aurobindo's stay in Chandernagore would last for a month and a half. To guarantee his security, Motilal's friends took turns hiding him. Making do with very modest accommodations and a frequent diet of dried fruit, Aurobindo maintained his concentration.

His visions became more frequent. Ethereal characters and alphabets now formed before his eyes as if superimposed in the air.

This phenomenon (*akasha lipi*) was repeated every day, eventually revealing that these cryptograms were a transcription of past, present or even future events. This 'virtual memory' of the invisible world did not seem to make any difference between the tenses: the future coexisted with the past or the present. Aurobindo, who sensed a rare receptivity in Motilal, confided to him:

> The gods of the invisible world become visible. They are as significant as the alphabet, and want to communicate something which I endeavour to discover.

Three divine figures from the ancient Indian tradition appeared to him. Well-known to yogis, Ila, Saraswati and Sarama personify three levels of the powers of intuition: revelation, inspiration and intuition itself.

The three goddesses whose light illuminate the cave of the 'Powers of Darkness' are figures from India's Vedic heritage. Dating back to several millennia before our era, prior to the Upanishads, they helped the fathers of the spiritual tradition, the Vedic rishis, to explore the den of the subconscient with the goal of initiating a revolution of human life.

Aurobindo had thus taken his first steps in the footprints of the Vedic rishis. He had retraced the course of his legendary ancestors. From his arrival in Bombay 17 years earlier, with the revelation of the Atman, to this insight of the first Vedic attempts, his course made perfect sense: he must take up the torch where his great predecessors had left it.

Virtually at the same moment, he again heard the inner voice utter three words within his heart:

> Go to Pondicherry.

This is what impelled him to put a close to life in Bengal.

> I came away because I did not want anything to interfere with my yoga and because I got a very distinct adesh (command) in the matter. I have cut connection entirely with politics, but before I did so, I knew from within that the work I had begun there was destined to be carried forward, on lines I had foreseen, by others, and that the ultimate triumph of the movement I had initiated was sure without my personal action or presence.

Last Days in Chandernagore

In Calcutta, despite police surveillance around his uncle's house, his cousin Sukumar Mitra (Krishna Kumar's son) had been able to send news and forward his mail. As to Mrinalini, mercifully, her life had been spared further emotional upset. Nivedita had managed to publish four issues of the *Karmayogin*. Meanwhile, Calcutta was rife with the most absurd speculations about his absence. To put a stop to the rumour mill, Aurobindo sent this following tongue-in-cheek 'clarification':

> We are greatly astonished to learn from the local Press that Sj. Aurobindo Ghose has disappeared from Calcutta and is now interviewing the Mahatmas (Great Initiates) in Tibet. We are ourselves unaware of this mysterious disappearance. As a matter of fact, Sj. Aurobindo is in our midst and if he is doing any astral business with Kuthumi (who is presumed to have inspired the Theosophical Society) or any of the other great rishis, the fact is unknown to his other *Koshas* (sheaths). Only as he requires perfect solitude and freedom from disturbance for his Sadhana for some time, his address is being kept a strict secret. For similar reasons, he is unable to engage in journalistic works, and *Dharma* has been entrusted to other hands.

Nevertheless, gossip about legal proceedings against him continued to do the rounds. One day, he received a letter from a reader exhorting him to leave his retreat and confront his judges. This man, a notorious police informer, ironically provided

Aurobindo with the opportunity to turn the situation to his advantage.

Aware that his escape through the police net was a blow to the authorities, he replied that he had no reason to go to court or to leave his retirement since no warrant had been issued against him. An irate government took the bait and initiated a new prosecution against him. However, the bureaucratic behemoth was to take weeks to produce a legal warrant—enough for Aurobindo to leave the jurisdiction of British India and begin a new life in the French territory of Pondicherry.

The only way to reach Pondicherry, 1,200 miles from Calcutta on the southeastern coast of India, was to take the maritime route. All road and rail links would be far too risky for a man whose description was by now displayed everywhere. A ship of the Messageries Maritimes, the SS *Dupleix*, was due to leave Calcutta on 1 April and to stop in Pondicherry on its way to Ceylon. There was enough time to organise the voyage. Aurobindo's cousin Sukumar bought two tickets for him and Bijoy (an ex-member of the Maniktala Garden).

Moni, the only boy not listed on police files, would travel ahead by train, carrying a letter from Aurobindo to his nationalist friends in Pondicherry.

The departure from Chandernagore was scheduled for 31 March. Sukumar had planned the voyage to Calcutta in three stages aboard three boats. The final stage would allow the passengers to board the *Dupleix* from the river, avoiding the ship's gangway, which was usually under police surveillance. In Bengal, which was prey to terrorist violence, two Bengali passengers would not fail to attract unwanted attention.

Unhappily, however, the third boat—with the trunks and tickets—was not at the appointed spot on the river. Aurobindo and his companions had to improvise a hurried trip to College Square (his uncle's house) to retrieve the tickets. Thus, as fate would have it, before leaving his native Bengal, Aurobindo drove past the headquarters of the British Empire, the Viceroy's residence in the centre of Calcutta. On that particular day, Lord Minto was absent, inspecting India's northeast territories and hunting tigers....

Thanks to Sukumar's resourcefulness, everything was resolved, and the passengers hastened back to the ship with their luggage. But time was running out to complete one last formality before being allowed to sail: a medical certificate.

At nightfall, as Aurobindo's vehicle with his three companions pulled up to the *Dupleix*, all the passengers had long since retired into their cabins, and the maritime medical officer had left the ship. So they again drove speedily through the European quarter in search of the doctor's home. Anxiety was palpable. What would happen if the medical certificate was unobtainable at this late hour? Aurobindo was silent, 'like a man in a trance', a witness recalled. In any event, the doctor delivered the precious certificates without any difficulty, though noticing with some surprise the perfect English accent of one of the passengers.

It was almost 11 pm when the travellers ascended the gangway, where police surveillance had long since ceased. While Bijoy busied himself with preparing their cabin, Aurobindo's two other companions bade him farewell, bowing silently before him, hands joined in the Indian fashion.

As scheduled, the SS *Dupleix* departed at dawn the following day, 1 April 1910, navigating through the Ganges Delta and out into the vast open sea, heading south.

Part II

THE LIFE DIVINE

Life is not entirely real until it opens into the sense of the infinite.

Sri Aurobindo, *Essays on the Gita,* CWSA, vol. 19, p. 128.

1910: Pondicherry

A New Life

After four days of uneventful navigation along the east Indian coast, the SS *Dupleix* came within sight of Pondicherry, the capital of French India. From the deck, Aurobindo and Bijoy watched a dinghy boat approach the ship to disembark the passengers. They immediately spotted Moni, who had reached Pondicherry by train two weeks earlier to prepare for their arrival. He was escorted by a man called Srinivasacharya, a nationalist militant whom Aurobindo had asked for help in finding accommodation.

On this late afternoon of 4 April 1910, the promenade along the seaside was practically deserted, and the carriage bearing the four men arrived without complication at the residence of Shankara Chettiar, a local notable and nationalist sympathiser who had accepted to lend a section of his house to the visitors. Aurobindo would have preferred an independent, more remote shelter, but he liked the house and the spacious, old-fashioned room allocated to him. An upper terrace, bordered by a high wall, would allow them to get some fresh air without being seen from the street. An ideal retreat for fugitives, Bijoy thought.

In Pondicherry, Aurobindo and his young companions had, thus, joined the ranks of the political refugees keeping out of harm's way from British police stationed in the neighbouring city of Madras. The most famous of them was the renowned Tamil poet and playwright Subramanya Bharati, whose 'extremist' politics had caused him frequent trouble with the authorities. He was the publisher of *India*, a weekly paper championing Indian nationalist policy in the vein of the late *Bande Mataram*. *India* had garnered in

Southern India the same popular attraction—and the same legal predicament—as Aurobindo's newspaper in the North.

Meanwhile, in Calcutta, and for the third time, a warrant had been issued for Aurobindo's arrest. This time, he was charged with sedition by the Government of India. In question was an article he had published three months earlier, in the *Karmayogin*, before leaving Bengal. Since the warrant could not be served, he was considered a fugitive, and his name was placed on a high-priority wanted list. Following a flurry of fanciful rumours as to his whereabouts (Tibet, Colombo, Bombay, Madras and even Europe), spies eventually located him in Pondicherry. Hence, a few days after his arrival, a party of plain-clothes police were stationed in front of Shankara Chettiar's house.

In London, Morley, the Secretary of State for India, was to learn of the warrant against Aurobindo in the *Times*. He immediately voiced his disapproval to Viceroy Minto: 'Does the article in question contain direct incitement to violence or assassination?' Throughout April, he tried to have the charges dropped. He feared the reactions of British opinion—and he was not wrong.

In Parliament, Ramsay McDonald—one recalls his inspirational encounter with Aurobindo in Calcutta—challenged the British government and demanded to know the real motives of the latest accusation. He had understood Aurobindo's decision to leave public life and pleaded with the government 'to show more generosity, some catholicity of sentiment, and some real effort to associate themselves with men like Mr Aurobindo Ghose'.

However, all these efforts were in vain. Neither MacDonald nor Morley could head off the authorities' obsession with the presumed danger Aurobindo represented to India. The tone even soured between Minto and his superior Morley, who now called the warrant 'an outright mistake'—to which the upset Viceroy replied: 'I can only repeat that he is the most dangerous man we have now to reckon with.'

Aurobindo had read in the *Hindu* an account of MacDonald's intervention in the House and had concluded that he would not be able to leave Pondicherry so long as the accusations against him were in force. Of course, he would ask his friends in Calcutta to challenge the legality of the charges against his article, but that procedure would take time.

Despite these life conditions fraught with uncertainty and peril, the little group settled into a routine at Shankara Chettiar's house. Aurobindo shared a common vegetarian meal, always the same, prepared by his two companions and served on banana leaves. Whereupon he returned to his room and immersed himself in his studies. Two boiling cups of tea and a small serving of a curry dish completed the daily food intake. At night, he slept on a thin mattress on the floor. But despite the frugality of these conditions, the sum of money brought from Calcutta was decreasing rapidly, and it was urgent to find some income.

In the evening, Aurobindo received visitors, often Bharati with Srinivasacharya. Another occasional guest of these meetings, V. Ramaswami Iyengar, remembered:

> In Bharati's speech there was the aggressiveness of the smell of jasmine. Aurobindo's had the beauty of the full-blown lotus. In the talk of both, new ideas and images appeared like dazzling fireworks. It was as if Bharati had caught the words as they flew in the sky; it was as if Aurobindo had scoured earth's buried treasures and brought them to our gaze. And the speech of both was equally flavoured with poetry, and both could laugh without reservation.

One day, Rangaswami Iyengar, the mayor of a nearby suburb, called on Aurobindo and unexpectedly declared his willingness to offer financial help to the fugitives. He justified his intention by relating a prophecy uttered by his grandfather's Guru, deceased 30 years earlier. According to the Guru, a yogi travelling from the north would come to seek refuge in the south with the aim of practising an 'integral yoga'. The mayor saw in Aurobindo's arrival the incarnation of that ancient prophecy.

Not long afterwards, Aurobindo received another visit which would have far-reaching consequences. At Bharati's suggestion, a meeting was arranged with Paul Richard, a newly- arrived Paris lawyer seeking election to the French Parliament. Initially hesitant to play the role of a tourist attraction, Aurobindo was convinced by Bharati that a political ally in Paris could only be beneficial to the refugees living under the constant threat of British police.

Paul Richard was a Protestant pastor involved in politics. He was also fascinated by occultism. In Paris, he shared his life with a young woman, Mirra Alfassa, who exercised her rare gifts of clairvoyance among a small spiritual group she gathered weekly in her house.

The two men were not long in broaching topics of conversation of common interest. Aurobindo disclosed his project of inner transformation through the practice of integral yoga. The interview convinced Richard to come back four years later to contest the election in earnest and to bring along his companion, Mirra. Returning to France, he wrote:

> All my life I have sought great men throughout the world, for all my life I felt they must be somewhere in this world; they are its light, its fire, its life. It is in Asia that I found the greatest of them all—the leader, tomorrow's hero. He is Hindu. His name is Aurobindo Ghose.

Integral Yoga

Actively concerned by current events and cordial in his communications with others, Aurobindo always remained silent about his 'Sadhana', that is, his practice of yoga. He shared with no one the development of his inner life. Once isolated in his room, the discipline he pursued and the world he embraced made sense to him alone. Every day, he succinctly noted the steps of his investigation in a journal, *Record of Yoga*.

> Essentially, yoga is a generic name for the processes and the result of processes by which we transcend or shred off our present modes of being and rise to a new, a higher, a wider mode of consciousness which is not that of the ordinary animal and intellectual man.... Yoga is the passage of the human thinking animal towards the god-consciousness from which he has descended.

Since earliest times, many schools of yoga have flourished in India, each focusing its application on one constituent of the human being: Hatha Yoga (the discipline of body postures or *asanas*), Raja Yoga (psychological disciplines and mind control), Karma Yoga, Jnana Yoga, Bhakti Yoga (triple path of the Works, Knowledge and Love). Aurobindo's aim was to synthesise these disciplines into an 'Integral Yoga' by concentrating on their central principle and secret dynamism: the Divine.

> The method we have to pursue, then, is to put our whole conscious being into relation and contact with the Divine and to call Him in to transform our entire being into His.

His efforts were to surrender to the Divine: all desires had to disappear; reason had to fall silent and reach a perfect self-abdication. The only way to create a being based on the extinction of the ego was to reveal him within oneself. Such was the character of Aurobindo's immersion.

> I want the Divine and nothing else. I want to give myself entirely to him and since my soul wants that, it cannot be but that I shall meet him and realise him. I ask nothing but that and his action in me to bring me to him, his action secret or open, veiled or manifest. I do not insist on my own time and way; let him do all in his own time and way, I shall believe in him, accept his will, aspire steadily for his light and presence and joy, go through all difficulties and delays relying on him and never giving up.

Passivity was to become the golden rule: no attempt could be made to know, to judge, to act, to will or even to move the body by self-action. Trust became the alpha and omega of life.

When his surrender reached a culmination, Aurobindo experienced unwavering joy at the beauty of the world:

> All sights, sounds, smells, tastes, touches, movements, actions, are now pleasurable or give pleasure.

In each person he met, he perceived the presence of the Supreme Being and His relation to the unchanging soul.

A few months after arriving in Pondicherry, he was able to write to one of his unfrequent correspondents:

> My subjective sadhana may be said to have received its final seal and something like its consummation by a prolonged realisation and dwelling in Parabrahman (the Absolute) for many hours. Since then, egoism is dead for all in me except in the physical self which awaits one farther realisation before it is entirely liberated from occasional visitings or external touches of the old separated existence.

Despite the liberation pervading his being, his consciousness kept a trace memory of 'the old separated existence' through which the egocentric personality exerts its control over material life. In other words, the world's physical reality continued to exert its presence in him through a set of age-old, pragmatic rules making up an existence seemingly devoid of the Divine.

Some 5,000 years ago, the Vedic rishis, the fathers of Indian civilisation, had faced the same problem while pursuing their dream of making 'Heaven and Earth equal and one', but they had failed to materialise their intuition. After the Vedas, the Upanishads, the Bhagavad Gita and the Mahabharata had celebrated the enlightenment of the mind, the exultation of the heart, and the release of the soul. However, the physical conversion had remained out of reach. The old dream of transforming material life had been abandoned. The problem remained entire: how to invest Matter with the divine presence?

The attempt to penetrate the physical crust and bring Matter to respond to the Spirit would be Aurobindo's battle, his ultimate achievement. He would apply to this research in his bodily individuality all the standards of scientific enquiry: each step of his progression would be recorded for its stability, intensity and reproducibility; each regression analysed to better understand its implications and eventual merits.

> I have been testing day and night for years upon years more scrupulously than any scientist his theory or his method on the physical plane.

His method for transforming the nature of the physical relationship was masterful in its simplicity. Pursuing his concentrated observation in everyday life, he endeavoured to manage material circumstances by operations of consciousness instead of by the customary procedures of physical-mental intervention. In the evening, rather than consulting his watch to predict the return of his companions, he guessed their arrival, often to the minute. Or watching a bird in the sky, he predicted its trajectory by an act of 'determining illumination'—by penetrating the 'truth' of its flight. This vision of the bird-in-itself—in the Brahman—revealed the character of its movement.

These precognitive feats were sometimes accomplished with astonishing mind control that lent a surreal character to the occurrence. For instance, this steering of ants!

> While watching the movement of ants on the wall opposite, it was suddenly perceived that every slightest movement of the particular ant observed in each case followed the anticipatory observation; wherever

> my idea turned, there the ant, with but slight variations, immediately corrected, turned to follow it; when the forceful will was applied, there was sometimes a slight, but unavailing struggle. This observation covered some half hundred successive movements of various ants.

He meant to unlock new perspectives in handling material life, to expose Matter's direct responsiveness to the application of consciousness. While science wields indirect mental truths—equations—to improve our handling of material phenomena, Aurobindo explored another kind of science, one that stemmed from the phenomena themselves and had to do with their intrinsic existence.

> I am developing the necessary powers for bringing down the spiritual on the material plane... there is a sort of locked struggle in which neither side can make a very appreciable advance, the spiritual force insisting against the resistance of the physical world, that resistance disputing every inch and making more or less effective counter-attacks.

What 'powers' could unlock a passage obstructed since the dawn of time between matter and consciousness? Aurobindo tested the objectivity of his 'subjective' sadhana by applying his force of silent concentration onto all kinds of remote physical circumstances. On Bharati, whose health was failing, he focused the Force of peace and harmony to make him better. He strove to purify his two companions, Bijoy and Moni, to spur them on the path of yoga. He concentrated on Indian and world affairs, including the war in the Balkans, endeavouring to counteract its most sinister omens.

During these first months in Pondicherry, it seems that everything depended on the capacity of the force brought into play. There is only one Force in the world, and if it was capable of controlling and guiding the material of ants by an act of consciousness, might it be able to control all of human matter? It was this Force that Aurobindo strove to fathom and implement on earth. It had to possess a compelling power of 'conviction' to prevail over matter's inertia and convert resilience into flexibility and harmony. Driving this Force into action would lead to a new material paradigm, another way of living life.

> I am seeking to bring some principle of inner Truth, Light, Harmony, Peace into the earth consciousness—I see it above and know what it is—I feel it over-gleaming my consciousness from above and I am seeking to make it possible for it to take up the whole being into its own native power, instead of the nature of man continuing to remain in half-light, half-darkness. I believe the descent of this Truth opening the way to a development of divine consciousness here to be the final sense of the earth-evolution.

After undergoing innumerable silent experiences pertaining to the most varied physical or psychological fields of life, in his immediate environment as well as in more distant circumstances, Aurobindo ultimately apprehended through his daily practice of yoga a masterful Force capable of accomplishing the change he had in view. He called this force 'the Supermind'.

> The Supermind is the vast Truth-consciousness of which the ancient seers spoke; there have been glimpses of it till now, sometimes an indirect influence or pressure, but it has not been brought down into the consciousness of the earth and fixed there. To so bring it down is the aim of our yoga.

The Police

At the end of 1910, after eight months at Shankara Chettiar's, Aurobindo seemed determined to settle in Pondicherry, even though in Madras, just a few dozen miles to the north, the British police continued to suspect him. Two newcomers from Calcutta had joined the small group: Saurin, Mrinalini's cousin, and Nolini, acquitted in the Alipore trial. As promised, the mayor Rangaswami Iyengar had recently donated 1,000 rupees to cover current expenses for a year, making it possible to rent an airy house closer to the sea. A servant was hired for housework, and a dog completed the household. Every evening, the boys took a leisurely stroll alongside the beach.

Aurobindo decided to make his presence in Pondicherry official. He wrote to the *Hindu* newspaper.

> I left British India over a month before proceedings were taken against me and, as I had purposely retired here in order to pursue my yogic sadhana undisturbed by political action or pursuit and had already severed connection with my political work, I did not feel called upon to surrender on the warrant for sedition, as might have been incumbent on me if I had remained in the political field. I have since lived here as a religious recluse, visited only by a few friends, French and Indian, but my whereabouts have been an open secret, long known to the agents of the government and widely rumoured in Madras as well as perfectly well-known to everyone in Pondicherry.

The next day, as he opened his copy of the *Hindu*, he learned that two judges from the Calcutta Court of Appeal had recently cleared him of sedition charges. He was now free to move where he pleased and even to return to Bengal, but he had decided to stay.

Against all odds, his legal saga with the British authorities began to earn him a growing reputation in Pondicherry. Unwanted visitors flocked to see him, and the intrusions became so brazen that he had to write a new letter to the *Hindu* to try to put a stop to the flood. He described the siege of these strange 'pilgrims' who had crossed India, prowling around his house and climbing on his windows to catch a glance of him. He also made a point of rejecting in advance all stories or fictitious news about him that these fake devotees might be tempted to peddle.

In reality, these intrusions were part of a destabilisation programme contrived by British police. After being turned away, one of the 'pilgrims' began to shout that he knew the bomb formula used at the Maniktala Garden and threatened to use it; he later turned out to be a spy in the pay of the police. The Bengal authorities, including the Viceroy, continued to suspect Aurobindo's retirement to be a cover-up for occult political activities, and it did not matter that he had been recently cleared by British courts. Police provocations went on for weeks and months with a view to ruining the protection he enjoyed in French India.

In April 1911, Aurobindo signed a two-year lease for a new home at 10 Rue St Louis. In the light of candles and a single oil lamp, the little group met in the evenings to receive lessons in French and Italian, and also in Greek and Latin, offered by Aurobindo, who opened his companions to universal literature.

In June, Pondicherry was shaken by the assassination of William Ashe, the English Chief Constable of a neighbouring district of Madras. It was the first time a terrorist act of this scale was perpetrated in South India. The investigation revealed that the young assassin, who took his life after the attack, was trained by a Tamil revolutionary residing in Pondicherry. The British launched a series of haphazard arrest warrants against Bharati, Srinivasacharya and four other refugees. Aurobindo was not directly targeted nor mentioned in the investigation, but he felt that the incident could jeopardize his retreat as the climate against political refugees in Pondicherry grew increasingly hostile. He again used an open letter to the *Hindu* to reiterate his position: since he had given up political action months ago, why should he feel compelled to spend most of his time refuting accusations supported by flawed evidence that partisan minds were only too prone to accept?

However, police suspicion remained. No less than 50 British officers turned up in Pondicherry. Ranked high-risk, Aurobindo and his four companions were continually tracked in their every move. A rumour even circulated about a possible kidnapping project; as a precaution, the young men armed themselves with bottles of acid and stood guard.

Aurobindo generally declined to receive visitors stopping by in Pondicherry, but in November 1911, he made an exception for Alexandra David-Néel, the Parisian writer and singer, who would later gain notoriety when she became the first Western woman to enter Lhasa disguised as a Buddhist monk. In Paris, she frequented the group of spiritual seekers meeting at Mirra Alfassa's home, which is probably why Aurobindo decided to extend a cordial welcome to her. 'In a French language of great purity, he spoke of the high philosophical ideas of ancient India.' As a fervent Orientalist, Alexandra was conquered:

> He thinks with such clarity, there is such lucidity to his reasoning, such lustre in his eyes that he leaves one with the impression of having contemplated the genius of India such as one dreams it to be after reading the noblest pages of Hindu philosophy.

He confided in her some of his 'experiments' in consciousness. She was struck by the 'careful and meticulous control' with which he conducted them.

On her return to Madras, she was met at the train station by an elegant Englishman, the chief of British police, who wanted to know everything about her visit with Aurobindo. She feigned to be surprised: 'I had heard of Aurobindo as a distinguished philosopher.' 'That he is,' admitted the police chief, 'but he is a dangerous man. We hold him to be responsible for the assassination of Mr Ashe.'

Alexandra would not be further bothered; a few days later, she received a letter of apology from the Viceroy.

Blueprint

Aurobindo went on with his research for a new life based on divine Nature.

His journal reveals that he structured his goal into a system of yogic accomplishments: a road map comprising seven major themes, or *chatusthayas*, each of which graded into four 'perfections' or *siddhi*. This full system of 'seven quaternaries', featuring a total of 28 yogic disciplines, became his blueprint of spiritual achievements, through which he would follow his progression. Achieving perfection in every *chatusthaya* would thus result in establishing the full divine life in the body.

The first theme of yogic perfection (*Shanti-Chatusthaya*) pertained to equanimity or *Samata*. This is the inner equilibrium that enables a person to face the contradictions of existence—life's ups and downs—without being overwhelmed with grief or transported with joy. This equality of temper points to a fundamental composure of the soul when meeting the impacts of external nature.

> It is the sign of growing into an undisturbed spiritual poise of being in the Infinite… the sign of our having passed beyond the egoistic determinations of our nature, of our having entered into the calm and peace of liberation.

Once the perfection of *Samata* is attained and the soul is uniformly surrendered to the divine will, joy and grief, health and illness, failure and success become equally perceived as the Play of the Divine with the human soul, and therefore intrinsically lovable. All the experiential values of ordinary life are then reversed: adversity turns out to be good fortune; defeat and failure become steps towards ultimate victory; grief and pain mutate into hidden forms of pleasure.

> A stage arrives even, when physical pain itself, the hardest thing for material man to bear, changes its nature in experience and becomes physical ananda (bliss).

The second theme of perfection (*Shakti Chatusthaya*) affects the active components of our physical nature. The mind, heart, vital force and body must be raised to their highest capacity and ultimate power. They must expand into the instruments of a new momentum of the soul in daily action. In India, the divine energy capable of effecting this transformation of our human nature is called *Shakti*. *Sraddha*, or Faith, is its spur, the indispensable condition to awaken the power of transformation and convert human aptitude to mirror the higher divine aptitude.

The third theme of perfection (*Vijnana Chatusthaya*) breaks away from human limitation and aspires to stride upward into the next higher plane of our being. At its peak, this supraconscious region, *Vijnana*, rises to what Aurobindo called the Supramental consciousness, or Supermind, the power of fully effective knowledge and will. Between ordinary thought and Supermind lie various powers of vision and intuition, particularly *trikaldrishti*, the vision of the three times (past, present and future), which greatly helped him approach Supermind in the circumstances of daily life.

The fourth theme of perfection (*Sharira Chatusthaya*) involves the spiritualising of the physical consciousness and the divinising of the law of the body. It manifests in particular by freedom from disease, or *arogya*, and the release from the pressure of physical forces and gravity, or *utthapana*. The perfection of the body also includes its physical beauty, or *Saundarya*, and various forms of physical bliss.

The fifth theme of perfection, the *chatusthaya* of divine action in the world, is based on the Unity with Krishna and Kali:

> When the Unity has been well founded, the static half of our work is done, but the active half remains. It is then that in the One we must see the Master and His Power—Krishna and Kali as I name them using the terms of our Indian religions; the Power occupying the whole of myself

> and my nature, which becomes Kali and ceases to be anything else, the Master using, directing, enjoying the Power to his ends, not mine.

The sixth theme of perfection, the *chatusthaya* of the Brahman, bears on a life in union with the brahmic consciousness—a life conscious of the Brahman that is all, in the Brahman infinite in being and infinite in quality, in Brahman as universal knowledge and self-existent bliss.

The last or seventh theme (*Yoga Chatusthaya*) 'is at once the means, the sum and the completion of all the rest'.

Henceforth, each progression or regression of Aurobindo's sadhana was ranked within one of these themes. His journey towards a new life became an intertwined development of all the elements of the *chatusthaya*s simultaneously. For instance, a mental telepathic activity that had reached its perfection in a given situation could be challenged and further perfected when affected to a wider context or when the sadhana reached a higher level of progress. Ultimately, it followed that the divine life in the body could only emerge....

> .... by applying the spiritual knowledge utterly to the world and to the surface psychological and outer life and to effect its transformation both on the higher levels of Nature and on the ordinary mental, vital and physical levels down to the sub-conscience and up to the supreme Truth-consciousness or Supermind in which alone the dynamic transformation could be entirely integral and absolute.

Seven Years

As August 1912 drew near—Aurobindo was 40—he took stock of his yogic discipline, started 7 years before.

> It has taken so long to complete a long record of wanderings, stumbles, gropings, experiments—for Nature beginning in the

> dark to grope her way to the light—now an assured, but not yet a full lustre—for the Master of the yoga to quiet the restless individual will and the presumptuous individual intelligence.... In this yoga, at least nothing has been abrupt except the beginnings—the consummations are always led up to by long preparation and development, continual ebb and flow, ceaseless struggling, falling and rising.

Since the beginning of his practice, he had given particular attention to the evolution of his mental faculties. The mind seemed to be a major player and beneficiary of the endowments of yoga. Every breakthrough in the sadhana usually included an equivalent enhancement in mental capability. Over time, he experienced that the mind was not only an efficient transmitter but also a powerful receptor. He followed with great interest his reception and exploration of other people's thoughts.

> There has long been a free and successful telepathy and reading of the characters, feelings and states of mind of others and for longer still an elementary perception of their actions. But the thought contents of the minds of others have been hidden from me except occasionally. Today, however, the veil was lifted, the barrier finally broken. Not only did telepathy and thought-reading abound, but in a single day, the proof of correctness began to be ample.

Mental impressions did not only reach him in the form of thoughts from other human beings but also from animals or even remote events. For several days in November, he is said to have 'received' news of the war in the Balkans: the presence of an Austrian warship at Durrazo, rumours of the murder of the Austrian Consul, and the Turkish request for inclusion in the Balkan Confederation. The next day, the Pondicherry newspaper confirmed this information from Sofia and Constantinople.

To this power of telepathic reception was recently added a faculty of mental vision called *trikaldrishti*, or vision of the three times. It enabled him to 'visualise' the origin as well as to 'forecast' the progress of any event while it occurs.

> Things distant in time and place have also begun to yield up the secret of their present, future and immediate past, even in the rough of their distant past.

Aurobindo watched a squirrel climb the tiles on the edge of the roof, jump onto the wall of the neighbouring house, and then run on its roof. He mentally followed its movement, perceived in the squirrel's mind the intention of the first jump, and likewise for its jump on the wall. Finally, its run on the roof was 'received' in advance, predicted by the *trikaldrishti* vision, without any fact or any subjective data suggesting this last movement.

An insect spotted the day before in a garden shrub was nowhere to be found. Aurobindo examined the shrub for a long time without being able to locate the insect. Yet, against all odds, he had received a *trikaldrishti* suggestion that the insect was still there. Half an hour later, Nolini discovered the insect in the shrub.

Prediction errors sometimes affected the accuracy of the *trikaldrishti* vision. That was the case whenever the mind refused to admit *trikaldrishti* suggestions and reverted to its habitual intellectual ways.

However, it became increasingly clear to Aurobindo that the soundness of the power of reception and transmission, the progressive elimination of the mental imbroglios, flowed naturally from the mind's passivity, from its submission to the Divine. It was the confirmation that every action had to be associated with Krishna's satisfaction and pleasure, the recognition that the truth of the inner voice was more reliable than the lived experience.

> The stage now reached by the *trikaldrishti* is one in which sraddha, blind faith, is demanded in all suggestions which are not corrected by discrimination. The mind is to question nothing and correct nothing.

Henceforth, *trikaldrishti* would replace the activity of intelligence. In other words, nothing would be accomplished based on judgement, logical inference, speculative decision or past experience. Even the most negligible and insignificant action would proceed from the supra-intellectual consciousness. As a result, the power of distant *trikaldrishti* finally began to manifest steadily, with unsolicited, spontaneous knowledge proving to be truer than opinions and logical reasoning. Aurobindo summarised these results in a letter to Richard.

> What I perceive most clearly, is that the principal object of my yoga is to remove absolutely and entirely every possible source of error and ineffectiveness, of error in order that the Truth I shall eventually show to men may be perfect, and of ineffectiveness in order that the work of changing the world, so far as I have to assist it, may be entirely victorious and irresistible.

Another yogic practice that often accompanied mental telepathy and *trikaldrishti* vision was the remote control of actions. Called *aishwarya* by yogis, this occult influence acts by focusing a strong power of suggestion on a distant object or event. Although still limited to ancillary activities, this power of remote influence grew day by day. Of all the yogic disciplines that mobilised Aurobindo, he devoted the most intense concentration to *trikaldrishti* and aishwarya.

For instance, as he followed the flight of a kite describing a series of straight lines in the sky bounded by 180-degree revolutions, he anticipated the path of the bird through the *trikaldrishti* vision. Then he ordered the kite to veer in the other direction at the next turn. After a brief hesitation, the bird accepted the suggestion and turned the other way.

On 23 December 1912, Viceroy Hardinge was targeted for assassination at a ceremony in New Delhi. The bomb killed the mahout of his elephant, and metal shards struck the Viceroy's back, head and legs. As soon as he learned the news, Aurobindo decided to concentrate and use the *trikaldrishti* perception to help in the healing.

He wrote in his journal:

> The improvement in the Viceroy's health took place in the direction willed, viz elimination of fever and pain. A period must now be fixed for entire recovery and it must be seen whether the element of time can be controlled.

Then a few days later:

> The Viceroy's health is following exactly the movement of the Will which was that the pain should be relieved within 31 December and the healing of the wounds fulfilled in January. This morning's news is that there is no longer any discomfort from the wounds, although the healing will take some weeks. It is also announced that there is still a piece of metal in the neck. This confirms the *trikaldrishti* of two or three days ago which suggested the fact when reading the description of the state of the wounds.

The next day, the newspaper reported that the piece of metal had been removed without complications. However, impatient to resume his activities, the Viceroy got unnecessarily tired and revived the neuritis in his arms. The final healing would take longer than expected. Through Aurobindo's yogic concentration, the *trikaldrishti* had followed in silence the course of the healing, fortifying the patient's recovery by pressure from the *aishwarya*. That was, in any case, what Aurobindo perceived. And he could write:

> What I am attempting is to establish the normal working of the siddhis in life, i.e., the perception of thoughts, feelings and happenings of other beings and in other places throughout the world without any use of information by speech or any other data. Second, the communication of the ideas and feelings I select to others (individuals, groups, nations,) by mere transmission of willpower; Third, the silent compulsion on them to act according to these communicated ideas and feelings; Fourth, the determining of events, actions and results of action throughout the world by pure silent will power. When I wrote to you last, I had begun the general application of these powers which God has been developing in me for the last two or three years, but, as I told you, I was getting badly beaten. This is no longer the case, for in the first, second and even in third, I am now largely successful, although the action of these powers is not yet perfectly organised. It is only in the fourth that I feel a serious resistance.

Having confirmed the subjective reality of the mind's psychic powers and validated some of their more objective effects on the physical plane, it was now time to extend their application to all material existence, to substantiate the proposition: matter = consciousness.

> The theory of the yoga has been proved. The perfectibility of the human being, *trikaldrishti*, Power, the play of the Divine Force in the individual, the existence of the other worlds, and of extra-mental influences, even the possibility of the physical perfections are established facts. What is wanting is the perfect application, free from the confusions of the falsehood which result from the play of mind.... The yoga has now reached a stage when the test of its positive worldward side has to be undertaken.

Yoga and the World

The physical body and its functions must be the first and foremost field of yogic mastery. In contradiction with the customary representation of a yogi, Aurobindo spent most of his time walking. From early morning, he paced up and down his room and veranda, sometimes for 10, 12 or even 16 hours a day, only pausing for a quick meal or to read the newspaper. He also carried out the exercises he had begun in Alipore jail, keeping his arms raised for two hours or more, then repeating the movement when sitting or lying down or else holding his legs horizontally for 45 minutes. His aim was to control and eliminate body fatigue and muscle stiffness. He accustomed his body to sleeping without a blanket at night or walking in the full sun during the day. Hunger and thirst were eliminated by a simple act of willpower. A sore throat or the onset of a cough was cured by consciously lowering the body temperature. Mild digestive troubles were appeased in the same way.

The beauty of the body (*saundarya*) was an imperative requirement of the divine perfection to be fulfilled by yoga. It rested on the ambition to recast the material appearance in the image of its spirit. The curvature of Aurobindo's foot gradually acquired a naturally more perfect and elegant form. His teeth kept their whiteness without artificial means. His hair recovered its lustre and smoothness; its tendency to entanglement decreased, but it became extremely fine and slightly greying at the temples—he was 40.

Most importantly, he had achieved significant progress in the quality of his surrender to the Divine 'by the disappearance of all questioning, revolts or self-action'. If one of these human reactions arose in him, it found no support in his deeper being. When an occasional lapse occurred in the yoga, it provoked neither revolt nor retreat. Henceforth, the improvement of his being was abandoned over to the divine action as it dealt with the contradictory forces of nature; he did not even try to interfere or insist on a coherent method. The use of the intellect was discouraged, and he had renounced all personal want.

Beyond the submission as God's servant and as God's lover, he had reached the supreme perfection of surrender: a state of 'helpless obedience' to the direct urge of the Master. This new intensity manifested itself in an increase of light and faith in the body. All efforts were ended, and no compulsion was used to change nature, which remedied its defects by itself. All this had become possible because every thought and feeling was now guided by Krishna's divine hand.

> Life is a great mass of existence moulding itself through its own conscious energy (*tapas*). All that has to be done is for our own divine being (*jiva*), the knowledge centre of this existence, to sit fast in his city (the body) and allow the infinite tapas to manifest through him, accepting it, sanctioning it, holding up the whole system and its working and watching and enjoying the results.

Ananda, or Divine Joy, was Aurobindo's principal physical support throughout his quest. Celebrated by the Vedic rishis as the elixir of immortality, or *amrita*, this blissful sensation can reveal itself in any part of the being, mental or physical, and stems from the perception of divine Unity. Aurobindo sought *ananda* above all else as he drew from it the energy to pursue his work. Thus, he had learned to 'expel' any physical discomfort by replacing it with the 'Ananda of discomfort'. Similarly, if he suffered a mishap in a particular yogic attainment, he transformed it with what he called the 'Ananda of defeat'. The worst was metamorphosed into the best. At its most intense, *ananda* could become so ecstatic that it completely obliterated physical pain. Only extreme discomforts, brutal cold or oppressive heat still resisted the transformation, but their 'expulsion' was only a matter of time.

At night or during the day, with eyes open or closed, images and words appeared to Aurobindo. Outside the normal range of sensory perceptions, these floating snapshots expressed the esoteric substance of his experiences. Figures in colour and relief (*rupa*) gradually elucidated their divinatory meaning. Words and etheric verbal expressions (*lipi*) disclosed premonitory signs or secret significances.

Other prophetic insights arose from his automatic writing or 'scripts', which he composed under the dictation of occult entities—sometimes, he felt, from God Himself—who stipulated the intricacies of a particular yogic process. He also used the simple divination technique of the sortilege: by drawing a random word or a sentence from a book.

He regularly used his powers to cure his companions when they were ill or to hasten their spiritual progress. Bharati, Bijoy, Nolini, Saurin, readily responded to his yogic influence. Bijoy exposed his own occult channel of communication and was enabled to receive personal telepathic messages and inspiration from supra-intellectual planes. He began to have visions. Bharati was encouraged to intensify his surrender to the Divine and make it 'more concrete'. For weeks, he had been vainly trying to help a friend suffering from hysteria. In two days of applying a 'moderate' intensity of power upon him, the man was completely cured by Aurobindo.

World events continued to reach Aurobindo by telegrams and newspapers, while telepathic connections made him feel as if he were present in the field. In January 1913, on the Balkan War front, he could thus follow Austro-Italian claims on Janina, Scutari and Prizrend in Albania; Romanian threats on Bulgarian territory; the Turks' firm attitude and their refusal to be intimidated by the threat of naval attack; the relatively moderate action of the Great Powers with regard to Andrinople in Turkey.

At about the same time, he received the prediction of the quick demise of four influential members of the Indian National Congress. Krishna Gokhale, Surendra Banerjee, Baikuntha Sen and Pherozshah Mehta were the 'moderate' congressional leaders whom Aurobindo had been battling in Bengal when he championed Indian nationalism with his colleague Tilak.

Their policy stance in favour of the British colonial regime was now terminally depressed, and the four men would soon disappear—not, however, without first promoting their suitable replacement in the person of Gandhi, returning to India in 1915.

Lack of funds, however, remained the perpetual challenge. The financial situation was worse than ever. A 300-rupees loan was almost exhausted, and all other sources of income were either closed or suspended. Even Rangaswami Iyengar, who had promised regular support at the beginning of the stay, had vanished. Aurobindo appealed to Motilal, the companion who had sheltered him in Chandernagore, before leaving Bengal:

> I must ask you to procure for me by will power or any other power in heaven or on earth ₹50 at least as a loan. The situation just now is that we have ₹1½ or so in hand. Srinivasa is also without money. As to Bharati, living on nothing a month means an uncertain quantity. [...] No doubt, God will provide, but He has contracted a bad habit of waiting till the last moment. I only hope He does not wish us to learn how to live on a minus quantity, like Bharati.

Worse than the actual shortage of money were the doubts, which kept creeping into Aurobindo's mind as to the soundness of the injunction he had received before leaving Bengal: was he really intended to carry out God's mission as the Voice seemed to have declared? This recurrent hesitation touched the core of his faith and yoga.

In early February 1913, a critical period loomed.

> All is petty, hampered and limited. A perfection (siddhi) rapidly established becomes otiose for days together. Continuity in the higher states seems as yet impossible, and from accomplishment there is always a relapse into a condition of partial imperfection. The whole yoga is continually beset with inertia and uncertainty and seems unable to rise permanently into clearness and perfect joy and assurance. There is no grief or acute trouble or even anything that can really be called trouble, but a dull

> depression never acute and a certain weariness and lack of interest has settled down on the system and is only lifted for short intervals.

For two whole months, all progression was halted. The *trikaldrishti* perceptions were perturbed; the intensity of the *ananda* drastically reduced; the body felt weary. The siege was primarily physical, but it soon affected the progress accomplished in yoga. Aurobindo lived in near-prostration and shaky health. He nevertheless managed to recover and resumed his journal on 1 April 1913.

Failing to renew the lease at Rue St Louis, the little group moved downtown, to Rue Foreign Missions, in a Tamil-style house built around an enfilade of three small courtyards—particularly convenient for walking. Bharati lived in the neighbourhood and resumed his daily visits. The household grew with two new arrivals. Nagen, the first newcomer, was a relative of Bijoy who suffered from tuberculosis. Aurobindo immediately attempted to cure him. The second newcomer, Amrita, had severed his ties with his Tamil Brahmin caste to be closer to Aurobindo:

> Aurobindo's eyes, it seemed, burned brighter than the lamplight for me; as he looked at me, in a trice all gloom vanished from within me and his image was as it were installed in the sanctum sanctorum of my being. I felt within that he had accepted me.

Since mid-September, Aurobindo had stopped his journal after noting that 'the habit of miscalculation still persists, temporary success being mistaken for final fixity'. He admitted:

> None of the perfections (siddhis) are yet finally perfect. Even the first one (equanimity) which is nearest to absolute finality has been disturbed yesterday and has not yet recovered its balance.

It followed from these setbacks that 'Faith in the rapidity of the yogic perfection and in God's command has been again shaken'.

The opportune arrival of a small sum of money—enough to cover three months of expenditure—relieved the pressure. But the yogic powers no longer seemed to work, neither against the spread of terrorism in Bengal nor against the capture of the strategic Turkish city of Adrianople by the Bulgarian armies (which marked the end of the Balkan War).

Thanks in part to Nagen, who had his own resources, the small group then relocated to the European sector of Pondicherry. On 11 October 1913, they moved to Rue François Martin, close to the governor's mansion. Living conditions were still precarious, but the house was spacious enough to accommodate its eight occupants and offered two rooms and a veranda on the first floor for Aurobindo.

Trying to analyse the reasons for the opposition arising against a perfect mental vision, free of errors, he figured out that it was not so much the internal enemies that disturbed his yoga—particularly the *trikaldrishti* vision—as external enemies, which 'acted from a great distance'. To thwart them, the *ananda* attempted to perceive their opposition as emanating from God, as a means of progress, so as to relieve suffering and allow the struggle and the intellectual activity to be exhausted in joy, but the mind was not ready to accept this scenario because it lacked faith in divine protection and help, and this defect allowed the external enemy to sow complete confusion inside the mind and shut down the ananda.

However, a new set of 'instructions' were communicated to Aurobindo in the form of a script:

1. Do accept error or falsehood, but let them not disturb such faith as is established. They are permitted, not enjoined. Accept all error as a disguise of truth; penetrate the disguise.
2. Accept all failure as a link in the process of success; place the link.
3. Accept the rapidity of the perfection as a certainty of the future and a growing certainty. Perceive all retardation as a help to the growth of the rapidity; fix the nature of the help.
4. Will pertinaciously whatever you are enjoined to will.

Mirra

Almost four years had elapsed since Paul Richard visited Aurobindo in Pondicherry. Along with Mirra Alfassa—whom he had married—he was preparing to return to run his campaign for French Parliament.

Born in Paris on 21 February 1878, Mirra had grown up in a well-to-do family in the comfortable settings of Boulevard Haussmann and Square du Roule in Paris. Her artistic sensibility had led her to Art school and to a first marriage with Henri Morisset, a pupil of Gustave Moreau. She rubbed shoulders with artists, musicians and writers of the time, including Matisse, Auguste Rodin, César Frank, Anatole France and Émile Zola. What gave her personality a wholly distinct character stemmed from her faculties of clairvoyance, from her aptitude to connect with extrasensory worlds beyond the physical realm.

At barely six, Mirra could sense above her head a light whose bright intensity seemed to increase month after month. Her rationalist mother did not hide her concern. One day, as she asked her daughter why she was crying, Mirra replied that she was crying at the world's misery and falsehood. She would forever refuse to accept that a sole God might alone be responsible for this misery. Such proclamation, she felt, would even make her 'a complete atheist!' Mirra combined painting with piano. She also communicated with the trees in the Fontainebleau Forest. At the age of 13, she had her first visions and out-of-body experiences when almost every night....

> .... as soon as I had gone to bed, it seemed to me that I went out of my body and rose straight up above the house, then very high above the city. I saw myself clad in a magnificent golden robe, much longer than myself; and as I rose, the robe would stretch, spreading out in a circle around me to form a kind of immense roof over the city. And then I would see men, women, children, old men, the sick, the unfortunate

> coming out from every side; they would gather under the outspread robe, pleading for help, describing their miseries, their suffering, their hardships. In reply, the robe, supple and alive, would extend towards each of them individually, and as soon as they had touched it, they were comforted or healed, and went back into their bodies happier and stronger. Nothing seemed more beautiful to me, nothing could make me happier; and all the activities of the day seemed dull and colourless and without any real life, beside this activity of the night which was the true life for me.

Between 18 and 20, without a guide or even books, she 'realized the conscious and constant union with the divine Presence'. She began reading Vivekananda's *Raja Yoga* before being introduced to the Bhagavad Gita by an Indian friend. Krishna became the figure of the immanent God within her. As her natural practice of occultism grew year after year, there was no danger of her going astray on these paths because, for Mirra, the primacy of truth went hand in hand with her consecration for the Divine.

> In true occultism, one must have the quality, the ability, the inner gift in order to use it, and that is the safeguard. This is no longer magic—neither white magic nor black nor golden—is not magic at all; it is a spiritual power. This means that as soon as one draws near the Truth, one is safe from all charlatanism, all pretension and falsehood.

At barely 20, she began to investigate her nights, training herself to remain aware and remember every phase of her sleep. Her explorations led her to the sheer evanescence of forms, the utter limits of the 'formless' reality.

A major event in her spiritual development occurred when she met, in Paris, the Cosmic Movement, an esoteric group headed by Max Théon, a mysterious character residing in Algeria. In 1906, having left Europe for the first time, she stayed for three months in Tlemcen with Théon and his wife, Alma, both fervent adepts of the occult. Mirra was dazzled by Alma's aptitudes:

> Her powers were quite extraordinary; she had received an extremely complete and rigorous training and could exteriorise herself, that is, bring out of her material body a subtle body, in full consciousness, and do this 12 times in succession, to the ultimate limit of the world of forms.

Initiated by Alma, Mirra eventually acquired the gift of ubiquity: to be present in two physical locations at the same time. While her physical body rested in Tlemcen, she could make her presence felt by a group of friends in Paris and even jot down a few words and sign her name on a piece of paper.

Back in France, she gathered a small group of spiritual seekers in her home. After her divorce from Henri Morisset, she shared her house with Paul Richard rue du Val-de-Grâce, near the Luxembourg Garden. There she lent her talents for the occult to an appreciative audience. Alexandra David-Néel wrote wistfully of the atmosphere of these meetings:

> We used to spend wonderful evenings among friends conversing about the great future.... I recall Mirra's elegance, spiritual realisations, and intelligence brimming with mystical passion. Despite her deep love and sweetness, despite her natural tendency to cede the spotlight to others, she could not hide the extraordinary force driving her.

Through her study and translation of the Gita and the Upanishads, Mirra sought to realise a spiritual life calling into question man's ordinary nature. Two years after Richard's meeting with Aurobindo in Pondicherry, she wrote in an essay entitled *The Supreme Discovery*:

> When in each atom of Matter men shall recognise the indwelling thought of God, when in each living creature they shall perceive some hint of a gesture of God, when each man can see God in his brother, then dawn will break, dispelling the darkness, the falsehood, the ignorance, the error and suffering that weight upon all Nature.

Even though she had not yet met Aurobindo, she had seen him in her visions.

> In these visions, I saw Sri Aurobindo just as he looked physically, but glorified; that is, the same man I would see on my first visit, almost thin, with that golden-bronze hue and rather sharp profile, an unruly beard and long hair, dressed in a dhoti with one end of it thrown over his shoulder, arms and chest bare, and bare feet. At the time, I thought it was a 'vision attire'! I knew nothing about India. And in these visions I did something I had never done physically: I prostrated before him in the Hindu manner.

On 29 March 1914, Mirra and Paul Richard arrived in Pondicherry. That same day, on her own, Mirra met Aurobindo. He was exactly the man of her vision. She wrote in her journal:

> It matters little that there are thousands of beings plunged in the densest ignorance, He whom we saw yesterday is on earth; his presence is enough to prove that a day will come when darkness shall be transformed into light, and Thy reign shall be indeed established upon earth.

Within just a few days, she recorded her own stupefaction:

> It seems to me that I am being born to a new life and all the methods, the habits of the past can no longer be of any use. It seems to me that what I considered results is nothing more but a preparation. I feel as though I have done nothing yet, as though I have not lived the spiritual life, only entered the path that leads to it.

1914–1919: First World War

Onset

Aurobindo endorsed Paul Richard's candidacy to the French Parliament. At the same time, he harboured no illusions. There was not enough time for Richard to run an effective campaign while tackling widespread political corruption. The results were announced on 5 May: Bluysen, the candidate most popularly disliked, won the election with 33,154 votes. Despite the sympathy of Hindus and Muslims, Richard collected only 231 votes, a poor showing largely due to a shamefully rigged vote counting.

Mirra and Paul had found a house to rent not far from Aurobindo's. Every afternoon at four o'clock, they visited him, and Mirra brought homemade candies and a chocolate drink. On Sundays, Aurobindo walked to the Richards' with the boys, who then proceeded to their soccer game. Later, everyone shared a vegetarian dinner while engaging in conversations lasting till late in the evening.

On 28 June, Archduke Francis Ferdinand, presumptive heir to the Habsburg Empire, was assassinated in Sarajevo. All European chancelleries were thrown into utter disarray. Austria declared war on Serbia on 28 July, then Germany declared war on Russia on 1 August, and France on the 3rd. England entered the conflict on 4 August.

The Richards and Aurobindo were shocked by the suddenness and brutality of the confrontation. In her prayers of 21 August, Mirra took the Divine to witness:

> O Lord, Lord, the whole earth is in an upheaval; it groans and suffers, it is in agony.... Out of the depths of this abysm of darkness, the whole being of the earth cries to Thee that Thou mayst give it air and light; it is stifling, wilt Thou not come to its aid?

Between 12–26 August, Aurobindo followed the episodes of the war with the *trikaldrishti* vision, adding, whenever possible, his concentrated influence through the yogic *aishwarya*. He thus 'saw' the arrival of the German armies in Liège, the movements of French troops in Alsace, the French success in Mülhausen, and the retreat of the same French a few hours later; he sensed the hesitation of England to engage its fleet in war. He was present through the yogic connection at the German retreat in Liège and Tongres, at the French conquest on the Lorraine border, at the Russian success on the Boug and Dniester rivers, and at the socialist riots in Berlin.

The German plan, which had forecasted the annihilation of the French army in less than two months, turned out to be a failure. The Germans now had to fight on both fronts: in the west against the Franco-Belgo-British alliance and in the east against the Russians, the prelude to a four-year quagmire.

By the end of September, the war made a brief foray into India when the German cruiser *Emden* shelled oil tanks in Madras, causing firestorms and panic in the city. Later on, while walking on the Pondicherry beachfront, Bharati saw the enemy ship approaching. He knew that the city possessed only a few small artillery pieces to counter the *Emden's* 105 guns. The stampede of the wealthiest residents towards the suburbs had already begun. But following what appeared as an interminable intermission, the German captain decided that the small French territory was not worth the cost of ammunition and withdrew.

If direct confrontation was avoided, the war affected the strategic alliances and altered the balance of power: Indian political refugees could no longer take the French authorities for granted. The British government insisted that its wartime ally expel all revolutionaries from French India. Fortunately, in Aurobindo's case, a government bureaucrat in Bengal did not see things so simplistically:

> If he were driven out now, he would almost certainly make straight for Bengal, and be received with enthusiasm. The risk is too great; and it is understood that there are suitable arrangements for watching him in Pondicherry.

The refugees themselves were sometimes tempted to take the lead and leave Pondicherry for a more hospitable shore. Maybe another French colony—Djibouti or Algeria—would be safer? When Bharati conveyed this suggestion to Aurobindo, the latter responded:

> Mr Bharati, I am not going to budge an inch from Pondicherry. I know nothing will happen to me.

Arya

In early 1914, Aurobindo and Paul Richard came up with the idea of launching a magazine called *Arya*. Its object would be 'to feel out for the thought of the future, to help in shaping its foundations and to link it to the best and most vital thought of the past'. During the next six years, Aurobindo would produce almost all his written work, nearly 5,000 pages, on the study and forecast of humanity's future trends and the evolution of mankind. A French version, under Paul's and Mirra's responsibility, was to be released in parallel and distributed in the French-speaking world.

The circulation anticipated 850 English-speaking and 250 French-speaking subscribers. The launch took place on 15 August 1914, Aurobindo's 42nd birthday.

Thus, just as one of the worst bloodbaths in history broke out, the first volume of *Arya*, with its energy of light, got underway.

> The world today presents the aspect of a huge cauldron of Medea in which all things are being cast, shredded into pieces, experimented on, combined and recombined either to perish or provide the scattered material of new forms or to emerge rejuvenated and changed for a fresh term of existence.

Aurobindo now had 64 pages of philosophy to produce every 15th of the month. Two full weeks were necessary for writing and preparing the galley proofs. What's more, he did not write one work at a time but four or even five different works concurrently in the same monthly issue. As he explained:

> I have simply left the higher Power to work and when it did not work, I made no efforts at all.... It is out of a silent mind that I write whatever comes ready-shaped from above.

The major works published in *Arya* included *The Secret of the Veda*, *The Life Divine*, *The Synthesis of Yoga*, *The Human Cycle*, *The Ideal of Human Unity* and *Essays on the Gita*.

The Secret of the Veda

Dating back from two to three millennia BC, the Veda is the foundation of Indian civilisation and Hinduism. A corpus of texts revealed by audition to the Vedic sages or rishis, it embodied a spiritual 'knowledge' that has been transmitted orally until the present day. It was later followed by the Vedanta, featuring the Upanishads, which crowned the Veda's inspiration in a more philosophical manner.

Aurobindo approached the Veda in Pondicherry by delving into the hymns of the Rig Veda, the oldest and most complex Vedic text. By comparing the original Sanskrit with later

Indian and modern translations, he realised that scholars had often overlooked essential inward aspects of the hymns. His work would bring to light 'a considerable body of profound psychological thought and experience lying neglected in these ancient hymns'.

His endeavour to make his translation accessible to modern intelligence without distorting the original significance gave birth to a text restored to its brilliance and internal harmony. To his surprise, the ideas and doctrines thus highlighted turned out to be ancient forms and expressions of the Upanishads' subsequent spiritual experiences. The natural relation with the Vedanta was thereby established.

The hymns of the Rig Veda investigate the transition of the human soul from a state of death to a state of immortality—not the physical survival to death, but a consciousness exceeding both birth and death. *Agni*, the Fire, is the central Power of this transformation of consciousness. He is the most omniscient, the most universal of the Vedic Gods, as he rules over the accomplishment of the inner sacrifice. When a man awakens from his night and aspires to offer his inner and outer activities to the gods of a truer existence, it is this flame of Force and Willpower that he must kindle; it is to this Fire that he must present the offering of his life.

The Life Divine

The Life Divine appeared in *Arya* from the first issue in 1914 until January 1919, coinciding almost exactly with the duration of the First World War.

Over 1,000 pages, Aurobindo affirmed the possibility of a divine life on earth. In the course of what we call evolution, hasn't Nature produced life from inert matter before developing the mind from life? It is, therefore, entirely plausible that human aspiration will pursue 'the imperative impulse by which Nature is seeking to evolve beyond Mind' towards the Divine.

The first part of the book sets out to describe 'the scale of substance' that connects Spirit to Matter: the upper hemisphere of the cosmos, the Brahman, to the lower hemisphere, comprising the ordinary principles of matter, life and mind. Between these two hemispheres rises the Supramental, or Supermind, which manifests the Brahman's fundamental unity as well as the multiplicity of the universe. It is, therefore, by tearing the veil between mind and Supermind that humanity would gain access to the divine life.

In the second part of the book, Aurobindo addresses the question of the why. Why is humankind overcome with ignorance, error and suffering? According to him, the reason lies with the individualisation of the soul, its propensity to consider everything in the universe according to its own point of view to the exclusion of all others.

What is the justification for the 'fall'? The plunge into the fragmentation of ordinary life is not 'a blunder and a fall, but a purposeful descent, not a curse, but a divine opportunity'. Brahman is embodied in the lower hemisphere to take part in what Aurobindo calls 'the adventure of consciousness and joy'.

The last part of the book is devoted to the conditions enabling the advent of the divine life. Brahman's blind plunge into fragmented matter must be followed by his re-emergence into the Light, his full recovery of Knowledge.

> But this is not an intellectual knowledge which can be learned and completed in our present mould of consciousness; it must be an experience, a becoming, a change of consciousness, a change of being.

This Knowledge is acquired through the process of yoga. Contrary to past evolutionary transitions, humanity can now participate in this ascent for 'evolution has become conscious'.

The Synthesis of Yoga

The book opens with this epigraph: 'All life is yoga.'

However, what is yoga? The book examines the spiritual experiences justifying and establishing the conversion to a divine life.

> Yoga is the exchange of an egoistic for a universal or cosmic consciousness lifted towards or informed by the supra-cosmic, transcendent Unnameable who is the source and support of all things. Yoga is the passage of the human thinking animal towards the god-consciousness from which he has descended.

From the mind's intellectual processes to the body's material functioning through the senses and emotional activities, everything essential to life is impacted by yoga. For life is nothing more than a 'vast yoga of Nature who attempts in the conscious and the subconscious to realise her perfection in an ever-increasing expression of her yet unrealised potentialities and to unite herself with her own divine reality'.

Delving into his 'Integral Yoga', Aurobindo revisits the traditional forms of yoga and their specific transformations: Hatha Yoga, Raja Yoga, the triple path (Karma Yoga, Jnana Yoga and Bhakti Yoga) and postulates a synthetic harmony between these disciplines by concentrating on the common dynamic principle in each.

The *Synthesis of Yoga* culminates with 'the yoga of Self-Perfection'. This new way of yoga, without equivalent in India's spiritual literature, is the very one the reader discovers in Aurobindo's journal, *Record of Yoga*—it is the first practical step of a new being after the human.

The Ideal of Human Unity

In September 1915, Aurobindo began writing for *Arya* a new volume called *The Ideal of Human Unity*, whose publication he announced to Mirra:

> I intend to proceed very cautiously and not go very deep at first, but as if I were leading the intelligence of the reader gradually towards the deeper meaning of unity—especially to discourage the idea that mistakes uniformity and mechanical association for unity.

His idea is that if we postulate that humanity's social and political unity is part of Nature's ultimate purpose, then the course of history can be seen as a progression towards more encompassing collective gatherings. However, if this union is obtained by 'mechanical means', that is, through 'social and political adjustments', the result is likely to be an 'impoverishment of individual life and therefore of the community'. The challenge is to keep the benefits of a stable organisation without sacrificing the richness of cultural diversity. For if social life consists of the interaction between the individual and the community, perfection of human life 'must involve the elaboration of an as yet unaccomplished harmony between these two poles of our existence, the individual and the social aggregate'.

Aurobindo's words may seem abstract or benevolent, but it is remarkable that—one century after he wrote these words—the questions of social integration resurfaced in France on the occasion of a recent debate on the European Union, when a political speaker was heard reading aloud this excerpt from *The Ideal of Human Unity*:

> In the present state of human egoism, it is evident that if European unity could be formed, it would become a tremendously powerful instrument for the domination and exploitation of the rest of the world by the group of nations which are at present in the forefront of human progress. It would inevitably awaken in antagonism to it an idea of Asiatic unity and an idea of American unity, and while such continental groupings replacing the present smaller national unities might well be an advance towards the final union of all mankind, yet their realisation would mean cataclysms of a kind and scope which would dwarf the present

> catastrophe (WWI) and in which the hopes of mankind might founder and fatally collapse rather than progress nearer to fulfilment.... If, therefore, any new supra-national order is to evolve sooner or later as a result of the present upheaval, it must be an association that will embrace Asia, Africa and America as well as Europe and it must be in its nature an organisation of international life constituted by a number of free nations.

To survive, this 'confederation of free self-determining nationalities' should submit to 'an intellectual and psychological change' whose motive would be 'the growth of the religion of humanity', ushered during the French Revolution:

> Mankind is the godhead to be worshipped and served by man and the respect, the service, the progress of the human being and human life are the chief duty and the chief aim of the human spirit.

Yet according to Aurobindo, if this remains an intellectual and sentimental ideal, the religion of humanity can never establish a lasting world union. To do this, it must spiritualise itself and become 'the general inner law of human life'.

> A religion of humanity means the growing realisation that there is a secret Spirit, a divine Reality in which we are all one, that humanity is its highest present vehicle on earth, that the human race and the human being are the means by which it will progressively reveal itself here. It implies a growing attempt to live out this knowledge and bring about a kingdom of this divine Spirit upon earth.

In this conclusion of *The Ideal of Human Unity*, we find again the principles of the evolutionary philosophy of *The Life Divine*.

The content of *Arya* did not stop with the four books presented here. Aurobindo wrote *Essays on the Gita*, his masterful treatise on Krishna's teaching to Arjuna; he produced translations, reviews, aphorisms and epigrams; various essays and memoirs on the progress of the war; dissertations on materialism, meditation, astrology; studies on reincarnation, art and poetry—nothing seemed to elude the *Arya's* reach.

In January 1915, the French version of *Arya* was suspended when Paul Richard learned that he must return to France to join his regiment. The Richards packed their bags and sailed on 22 February for Europe. On 3 March, on board the *Kamo Maru*, Mirra wrote in her diary:

> SOLITUDE... a harsh, intense solitude, and always this strong impression of having been flung headlong into a hell of darkness! Never at any moment of my life, in any circumstances, have I felt myself living in surroundings so entirely opposite to all that I am conscious of as true, so contrary to all that is the essence of my life... each passing hour seems to plunge me deeper into that past with which I had broken.

Why did she have to depart from India and leave Aurobindo?

For Aurobindo, a new phase began. Since 6 February 1915, he had abandoned his journal. He resumed it on the 25th, after Mirra's and Paul's departure, with this preamble:

> The record has been suspended because of an almost entire suspension of all progress in which the hostile forces have seemed to take possession and only the literary and intellectual activity has continued to progress.

Gandhi

The war also brutally brought back the problem of independence as a central issue among the Indian political class: if India cooperated with England by sending her young men into battle, how would that affect the fate of colonialism? In a letter of August 1914 to a nationalist correspondent, Aurobindo had suggested that India could benefit from the war by offering limited cooperation to the British in exchange for some concessions and military training. From his point of view, defending the British regime against an aggressor amounted to defending India's future independence.

Gandhi's personality would soon come to dominate the Indian political landscape. To comprehend Gandhi's meteoric rise to lead the Indian Congress, we have to return a few years back to South Africa. In 1893, we recall that he had left India as an attorney to flee racial prejudices and authoritarianism in India's judiciary. His professional success in the South African law firm that recruited him, strengthened him and cured his stage fright. Narrowly escaping a lynching by South African white settlers, he refused to file a complaint; the activist began to emerge in him.

He decided to change his life. He cut his hair, practised fasting, and became a strict vegetarian—and a pacifist after devouring Tolstoy. In *Letter to a Hindu*, the famous Russian writer maintained that only the energy of love could free India from the British yoke. Gandhi was conquered. He found in the words of Christ, and also from Buddhism and Jainism, the doctrinal confirmation of his pacifist zeal. Hinduism, his own religion, was the one creed in which he sought in vain a direct validation of his ideas. The Bhagavad Gita collided with his pacifism, and he spurned Krishna's admonitions to Arjuna on the need to take up arms.

In India, meanwhile, the moderate-loyalist party of Congress had still not recovered from the Surat explosion of 1907 and the secession of the nationalist party led by Aurobindo and Tilak. Its leaders, Gokhale, Mehta, Banerjee and Naoroji, eagerly observed Gandhi's tribulations in South Africa; they approved of his principles and, beneath his exterior of 'Hindu Nationalist', they knew his attachment to British civilisation and its Christian foundations. They prompted Charles Freer Andrews, an Anglican pastor friend of Gandhi's, to travel to South Africa to convince the Mahatma to put his talents into reviving the Indian National

Congress. These men with strong anglophile views were to become Gandhi's guides in the corridors of Indian politics.

In January 1915, a few months after the outbreak of the First World War, Gandhi landed in India in a halo of incandescent popularity. His plan was to apply non-violent protest on Indian soil. Gokhale's patronage was a guarantee of respectability, and even Viceroy Hardinge was favourable to his 'passive resistance'.

However, first, he needed to check the pulse of Congress to convince the delegates of his new approach in which non-violence would be the prerequisite to any action of protest. 'If India made violence its creed, I would not want to live in India. My patriotism is subordinated to my religion of non-violence,' he stated.

Two incidents helped him assert his influence. In Champaram in the state of Bihar and in Kheda in Gujarat, he joined a campaign to repeal the taxes of the poorest farmers. As young men were falling by the thousands on the death fields of the Marne in France, he offered the British a deal that was hard to refuse: if tax repeal was granted, it would be interpreted as a victory for non-violence and, in return, he would enlist all able-bodied young Indians to fight alongside England. Although a newcomer on the political scene, he addressed the viceroy with leading authority:

> At this critical hour, I will make sure that India offers all her able-bodied sons as a sacrifice to the Empire. [...] The events of Champaram and Khoda will be my direct, determined and personal contribution to the war effort.

This was a compelling proposition in the mouth of the apostle of non-violence.

He was propelled onto the national stage—and into the heart of his compatriots—as the undisputed challenger to the British

Goliath. But his fame did not yet affect the distribution of votes in Congress. His next problem was to tip the scales in his favour.

The war had now ended in Europe, ratifying the defeat of the Sultan of Turkey, an ally of Germany, and the breakup of the Ottoman Empire. In India, a radical fringe of Muslims rose to demand that the British restore the sultan to his function as the natural head of the caliphate, resulting in the nominal authority over all Muslims in the world. This demand was clearly political, the authority of the caliph having fallen into disuse since the 13th century. Two leaders of the Muslim League—created by the British to counterbalance the Hindu influence in Congress—the Ali brothers then launched the 'agitation of the caliphate' and dared Gandhi to support their claim. His reaction exceeded their wildest expectations.

Gandhi speculated that a rapprochement with Muslims would further broaden his political base as he would become the champion of Hindu-Muslim unity:

> As a man of truth, I honestly believe that Hindus should give Muslims whatever they want, and rejoice in doing so.

From one day to the next, he was to commit the majority of his people to the pan-Islamic demands of the Ali brothers.

It was a calamitous decision for which India would pay a heavy price of blood: 27 years later, the wild horse of radical Islam would bring about India's dismemberment and the creation of Pakistan.

Yet Gandhi's political calculation proved right: Muslim congressional delegates lined up in droves behind him. Meanwhile, he was laying the foundation of a massive campaign of non-violent non-cooperation in which both communities, Hindu and Muslim, would struggle shoulder to shoulder for … the Muslim caliphate.

Overnight, the popular aspiration for independence, the efforts and hopes of Tilak, Bipin Chandra, Lajpat Rai and the perspectives of revival predicted by Aurobindo were 'postponed' and diverted towards a programme completely foreign to India's interest. It would take nine years for Swaraj (independence) to return to the agenda of Indian politics.

Now that he controlled Congress, Gandhi asserted his ideas with force. As a test of independence from British cotton mills, all Congress delegates would manufacture their own clothes by weaving them with a portable spinning wheel (charkha), which Gandhi exhibited for the media, stating:

> Before returning to India, I felt a conviction that only by resuming hand spinning would India be restored to its original glory.

With Tilak's death in August 1920, the last opposition to Gandhi's ideas disappeared from Congress:

> My life is dedicated to the service of India through the religion of non-violence.

Like his mentor Tolstoy, he could now proclaim that India would win her independence by choosing the path of love and by not responding to violence with violence, which would ultimately dry up from unfailing kindness.

With Gandhi at the helm of Congress, India's political class was to founder in the phantasmagoria of non-violence for 30 years. No strategy was formulated, and no decision was approved if they had not initially passed through the filter of this collective illusion. Programmes were launched that involved the fate of entire populations; direct incitements triggered communal riots (91 for Uttar Pradesh alone in 1924), but Gandhi the Saint would invariably manage to justify the miscalculations of Gandhi the Politician. When at a loss for words, he resorted to hunger strikes—35 in 30 years—which strengthened his image of holiness.

For Aurobindo, Gandhi was not Indian but European—specifically, a Christian Russian in an Indian body. The gospel of suffering he advocated had its roots in Russia more than anywhere else in Europe. Westerners praised him as more Christian than most Christians, some even calling him the Christ of modern times.

Japanese Interlude

Torn from leaving India and separating from Aurobindo, Mirra had returned to France.

Arriving in Lunel, where Paul was posted, she fell gravely ill, and her condition grew critical. Lying on a lounge chair in her garden, despite the inflammation affecting her nerves and almost total paralysis of her body, she discovered that she was still quite capable of feeling inward connections with people. She could answer calls from anywhere in the world and even clearly perceive the face of individuals with whom she established contact.

In 1915, the war redoubled in horror. The Germans used mustard gas on the Western front, and the sinking of the *Léon Gambetta* by a submarine caused 700 deaths, while that of the *Lusitania* killed 1,200 passengers and contributed to drawing America into the war in 1917.

In his first letter sent to Mirra from Pondicherry, in May 1915, Aurobindo alluded to the battle of his yoga, 'The daily struggle between the spiritual and the physical':

> One needs to have a calm heart, a settled will, entire self-abnegation and the eyes constantly fixed on the beyond to live undiscouraged in times like these which are truly a period of universal decomposition.

Highlighting the parallel with the stagnating conflict in Europe, he emphasised, in another letter of 28 July, the complexity of his internal struggle:

> If there were not the strength and Ananda within, it would be harassing and disgusting work; but the eye of knowledge looks beyond and sees that it is only a protracted episode.

In November, Mirra again had a powerful body experience. In a long letter, she described to Aurobindo her consciousness immersed in divine contemplation:

> The whole being enjoyed a supreme and vast felicity. The physical body was seized by a sacred trembling which made all personal limits fall away even in the most material sensation. The being grew in greatness progressively, methodically, breaking down every limit, shattering every obstacle so it might contain and manifest a force and a power which increased ceaselessly in immensity and intensity. It felt like a progressive dilatation of the cells until there was complete identification with the earth: the body of the waking consciousness was the terrestrial globe moving harmoniously in ethereal space.

Aurobindo soon replied:

> The experience you have described is Vedic in the real sense. It is the union of the 'Earth' of the Veda with the divine Principle, an earth which is said to be above our earth, that is to say, the physical being and consciousness of which this world and the body are only images.

Returning to Paris, Paul was declared medically unfit and released from military obligations—'a yogic heart disease!' later rectified Mirra. He looked around for a new post that would allow him to leave France. In February 1916, the Ministry of Foreign Affairs appointed him as a delegate of the Union for the Export of

French Goods. On 14 March, he embarked with Mirra for Japan. Their stay there would last four years.

Despite the distance, Mirra kept informing Aurobindo of her yogic progress, also mentioning her relapses, the drops of intensity that sometimes brought her back to ordinary consciousness. He was long accustomed to these relapses—they were his daily fare:

> The difficulties you find in the spiritual progress are common to us all. In this yoga the progress is always attended with these relapses into the ordinary mentality until the whole being is so remoulded that it can no longer be affected either by any downward tendency in our own nature or by the impressions from the discordant world outside or even by the mental state of those associated with us most closely in the yoga.

Aurobindo also kept her abreast of his own advances, particularly with regard to the relationship within himself between the Presence of Krishna (the Master) and his Power (Kali):

> When the Unity has been well founded, the static half of our work is done, but the active half remains. It is then that in the One we must see the Master and His Power—Krishna and Kali as I name them using the terms of our Indian religions; the Power occupying the whole of myself and my nature which becomes Kali and ceases to be anything else, the Master using, directing, enjoying the Power to his ends, not mine, with that which I call myself only as a centre of his universal existence and responding to its workings as a soul to the Soul, taking upon itself his image until there is nothing left but Krishna and Kali. This is the stage I have reached in spite of all setbacks and recoils.

In Tokyo, Paul's mission turned out to be devoid of any practical substance because of the war conditions. He spent his time writing and sending his texts to Aurobindo for translation in the *Arya*. Mirra resigned herself to wait for the end of the war. She adopted the Japanese lifestyle, wore kimonos and learnt the art of flower arrangement. She painted, learnt Japanese, communicated, in her own way, with the vegetables in her garden and meditated among a circle of friends. For her, the true Japanese were those who kept in touch with the righteousness and bravery of the Samurai tradition:

> They know how to remain silent; and though they are possessed of the most acute sensitiveness, they are, among the people I have met, those who express it the least. A friend here can give his life with the greatest simplicity to save yours, though he never told you before he loved you in such a profound and unselfish way.

Yet, despite her admiration for Japan, she felt something was missing from this perfection and found 'a dearth of spirituality as entire as could be'.

However, her diary reveals that, from meditation to meditation, she advanced on the path, opening up to the consciousness of her own destiny:

> The whole being began to love, to love ever more and more, without any definite aim, nothing and everything at the same time, what it knows and does not know, what it sees and has never seen; and gradually this potential love became an effective love, ready to pour itself out upon all and everything, in beneficent waves, in an active effulgence....

In 1917, Mirra and Paul left Tokyo for Kyoto, the ancient imperial capital of Japan and the centre of her millennial culture, where Mirra 'lived from wonder to wonder', prompting her to paint and draw using the technique of Japanese prints. However, nothing could distract her from her inner research:

> Thou hast subjected me to a hard discipline; rung after rung, I have climbed the ladder which leads to Thee and, at the summit of the ascent, Thou hast made me taste the perfect joy of identity with Thee.... And

> now that I have come back to the bottom of the ladder, all is so dull, so mediocre, so neutral, in me and around me, that I understand no more.

She did not give up and pursued her quest until this day when she could exclaim:

> O Lord, because in an hour of cruel distress I said in the sincerity of my faith: 'Thy Will be done', Thou camest garbed in Thy raiment of glory. Agni is rekindled in my fortified heart, and his splendour shines out and sets aglow the atmosphere and purifies it.... Thou hast said to me: 'I have returned to leave thee no more.'

In January 1919, Japan was struck by the influenza pandemic that caused unprecedented devastation worldwide. People died by the thousands every day, and no one went out without a mask. When Mirra had to go to town, she was shocked by the dreadful atmosphere she felt everywhere around her. When she returned home, she knew she was contaminated. She laid down but refused to take the medication prescribed by the doctor. The fever rose.

> Suddenly I felt seized by trance—the real trance, the kind that drives you out of your body—and I knew. I knew: 'This is the end; if I can't resist it, it'll be the end.' So I concentrated and I saw inwardly a being whose head had been half severed by a bomb and who didn't know he was dead. So he was attaching himself to anybody he could suck life from. Each of these beings spread out a terrible atmosphere of human decomposition, utterly pestilential, and that's what gave the illness. So once I saw and knew, I collected all the occult energy, all the occult power I could muster, and I turned over on my bed, awake. And it was over. Not only was it over, but I began to work in the atmosphere.... From that moment on, there were no new cases! It was so surprising that it appeared in the Japanese papers.

This post-war flu pandemic—which spread worldwide and claimed fifty million lives—also had a dramatic impact on

Aurobindo's life. Since his departure from Bengal, his wife, Mrinalini, had led an isolated, almost monastic life with her parents in Assam. In December 1918, as the end of the war finally made it possible to join her husband in Pondicherry, she travelled to Calcutta to prepare for her trip. There she was contaminated by the flu virus and passed away three days later. In his letter to her father, Aurobindo revealed the sadness Mrinalini's disappearance caused him.

> I have not written to you with regard to this fatal event in both our lives; words are useless in face of the feelings it has caused, if even they can ever express our deepest emotions. God has seen good to lay upon me the one sorrow that could still touch me to the centre. He knows better than ourselves what is best for each of us, and now that the first sense of the irreparable has passed, I can bow with submission to His divine purpose. The physical tie between us is, as you say, severed; but the tie of affection subsists for me. Where I have once loved, I do not cease from loving.

In Japan, Mirra's stay was drawing to a close. Although she systematically removed from her journal the most private circumstances of her life, yet this confidence of 3 September 1919 was kept:

> Since the man refused the meal I had prepared with so much love and care, I invoked the God to take it.

This sentence alluded to the growing distance with Paul Richard, which would lead to the breakup of the marriage. Sensing the inevitable rupture, she asked the Lord:

> Now tell me, what must I do?

In a vision, she felt carried towards India:

> I felt it physically. I saw—my eyes were closed but I saw.... This vision literally gathered me into its arms; it turned towards the West, towards India, and offered me—and at the other end I saw Sri Aurobindo. Not a word, nothing else, only that.

The next day, she began preparing to return to India.

1920–1926: The World as It Is

A Lull?

On 28 June 1919, the Treaty of Versailles brought an end to the war. Initially refusing to accept the draconian conditions demanded by the Allies, Germany finally bowed to their 'diktat'. Aurobindo harboured no illusions about this 'Carthaginian peace', nor did he put any trust in the power of the 'League of Nations' to prevent future conflicts:

> The new fair and peaceful world order that was promised us has gone far away into the land of chimeras. The League of Nations that was to have embodied it hardly even exists or exists only as a mockery and a byword.

The Allies clearly won the war, but they were just as clearly in the process of losing the peace. A humiliated Germany vowed revenge. New conflicts, which were thought inconceivable, would soon arise. Always clairvoyant, Aurobindo saw the grim future ahead:

> This year (1919) may be only the end of an acute phase of a first struggle, the commencement of a breathing time, the year of a makeshift, the temporary halt of a flood in motion. That is so because (the peace) has not realised the deeper mind of humanity nor answered to the far-reaching intention of the Time-Spirit.

For him, the time had come to work for another kind of future. Between 1915 and 1920, as far as his yogic progression was concerned, he admitted that he could have been described as 'sitting on the path'. However, he added: 'The sadhana and the work were waiting for Mirra's coming.'

Waiting for Mirra

Aurobindo devoted his days to writing for *Arya* and keeping abreast of the latest news, notably from the *Hindu* newspaper. The evenings were spent with his usual companions, Bharati, Srinivasacharia and a few others. Casual visitors such as C.R. Das, his friend and lawyer from the Alipore trial, or Khasirao Jadhav, his colleague of the Baroda government, made brief appearances. The visits and conversations were not just an exchange of courtesies: a deeper interchange took place with his guests.

> I am now able to put myself into men and change them, removing the darkness and bringing light, giving them a new heart and a new mind. This I can do with great swiftness and completeness with those who are near me, but I have also succeeded with men hundreds of miles away.

His brother, Barin, had just been released from the penal colony in the Andaman Islands after serving his sentence. In a long letter in Bengali, Aurobindo described the progress of his own sadhana and outlined the ideal future community he had in view.

> I do not want hundreds of thousands of disciples. It will be enough if I can get a hundred complete men, empty of petty egoism, who will be instruments of God.

Barin joined his brother in Pondicherry.

With the conclusion of the war and Gandhi's recent dominance over Congress, politics had returned to centre stage. Gandhi launched a campaign of passive resistance against the repressive measures put in place by the Indian government during the war. It mobilised huge popular support. At Amritsar, in North India, the British army faced a peaceful protest and fired on the crowd, killing hundreds of demonstrators. Gandhi skilfully combined this tragedy with the resentment felt by Indian Muslims about the breakup of the Ottoman Empire during the war. He assembled a march in which both Hindus and Muslims could join. It seemed that nothing could stop his ascendency.

Still, many political observers awaited Aurobindo's reaction. A majority in the nationalist ranks even hoped he would come back to politics. As the forthcoming Congress session of December 1920 was to be held in Nagpur, Balkrishna Moonje, a former nationalist colleague, asked Aurobindo to accept the presidency of the session to replace Tilak, who had died in September. Aurobindo's answer was unambiguous:

> Since my retirement from British India, I have developed an outlook and views which have diverged a great deal from those I held at the time (1906–1910) and, as they are remote from present actualities and do not follow the present stream of political action, I should find myself very much embarrassed what to say to the Congress. I am entirely in sympathy with all that is being done so far as its object is to secure liberty for India, but I should be unable to identify myself with the programme of any of the parties. The president of the Congress is really a mouthpiece of the Congress and to make from the presidential chair a purely personal pronouncement miles away from what the Congress is thinking and doing would be grotesquely out of place.

He added that he was all the more unavailable since he 'had commenced another kind of work with a spiritual basis, a work of spiritual, social, cultural and economic reconstruction of an almost revolutionary kind'.

As expected, the December session of Congress confirmed Gandhi's hold on public opinion. Between 1920 and 1922, his civil disobedience movement mobilised the country, and even hardened revolutionaries were tempted to join him. To his indecisive former political friends, Aurobindo predicted that Gandhi's civil disobedience movement would end 'in great confusion or a great fiasco'. A year and a half later, he was proven right.

The Return of Mirra

Mirra arrived in Pondicherry with Paul Richard on 24 April 1920. As in her first meeting six years earlier, she met Aurobindo alone.

> Physically there was hardly any contact, we were standing side by side, gazing out through the open window, and then TOGETHER, at exactly the same moment, we felt: 'Now the Realisation will be accomplished.' The seal has been given and the Realisation will be accomplished. From that moment on there was nothing else to say—no words, nothing. We knew that was it.

The Richards rented a house on Rue Saint-Martin, and they resumed their daily visits to Aurobindo. Stimulating conversations flowed—yet sometimes the meetings took place in 'a natural silence close to meditation'. Every Sunday, as before, Aurobindo and his young companions were dinner guests at the Richards.

In their verbal exchange, as in the silence, in what Mirra would call 'a mental miracle', Aurobindo and Mirra became closer.

With changing events and diverging priorities, even before going to Japan, Paul Richard and his wife were further growing apart, and their separation became eventually inevitable. Richard departed from Pondicherry in November and wandered for a while in the Himalayas before returning to France. Finally, he left for America, where he assumed a teaching position in New York prior to finalising the divorce from Mirra.

November is monsoon season in Pondicherry, sometimes even prone to cyclones. Violent downpours flooded the city, causing leaks and seepage in houses. One evening, it was reported that the roof of a nearby warehouse had caved in, and Mirra's house was also in danger of collapse. Aurobindo thought it best to offer her the shelter of his own house.

One can easily imagine the emotion caused by this foreign feminine intrusion among the group of young men. They were as curious as they were disconcerted.

However, Mirra's kindness, sensitivity and dedication to Aurobindo would soon assuage their fears. Although she was accustomed to a comfortable life in Paris, she adjusted to Pondicherry's harsher conditions and deprivation. After glancing at her new environment and the methodical chaos serving as a substitute for order, she set to work. Little by little, chaos gave way to order. To Purani, who visited Aurobindo after two years of absence, the improvement came as a surprise:

> The house has undergone a great change. There is a clean garden in the open courtyard; every room has simple and decent furniture—a mat, a chair and a small table. There is an air of tidiness and order everywhere.

The real amazement for him was in the physical transformation undergone by Aurobindo's body: 'His cheeks wore an apple-pink colour and the whole body glowed with a soft creamy white light.' Purani could not contain his stupefaction and asked: 'What has happened to you?'

Aurobindo explained: 'When the Higher Consciousness, after descending to the mental level, comes down to the vital and even below the vital, then a transformation takes place in the nervous and even in the physical being.'

Before leaving, Purani wondered: 'What do you expect now?' 'It is true that the Divine Consciousness has descended', Aurobindo replied, 'but it has not yet descended into the physical being. So long as that is not done, the work cannot be said to be accomplished.' The goal was to establish the full Supramental consciousness in the body.

Over time, Aurobindo entrusted Mirra with the administrative care of the house. For two or three more years, their spiritual relationship remained invisible to all; she was a practitioner of yoga among the others, a *Sadhika*. Yet, Aurobindo confided to Barin that her presence was crucial, that her influence helped him to materialise his subjective advances in outer life. Thanks to her, he was able to reduce several years of work into one. He now determined that a Shakti, the feminine counterpart of the divine Power, was indispensable to the transformation of the self and the world.

Traditional yoga systems aiming at self-perfection, such as Tantrism, regard woman as the incarnation of the divine Power. To them, the consecrated union of man and woman is the re-enactment of the cosmic act of creation. Aurobindo emphasised that this was not true for his yoga. 'How can the sexual act be made to help in spiritual life?' he asked a disciple who had raised the question.

'Sex is a degradation or distortion of the *ananda* Force.'

If the union of the male and female principles was necessary for the work of transformation, this had nothing to do with sex, he pointed out. This union was, in fact, possible in the case of Mirra and Aurobindo because they had both conquered the force of desire.

A Spiritual Community

In January 1921, as Aurobindo came to the end of what he intended to communicate in the *Arya*, he stopped its publication.

During six-and-a-half years, he had, on his own, produced 77 issues of the review. Although it would often be difficult for him to find time to revise these texts for publication in book form, he felt he had achieved 'the intellectual side of (his) work for the world'.

He was now free to devote himself to a new approach to yoga in a new spiritualised form of social organisation.

> Our business is not with the formless spirit. We have to keep life in motion. There is no effective motion of life without form.
>
> Not a fixed and rigid form like that of the old Aryan society, not a stagnant backwater, but a free form that can spread itself like the sea with its multitudinous waves.

From 1921 onward, a daily practice of collective meditations began. The dozen or so residents who were accepted as serious practitioners of yoga met at 4 pm on the first-floor veranda. Aurobindo came out of his room and sat among them. A 'talk' ensued on a topic that was not necessarily yogic. Half an hour later, a short meditation followed, at the end of which the Master returned to his room, and everyone else resumed their daily occupations.

Recalling these encounters, Barin emphasised that Aurobindo 'never cared to waste his breath in a long discourse on his yoga'. The same attitude was reported by the other companions. Suresh, who had been part of the household since the beginning, could not remember one instance when Aurobindo spoke to him about practising 'yoga'.

This would suggest that the 'talk' on the veranda took place outside any rational influence, within an invisible plane of energy, a Force indistinguishable by human senses. Attempts at words and explanations had come to an end.

> The spread of the idea is not sufficient; (we) must have real yogins, not merely men moved intellectually and emotionally by one or two of the central ideas of the yoga.

No instructions, no explanations, no mantra. People who came to Aurobindo 'were free to pursue any method or all methods'. When asked for guidance, he only suggested that they try to surrender to the Divine and invoke the Shakti to purify themselves. There was only one overt rule: the strict observance of celibacy (*brahmacharya*). Otherwise, the companions were free to lead their life as they pleased.

Such was the initial approach to what would develop into the future Ashram community: a dozen participants who had made the free choice of a 'serious yoga practice', founded on Aurobindo's presence and his inspiring silence.

This new collective yoga would soon need vaster grounds to house its members. Thanks to Barin, a large house was found minutes away from the current residence. At the end of October 1922, Aurobindo, Mirra and five of their companions moved to 9 Rue de la Marine, which would become the Ashram's main building and its present address. By the end of 1923, the community counted 15 full-time residents lodged in two houses.

The *Evening Talks* continued until 1926. From 1924 onward, formal meditation was discontinued to make room for a single questions and answers session. Members of the household would gather every day at the appointed time and start chatting in low tones. Aurobindo came out last, and only then would the session commence. Purani took notes:

> How much were these sittings dependent on him may be gathered from the fact that there were days when more than three-fourths of the time passed in complete silence without any outer suggestion from him,

> except an abrupt 'Yes' or 'No' to all attempts at drawing him out in conversation. And even when he participated in the talk, one always felt that his voice was that of one who does not let his whole being flow into his words; there was a reserve and what was left unsaid was perhaps more than what was spoken.

The conversation ranged from local news to philosophy, integral yoga and even politics. Yet Aurobindo felt that India should no longer place any hope for a breakthrough in politics.

> My one aim is to bring down the Supermind, allow it to organise itself in my being and life.

To one of the participants who asked if he carried out any external work, he replied:

> I am not doing any outward work at present. I have given up everything, even writing. Unless we realise the thing internally, no outward work will be possible.

Although the *Evening Talks* remained informal, Aurobindo began to accept the role of guru in his relationship with his companions. Up until now, while they admired and respected him as the prophet of nationalism and a spiritual leader, their relationship with him was one of familiarity and camaraderie. Under Mirra's influence, the tone gradually changed. She had set the house in material order; leading by example, she would now do the same with the code of behaviour. The boisterous comrades became respectful disciples of the Master from whom they had everything to learn.

Mirra's status and name also would change. Nolini recalled that in the beginning, Aurobindo would refer to her quite distinctly as 'Mirra'. Later on, everyone noticed that he would stop at the sound of 'M' and utter the full name 'Mirra' as if after a slight hesitation. Nolini felt that 'his lips were on the verge of saying "Mother", but we had yet to be ready for it, so he ended with "Mirra" instead of saying "Mother"'.

This was also the time when Aurobindo started using the prefix 'Sri' before his own name. Originally a Sanskrit sign of veneration found in the Rig Veda, this prefix has been applied in India for centuries. Sri Aurobindo—he thus signed his autograph for the first time in 1926—is the name by which he has been known ever since.

Among the fledgling community, no day was more memorable or celebrated more intensely than the 'Darshan', Sri Aurobindo's birthday, on 15 August. It was customary that each participant stopped before him to receive his steady gaze.

On the first such Darshan day, the *Evening Talks* assumed a special significance when a disciple felt emboldened enough to ask Aurobindo to describe the 'state' of his sadhana. He replied in a clear but low voice:

> I cannot call it a state, or a condition. It is, rather, a complex movement. I am at present engaged in bringing the Supermind into the physical consciousness, down even to the sub-material. The physical is by nature inert and does not want to be rendered conscious. It offers much greater resistance as it is unwilling to change. One feels as if 'digging the earth', as the Veda says. It is literally digging from Supermind above to Supermind below. The Veda calls it 'the two ends'—the head and the tail.

At the next birthday, in 1924, he again commented on the difficulties of the sadhana.

> All I can say is I am doing the same thing over and over again; only I am doing it each time better.... The physical layer is a very obstinate thing and it requires to be worked out in detail. You work out one thing then think it is done; something else arises and you have again to go over the

> same ground. It is not like the mind or the vital where it is easier for the Higher Power to work. Besides there—in the mind and in the vital—you can establish a general law leaving out the details; the physical is not so; it requires constant patience and minutia.

In 1925, as the disciples again pressed him for a date on bringing down the Supermind into the physical plane, he elicited bursts of laughter when he declared:

> I can say now, 'It is more possible this year than it was last year'!

The following months were spent struggling to overcome the resistance in the physical consciousness. Although the household was growing and 20 participants now took part in the evening meetings, Sri Aurobindo was less and less accessible, and the *Talks* were often postponed until late. He rarely mentioned his progress and exchanged little with the disciples.

1926–1950: The Life Divine

The Ashram

On 24 November 1926, Mirra personally summoned everyone onto the veranda at 7 pm. Very quietly, the door opened and she appeared, followed by Sri Aurobindo. They walked slowly and sat down. A hushed silence fell upon the assembly and prevailed for three-quarters of an hour. Then each of the participants stood up and bowed to Mirra, Sri Aurobindo placing his hand behind her head 'as if blessing through her'.

Three days later, Sri Aurobindo asked Barin to tell the disciples that 'the power had descended into the unconscious, in association with Krishna; it was now necessary to work out the detail with the help of that power'. He also added a more personal note about the new organisation he intended to adopt:

> Mirra is my Shakti. She has taken charge of the new creation. You will get everything from her. Give your consent to whatever she wants to do.

This was the spiritual foundation of the Ashram. Sri Aurobindo would no longer see his disciples on a daily basis, as had been the practice until then. His door would remain closed for everyone except for Mirra. For everyone, she became 'The Mother', guiding individual disciples in their spiritual journey as well as organising their material life. He would later substantiate his decision by offering this spiritual explanation:

> The Mother's consciousness and mine are the same, the one Divine Consciousness in two, because that is necessary for the play. Nothing can

> be done without her knowledge and force, without her consciousness—if anybody really feels her consciousness, he should know that I am there behind it and if he feels me it is the same with hers.

Sri Aurobindo could now devote his entire time to his sadhana, that is, incarnate the Supramental consciousness in his body. He soon realised that the great descent he had experienced on 24 November was not yet the final Supramental power but the intermediary manifestation of a transitional plane between Mind and Supermind proper. This intermediate realisation—which he called Overmind—was an essential stage in the conquest of the higher Supermind consciousness. His work was clearly laid out.

An Active Retirement: Record of Yoga

For the first time in years, Sri Aurobindo resumed recording his daily progress in his journal. Yoga had reached a climax in which the body consciousness had become the primary focus, and the prospective receptacle of a Force capable of recasting its physical activities in the world and its entire approach to life.

> When the fullness of the supramental life-energy is in the body, then all difficulties will be reduced to nothingness. It is the life-energy in all the body, not only in the seven centres, that is demanded. Once in all the seven centres, it cannot fail to pour through all the body. It must take possession of all the cells, the flesh, muscles, bones, blood, nerves, skin, hair; then the body will be ready for transformation.

The following weeks reinforced the reality of this transformation:

> (2-12 January) The flow of the energy has begun, but is still subject to interruption. Make way for the Supreme Force. It will take up your responsibilities. [...] The Supreme Power is taking up all the movements. It will turn them into the Truth. No effort is needed, no aid from the mind or any of the instruments; even the individual consent is no longer

> needed. [...] The final dealings with this body begin from today. The first stage of them finishes with the end of the month.

Remarkably, Mirra was associated with these experiences, as if the very same invisible Power affected her body as it did his.

> (12-29 January) And with her body, it begins from tomorrow. At present, it is the preparation of the forces. [...] For this body, the evidence is tomorrow; for hers it is veiled and will only appear day after tomorrow. [...] As predicted, there are the first signs of amelioration in her body, though nothing yet is complete or in appearance finally decisive. [...] The action on health in both bodies is more evident but not yet entirely conclusive.

As was revealed by the great Krishna experience, the key to establishing the Supramental Power in the body rested in the inconscient. Complete control over all unconscious body activities—including health—was the primary condition for incarnating the Supermind:

> When the hidden secret has been discovered and made effective, the human consciousness will be exceeded, the superconscient made conscient and the subconscient or inconscient which is the inevitable shadow of the superconscient filled with the true spiritual and supramental consciousness.

Sri Aurobindo tracked the incarnation of the Supramental by testing the activities of the higher faculty of intuition. Several notes from this period dealt with the evolution of *trikaldrishti* (vision of the past, present and future) beyond the classic form into a 'Gnostic' *trikaldrishti*, the very absolute Supramental influence he was trying to 'secure'.

He felt that the conquest of the Supramental plane and its 'descent' into our world was part of the evolutionary design.

For him, this new mental stage beyond humanity was analogous to the evolution of the mind among the hominids.

> Man is a transitional being, he is not final; for in him and high beyond him ascend the radiant degrees which climb to a divine supermanhood. The step from man towards superman is the next approaching achievement in the earth's evolution. There lies our destiny and the liberating key to our aspiring, but troubled and limited human existence.

The Psychic Being and the Force

For the disciples, it was as if, through the Mother, Sri Aurobindo had duplicated himself. She incarnated the power of transformation:

> If you desire this transformation, put yourself in the hands of the Mother and her Powers without cavil or resistance and let her do unhindered her work within you.

A disciple asked: 'Is our Mother the "individual" form of the Divine Mother whom you described in your book as embodying "the power of these two vast ways of existence—transcendent and universal?"'

He simply replied, 'Yes.'

A number of disciples would take time to adjust to this new relationship and practice of yoga. A few could not accustom themselves.

Indeed, the Mother's presence introduced a radical change in the approach to yoga. Most of those coming in contact with her felt carried away in their heart and soul by an emotion—never experienced before—which felt like 'a sort of inherent perception of the truth, akin to a soul-feeling'. This burning, flame-like sensation was what Sri Aurobindo named 'the psychic opening'.

The psychic opening triggered the entire movement of yoga. By livening up the psychic emotion and relying on its activities, the disciple was embarked upon yoga and automatically led towards spiritual transformation. As Sri Aurobindo described it, the Force was the driving impetus of this spiritual transformation:

> The Force works at the same time for perfection as well as liberation; it takes up the whole nature part by part and deals with it, rejecting what has to be rejected, sublimating what has to be sublimated, creating what has to be created. It integrates, harmonises, establishes a new rhythm in the nature.... All this is prepared, assisted, farthered by the work of the psychic being in the heart centre; the more it is open, in front, active, the quicker, safer, easier the working of the Force can be.

Ashram Members

The disciples arrived from everywhere. Some of the former companions of Alipore Jail paid a brief visit, such as Ullaskar, the former bomb maker who directed the prisoners' choir in the bus to the courthouse, and Abinash Battacharya, the faithful 'major-domo' from Calcutta. Other young men came to Pondicherry never to leave: Champaklal, the most loyal, arriving at 18 from his native Gujarat; Dilip Kumar Roy, the talented Bengali musician.

There was even a French civil Engineer from the famed École Polytechnique. Second Lieutenant Philippe Barbier de Saint Hilaire had fought in trench warfare in France. After the war, travelling to Japan and then to Mongolia in search of his spiritual destiny, he landed in Pondicherry in 1925. There, he first met Mirra, then Sri Aurobindo, who explained his yoga briefly before adding: 'Well, if you would like, you can stay.' He was given a new name, Pavitra, the Pure, and became Mother's personal secretary.

Margaret Woodrow Wilson, President Wilson's daughter, ran into *Essays on the Gita* at the New York Public Library. She sailed to Pondicherry to be accepted as a disciple by Sri Aurobindo, who called her Nishta ('One-pointed devotion'). Of him, she would say: 'Here is one on earth whom one can love all one's life and in whom one can lose oneself.'

Scholars and intellectuals occupied a prominent place among the newcomers. J.A. Chadwick (aka Arjava), professor of Mathematical logic and member of Trinity College, Cambridge, became a fine metaphysical poet under Sri Aurobindo's tutelage, producing over 3,000 poems in a few years. Prithwi Singh came from his native Bengal to tackle the entire analytical index of *The Life Divine*. Other writers—Nishikanto, Sisirkumar Mitra, K.D. Sethna, Rishabchand, Narayan Prasad—began composing poetry under the influence of yoga.

There was also Nirodbaran, a young medical graduate from the University of Edinburgh, who took over the Ashram dispensary and became the privileged recipient of Sri Aurobindo's humour. There was no shortage of lawyers either: Doraiswami Aiyar, attorney at the Madras bar, and Syed Mehdi Iman of the Supreme Court. Sir Akbar Hydari, prime minister of the state of Hyderabad, donated funds to build the Ashram Golconde residence in 1937.

Sri Aurobindo would have preferred to limit the membership until the community had reached spiritual maturity, but he was sometimes forced to accept new disciples, so great was their eagerness. At the end of 1928, the Ashram sheltered 70 men and women in 15 houses.

Ashram Life

Within a few years, Sri Aurobindo's correspondence with his disciples was to grow phenomenally. Letters conveying their questions and problems were dropped off daily before 11 pm—a pile often exceeding 100. Sri Aurobindo spent almost the rest of the night answering. Every day, he penned up to 70 responses of a few lines, but often of one page or more.

> Whenever I write these letters or replies, I never think or seek for expressions or try to write in good style; it is out of a silent mind that I write whatever comes ready-shaped from above.

Perhaps, as a concession to the significant increase of disciples, Sri Aurobindo decided to reappear regularly in public. For his birthday, on 15 August 1927, seated next to Mother, he gave the first of a series of what would become annual Darshans. Each attendee stood 1 to 2 minutes before him to receive his gaze. For many of those present, it became an unforgettable experience. This form of celebration was repeated on 24 November 1927, for the first anniversary of the Overmind descent; then three months later, on 21 February 1928, for Mother's anniversary. These three Darshans became the highlights of Ashram life. In 1934, the number of disciples and visitors thus admitted reached 700.

With the exception of these Darshans, for more than 20 years, Sri Aurobindo's retirement was strictly enforced. In 1928, he made a rare deviation for Rabindranath Tagore, who described this meeting the following day:

> At the very first sight I could realise that he had been seeking for the soul and gained it. His face was radiant with an inner light and his serene presence made it evident to me that his soul was not crippled or cramped to the measure of some tyrannical doctrine, which takes delight in inflicting wounds on life.... I felt that the utterance of the ancient Hindu rishi spoke from him of the equanimity which gives the human soul its freedom of entrance into the All. I said to him, 'You have the word and we are waiting to accept it from you. India will speak through your voice to the world.'

As Sri Aurobindo had warned Tagore that he would be unable to come out of his retirement before establishing the foundations of the Supramental life in his body, the poet had concluded that he would likely return to public life within a year or so. However, as the years went by and the 'retirement' seemed to last, Sri Aurobindo noted wryly, 'he is disappointed that I have not come out and started giving lectures in America and saving humanity'.

Gandhi, even though at the very peak of his influence in India, was unable to intrude on his solitude:

> Perhaps you know that ever since my return to India, I have been anxious to meet you face to face. Now that it is almost certain that I am to be in Pondicherry, will you spare me a few minutes and see me! I know how reluctant you are to see anybody. But if you are under no positive vow of abstinence, I hope you will give me a few minutes of your time.

Sri Aurobindo replied:

> It is true that I have made no vow, for I never make one, but my retirement is not less binding on me so long as it—and the reason for it—lasts. I think you will understand that it is not a personal or mental choice but something impersonal from a deeper source for the inner necessity of work and sadhana. It prevents me from receiving you but I cannot do otherwise than keep to the rule I have adhered to for some years past.

If he did not feel impelled to depart from his rule, it is also that he perceived that Gandhi's request 'was dictated by curiosity rather than anything else'.

> I don't think he would accept the Truth that is here. His mind is too rigid for it.... Gandhi has his own work, his own ideal and dharma—how can he open himself to receive anything from here?

Challenges

The Ashram development and its management under Mother's supervision aroused admiration and praise in Pondicherry but also suspicion. The French authorities—perhaps prompted by the British consul—launched an investigation into its operations.

Was it a properly registered organisation? Where were the account books? The inquiry was passed on to the colonial office in Paris, and the Pondicherry governor was requested to submit a report. Sri Aurobindo took the underlying threat very seriously: 'I am faced with a wanton and brutal attack on my life-work from outside.'

He issued a statement about what was and was not the Ashram, appending a summary of his teaching and his personal approach to spiritual transformation. This summation, combined with private explanations to the local authorities and a letter from Mother to her brother Mattéo, stationed at the Foreign Office in Paris, assuaged domestic concerns.

Years later, Mother offered this striking occult perception of what was going on in the disciples' existence at the time:

> Even till they reached 150… they were as if held in an egg-shell in my consciousness, so close, you know, that I could direct all their movements, both inner and outer, all the time. Everything was under control, at every moment, night and day. Naturally, I think in those days they made real progress. It could be said that I did the sadhana for them!

As for Sri Aurobindo, he had now reached a stage where, despite the constant challenges and difficulties he faced….

> …. the descent of the supramental is an inevitable necessity in the logic of things and is therefore sure.

He commented that people could not understand this 'because they did not realise the significance of the emergence of consciousness in a world of "inconscient" Matter'. This also implied that the Supramental descent did not depend on the readiness of the disciples: 'Everything depends on my getting through.'

In November 1934, the long-awaited 'general descent of the Supermind' seemed imminent. However, the process came to a brutal stop when it was met with considerable resistance from material Nature: 'an upsurge of subconscient mud,' declared Sri Aurobindo. The mind was overrun by 'old thoughts, old mental, vital and physical habits or an obscure stimulus to sensations, actions, emotions'—also by the body's long-forgotten diseases. For the disciples, it meant the resurgence of old problems and a general lack of progress. For six months, Sri Aurobindo remained busy with that subconscious surge before declaring:

> It is still there, but personally I have become superior to it and am travelling forward like a flash of lightning, that is to say zigzag but fairly fast. Now I have got the hang of the whole hanged thing—like a very Einstein I have got the mathematical formula of the whole affair (unintelligible as in his case to anybody but myself) and am working it out figure by figure.

The disciples could not help him; on the contrary, they delayed his progress with their revolts, their depressions and quarrels. 'The Supramental is coming down as fast as you fellows will allow,' Sri Aurobindo commented in 1936. Nevertheless, he continued helping them with his letters on every aspect of yoga. Whatever difficulties and obstacles, he felt that even....

> .... if I still saw the chance that it might come to nothing (which is impossible), I should go on unperturbed, because I would still have done to the best of my power the work that I had to do and what is so done always counts in the economy of the universe.

At the end of 1937, new disciples were admitted, and the Ashram grew to 200 members, who were lodged across many houses in the city. Whenever possible, newcomers were supposed to make the offering of their material possessions to compensate for the expenditures of their life maintenance. Most, however, were unable to contribute financially.

> It has been an arduous and trying work for the Mother and myself to keep up this Ashram, with its ever-increasing numbers, to make both ends meet, and at times, to prevent deficit budgets and their results.... Carrying on anything of this magnitude without any settled income could not have been done if there had not been the working of a Divine Force.

At this point, the pace of his correspondence began to slacken—to stop completely for six months when an eye condition developed as a result of the nights spent writing in poor electric light. He took this opportunity to work with an assistant on *Savitri*, the epic poem inspired by the Mahabharata, which would become, in the course of multiple revisions, the immense symbolic account of his yoga.

His reputation in India continued to grow. Newspapers frequently called him 'India's greatest living thinker'. Radio programmes cited his works. Essayists sought him out to contribute to their philosophical dissertations. Would-be biographers pestered his disciples to collect material about his life. In most cases, he dismissed all the requests.

> I do not care a button about my having my name in any blessed place.

Then his name began to spread in the West. The Ashram received European intellectuals and writers who lauded their visit. Maria Montessori and Albert Schweitzer sent their books with complimentary dedications. Yet, overall, Sri Aurobindo did nothing to cultivate Western interests towards himself.

The world was inexorably moving towards the second tragedy of the century. In September 1938, a disciple wrote in jest: 'By the way, you had better hurry up with your Supermind descent, Sir. Otherwise Hitler, Mussolini and Co. will gunfire it like—!'

Sri Aurobindo retorted sharply: 'What has Supermind to do with Hitler or Hitler with Supermind?'

Yet he was well aware of the global turmoil in preparation, as is evident in these lines composed in September 1938.

> I look across the world and no horizon walls my gaze;
> I see Tokyo and Paris and New York,
> I see the bombs bursting on Barcelona and on Canton streets.
> Man's numberless misdeeds and small good deeds take place within my single self....
> I carry the sorrow of millions in my lonely breast.

The 24 November 1938 Darshan was approaching. Although it was reserved for members of the Ashram and a few guests, around 400 people were expected. Beginning at 7:30 am, it would continue till the evening. Sri Aurobindo had stopped all correspondence three weeks earlier to prepare for the occasion. In the early hours of the morning of the 24th, while the Ashram slept, he got up from his table to go to the bathroom. On the way, he stumbled on a tiger skin spread on the floor and fell. He could not get up on his own. Several doctors were called in. An x-ray machine brought from Madras revealed that Sri Aurobindo's femur was badly fractured above the knee.

The recovery took time. Mother served his meals while a team of disciples took turns by his side. He conversed with them (some had yet to hear his voice), and these conversations were transcribed and published by Purani. One day, one of the attendants asked Sri Aurobindo if he had 'realised the Supermind'.

> I know what the Supermind is. And the physical being has flashes and glimpses of it.... I am not satisfied with the Supermind in the physical consciousness. I want to bring down the whole mass of it, pure, and that is an extremely difficult business.

Then the same doctor-disciple asked how it feels to live in 'the divine consciousness'.

> One feels a perpetual calm, perpetual strength, one is aware of Infinity, and lives not only in Infinity but also in Eternity. One feels Immortality and does not care about death of the body. And then, one has the consciousness of the One in all. Everything becomes the manifestation of the Brahman. For instance, as I look round this room, I see everything as the Brahman. No, it is not mere thinking, it is a concrete experience. Even the wall, the books are the Brahman. I see you as no more Dr Manilal but the Divine living in the Divine. It is a wonderful experience.

The Second World War

In 1939, the Second World War broke out in Europe. After Hitler invaded Poland, France and England declared war on Germany on 3 September. That same day, without consulting Indian leaders, Viceroy Linlithgow announced that India also was at war. Ignoring the storm of protest, he served notice to Gandhi and Jinnah (the Muslim leader) that all talks of self-government were now suspended until the end of the hostilities. The contrast in the reactions to this dramatic proclamation would summarise the coming four years for the Hindu and Muslim populations of India. While Jinnah willingly accepted that a global conflagration could impact India's destiny, Gandhi, along with a united Congress, demanded India's immediate independence from Britain and the appointment of a constituent assembly.

Hoping that a victory by Hitler would liberate the country from colonial rule, the Indian public opinion was mostly favourable to Germany. However, it did not take long for Sri Aurobindo to understand that the victory of Nazi Germany was too heavy a price to pay for the fall of the British Empire. He declared his unconditional support for the Allied effort, while Gandhi and Congress refused to side with the British. Sri Aurobindo was the only Indian leader to take an open stand in favour of the Western democracies.

Most of his former nationalist comrades disagreed with him. Some of his disciples even openly declared themselves pro-German—a stance that the Pondicherry government could have taken as an excuse to close down the Ashram. In May 1940, the Wehrmacht-controlled Poland, Denmark, and part of Norway; it broke through the French lines at Sedan, and the British and French troops narrowly escaped being encircled at Dunkirk. In a letter he circulated among his disciples, Sri Aurobindo explained the fuller scope of the conflict at hand:

> The victory of one side (the Allies) would keep the path open for the evolutionary forces; the victory of the other side would drag back humanity, degrade it horribly and might lead even, at the worst, to its failure as a race, as others in the past evolution failed and perished.

As he had previously recorded in his journal when chronicling the Balkan War and the First World War, he used his yogic powers on the current warfare. It would, no doubt, be interesting to know the details of what he did to address the conflict, but he simply offered this general commentary:

> I have avoided as much as possible writing about these subjects... because I might have to speak of laws and forces not recognised by physical reason or science.

Later on, by chance, talking to a disciple about the battle of Stalingrad, he confided 'to have to put his force on Russia, daily and concretely enough, in all conscience'.

From the outset, the British had been eager to enlist India's support in the war. That is what Jinnah and his Muslim League understood and managed to turn to their advantage, while the

Hindu majority in Congress, under Gandhi, was incapable of profiting from the opportunity.

In February 1940, Jinnah unexpectedly informed the Viceroy that the Muslim League had resolved to demand the partition of India to separate Muslims from Hindus and to refuse the federation premeditated by London. Two months later, the Muslim League confirmed their plan by requesting the autonomy of several Muslim-led north-western and eastern provinces. The vision of Pakistan was emerging. Feigning surprise, Gandhi declared himself 'baffled' by this news and erupted in sermons on the right of people to self-determination. His followers were stunned. 'This request (from Jinnah) is the sign of a sick spirit!' one of them cried out.

In May 1940, Churchill replaced Chamberlain as British prime minister and thus held the rein of the British war effort. In July, as England faced the imminent threat of a German invasion, Gandhi wrote this open letter to the British people:

> I appeal for cessation of hostilities… because war is bad in essence. I venture to present you with a nobler and a braver way. I want you to fight Nazism without arms, or with non-violent arms. I would like you to lay down the arms you have as being useless for saving you or humanity. You will invite Herr Hitler and Signor Mussolini to take what they want of the countries you call your possessions. Let them take possession of your beautiful island, with your many beautiful buildings. You will give all these but neither your souls, nor your minds.

In August, rejecting the advances of Viceroy Linlithgow to bring the communities closer together and prevent the dismemberment of the country, Congress embarked on a new campaign of civil disobedience. Renewing the Satyagraha credo, Gandhi's emissaries travelled the country to denounce the English war effort. In retaliation, the government put more than 15,000 demonstrators behind bars. It would take until December 1941, the Japanese attack on Pearl Harbor and the deterioration of the military situation in Europe, for Congress to admit the need to reassess its programme of non-cooperation and for Gandhi to cancel this new disobedience movement.

On 7 December 1941, the Japanese attack on Pearl Harbor brought America into the war. As a fallout, the Japanese armies began their progressive conquest in Southeast Asia; it became more urgent than ever for the British to win the support of Indians in the growing global conflict.

Despite his personal antipathy for Gandhi, Churchill sent a seasoned diplomat to India, Stafford Cripps, to try and win Indians to the cause of war. His proposals were simple enough: immediate creation of a new Indian Union associated with Great Britain under Dominion statute; at the end of the war, India would be free to choose her constitution; meanwhile, the defence of the country would remain in British hands as part of their overall war strategy, while human and material resources would be managed by the government and the people of India.

On 31 March 1942, the day after Cripps announced the details of his plan on Indian radio, Sri Aurobindo sent him a personal telegram welcoming his initiative and hoping it would meet with the approval of the Indian leaders. It was the first time since his withdrawal in 1910 that he publicly raised his voice in the political debate of his country:

> As one who has been a nationalist leader and worker for India's independence though now my activity is no longer in the political but in the spiritual field, I wish to express my appreciation of all you have done to bring about this offer. I welcome it as an opportunity given to India to determine for herself and organise in all liberty of choice her freedom and unity and take an effective place among the world's free nations.

Cripps' telegram reply was immediate:

> I am most touched and gratified by your kind message allowing me to inform India that you, who occupy a unique position in the imagination of Indian youth, are convinced that the declaration of His Majesty's government substantially confers that freedom for which Indian nationalism has long struggled.

Sri Aurobindo thought that if India accepted Cripps' proposal, this would commit her to fight alongside England against the Nazi destructive forces while also helping her to exorcise her communal problems. He sent an emissary to the Congress steering committee with the recommendation to accept Cripps' proposals. However, Gandhi held the key to the final decision. 'He has retired from political life; why does he interfere?' he riposted to Sri Aurobindo's envoy. Despite the efforts of a few independent delegates, the Congress finally rejected Cripps' offer, which Gandhi finished off by calling it: 'A post-dated check drawn on a failing bank.'

In reality, as Nehru would later reveal, 'Gandhi was convinced that Japan and Germany would win the war, and this conviction guided his decisions unconsciously.' This confidence by Nehru was leaked in London, then later reported to Roosevelt, who lambasted Gandhi as 'a traitor'.

After the war ended, K.M. Munshi, one of the Indian leaders of this period, lamented Gandhi's decision in these terms:

> Today, we realise that if Cripps' proposal had been accepted, there would have been no partition, no refugees and no Kashmir problem (still inflamed today).

Peril of Partition

In August 1942, four months after Cripps' departure from India, Congress launched another stubbornly misguided protest movement called 'Quit India', which demanded the immediate departure of the British. Although the government had more serious preoccupations to face—the Japanese capture of Singapore and the advance of the first enemy troops on the Indo-Burmese border—it confronted the crowds exhorted by Gandhi head-on: 100,000 demonstrators were arrested; all Congress leaders were jailed, and Gandhi was moved to house arrest in a palace of the Aga Khan.

The Quit India movement would soon collapse, but not without causing many casualties among the population. Congress leaders spent the rest of the war in prison (i.e., three years cut off from the world) while Gandhi was released on 6 May 1944, 'for health reasons'. In the political vacuum created by the Mahatma's initiatives, Jinnah had his hands free to prepare the future. For three whole years, he was the only Indian interlocutor of England, with a sole objective: the partition of India.

Hardly more than a social norm, Gandhism had now run its course. Since 1930–1932 and the glorious hour of the Salt March (which attempted to bypass the British salt imports), none of the Mahatma's initiatives had managed to tip the balance of power in favour of India. And the Quit India fiasco signed the coup de grace of Gandhi's political credibility, as the historian R.C. Majumdar summarised.

> Gandhi had fired his first shot (figuratively speaking) in 1932, and he had missed his target. For 10 years he had stayed on the sidelines. On 8 August 1942 (beginning of Quit India movement), he pressed the trigger again, but nothing happened because he had forgotten to put a bullet in the chamber. Then, he finally suspended his participation to the direct struggle for India's independence.

The days of Gandhism with Gandhi were over. His heirs—Nehru, Rajagopalachari, Rajendra Prasad—were looking to the future. They watched over Gandhi like an old uncle on a drip: the myth had to be preserved in order to claim the inheritance.

The personality at centre stage, the man whose political ambition held India's destiny in his hands, was Jinnah. The Muslim League he headed had won elective seats in predominantly Muslim regions and controlled these regions. 'The war, which no one looked forward to, turned out to be a blessing in disguise,' he acknowledged.

He had embraced the 'two-nation theory', according to which the Muslims' identity was derived from their faith in Islam, not from a specific territory. Hence, because Muslims and Hindus were of different 'identities', it was natural to envision two nations to house them. 'Pakistan is a matter of life or death,' Jinnah declared. His ambition was to become the supreme leader of a nation invented by him.

The legend depicts Gandhi as a last bastion against India's partition, yielding against his will to Jinnah's pressure in order to avoid a civil war. Yet the following casual conversation of Sri Aurobindo with a disciple betrays unmistakably that Gandhi's mind was made up in favour of partition as early as 1940.

> Have you read what Gandhi has said in answer to a correspondent? He says that if 80 million Muslims demand a separate State, what else are the 250 million of Hindus to do but surrender? Otherwise, there will be civil war.

In 1944, leaving his 'palace-prison', Gandhi paid a visit to Jinnah. As R.C. Majumdar later confirmed, this is when the two men agreed on the details of dividing India:

> The concrete proposal put forward by Gandhi was to partition India into Hindustan and Pakistan, under conditions which did not differ substantially from the plan finally adopted in 1947.

Thus, despite the fiction maintained by his followers, the principle of the partition was approved by Gandhi in 1940, then validated with Jinnah in 1944, in a private transaction that would be acceptable to the entire political class.

The Ashram during the War

After the fall of Singapore in 1942—'the worst defeat in British military history,' according to Churchill—it became clear that this was the first step in invading India. The Burma campaign, which involved nearly a million Japanese soldiers, would have to allow Japanese armies to penetrate into India through an almost impassable border area. Indeed, from December 1943 to November 1944, the strategic balance of the Burma campaign shifted decisively when the advance of Japanese troops towards India resulted in unbearably heavy losses and the eventual ejection of the Japanese. Using the concentration of his force against the armies on the ground, Sri Aurobindo 'had the satisfaction of seeing....

> The tide of Japanese victory, which had till then swept everything before it, changed immediately into a tide of rapid, crushing and finally immense and overwhelming defeat.'

The war also affected the conditions in the Ashram. As the Japanese armies advanced towards Assam and Bengal, the disciples living in these bordering areas requested to take refuge in Pondicherry. In late 1943, more than a hundred people arrived in the Ashram, including many children. With around 20 boys and girls to look after, Mother opened a school where she herself taught some courses. A playground was acquired where children and adults began practising exercises, including tennis and boxing.

Finally, the war came to an end on 15 August 1945. Emperor Hirohito announced the capitulation of Japan. In the Ashram, on this Darshan day, the Allied victory was celebrated with a meditation.

Partition of India

Clement Atlee, the new British prime minister replacing Churchill, had long campaigned for India's autonomy; he now had the means to make it happen. He first sent a special commission to Delhi, the Cabinet Mission, to try to unravel the tension between the Indian communities while submitting concrete proposals for the transfer of power.

The Cabinet Mission proposed to form an Indian interim government following the apportionment of the three main religious communities (Hindus, Muslims, Sikhs). That would have roughly amounted to assigning a territory the size of Pakistan to the Muslims but without formally partitioning the country. Unfortunately, the talks broke down. The Cabinet Mission, the Congress and the Muslim League could not reach an agreement. Jinnah feared that his project of an independent Pakistan would collapse. He warned:

> Do not expect me to submit with folded hands. I too can create troubles.

He resolved to appeal to the streets. On 16 August 1946, the Muslim League spearheaded the so-called 'Direct Action' day: each Muslim was called upon to demonstrate for an independent nation. In Calcutta, the parades turned into riots. In three days of carnage, more than 4,000 people lost their lives, while 100,000 residents fled the devastated city. The Muslim Bengali prime minister, H.S. Suhrawardy, vainly attempted to justify the non-intervention of police. At the end of August, the urban riots spread to the rural areas in Uttar Pradesh, Punjab, Bihar and East Bengal. At Noakhali, 5,000 Hindus were massacred by paramilitary gangs, while tens of thousands of others were forcibly converted to Islam.

Reaching genocidal proportions, these targeted massacres of civilian populations continued unabated for two months before they were quelled by the British army. In a delayed reaction, Gandhi himself visited Noakhali under a suitable escort and remained a few weeks to help the families of victims—but abuses against Hindus continued despite his presence. Touring the scene, the British Governor of Bengal had these words to express the futility of Gandhi's intervention:

> A dozen Gandhis will be necessary for the Muslim leopard and the Hindu kid to lie down again together in this part of the world.

There were more than 20 million Hindus in Bengal. 'Why don't they strike back ?' asked Sri Aurobindo.

The Noakhali massacres provided a radical demonstration that the two communities could not live together. The decision-makers and officials of the Congress could now take the path recommended by Jinnah. As Nehru admitted in 1960:

> The truth is that we were tired men, and who were not that young.... The partition plan offered a way out and we grabbed it.

The partition of India, they believed, had become the reasonable and civilised solution to avoid a civil war. But despite the stated rationale, Jinnah's stunning victory remained tainted by this fatal ambiguity: his resort to 'Direct Action' branded the new nation with an indelible stamp of violence, which is still present today.

In March 1947, the new Viceroy chosen by Attlee to organise the British withdrawal arrived in New Delhi. Louis Mountbatten was the man for the job. Grandson of Queen Victoria and Admiral of the Fleet, he particularly distinguished himself on the Burmese front during World War II. Attlee's instructions gave him much leeway to grant independence to India and negotiate a speedy transfer of power. Although Gandhi could still spout off: 'If Congress wants to consent to partition, they will have to do so over my dead body,' the partition was a fait accompli for the entire political class. In a final snub to historical coherence, Gandhi proposed to elevate Jinnah to the dignity of 'Supreme Leader of India', with a government of his choice and Muslim ministers. Even Gandhi's most loyal supporters pretended not to have heard.

In April, the Viceroy began the negotiations for partitioning India. Jinnah was a skilled, unrelenting negotiator. The following 15 August, nine months before the deadline set by Attlee, the terms of the settlement created two independent nations within the British Commonwealth—India and Pakistan. The real 'independence' of India would occur three years later since Nehru had agreed to keep the King of England as Indian head of state until January 1950.

Within just a few months, politicians of all stripes had done away with a vast country where Hindus, Muslims, Sikhs and Christians had managed to live together for centuries. In a private interview, Sri Aurobindo did not hesitate to qualify the new nation as 'fraud and cheating'.

When Jinnah landed on the tarmac in Karachi, the future economic capital of the nation he had just founded, his entourage could hear him whisper: 'That's the end of that.'

The masterful accomplishment of his objective also marked the end of his life. One year later, worshipped as a god, concentrating on his person all the powers of government, he died of tuberculosis—a medical condition he had concealed for the past 10 years.

Indian radio asked Sri Aurobindo for his reactions to the independence of his country.

> 15 August, 1947 is the birthday of free India. It marks for her the end of an old era, the beginning of a new age. [...] 15 August is my own birthday

> and it is naturally gratifying to me that it should have assumed this vast significance. I take this coincidence, not as a fortuitous accident, but as the sanction and seal of the Divine Force that guides my steps on the work with which I began life.

To a disciple, he confided with humour:

> I am getting a birthday present of a free India on 15 August, but complicated by its being presented in two packets as two free Indias: this is a generosity I could have done without, one free India would have been enough for me if offered as an unbroken whole.

The Death of Gandhi

The official ceremonies celebrating the independence of India on 15 August went almost unnoticed amid the unrest that attended the actual partition. What happened was the largest human migratory movement in history. Fourteen million people thronged the roads to cross the new border feverishly drawn by an English lawyer, Cyril Radcliffe, and his team of topographers imported from England. Baluchistan and the Sind went entirely to the Pakistan side, as did half of Punjab and Bengal.

Although the bulk of Muslims living in India chose to remain, about 7 million of them moved to Pakistan. The same number of Hindus and Sikhs living in Pakistan took the opposite direction. Logistically helpless to cope with such a gigantesque exodus, the two new nations were even more powerless to stem the massacres of civilians crossing the 'Radcliffe line'. One million people perished from illness, hunger or exhaustion and were often killed by opposite community members. For several years, India would have to absorb the human tide of millions of homeless people.

Confronted by this devastation of the border areas and unprecedented bloodbath, Gandhi wondered:

> Why do they all want to come here (to Delhi)? Why not die over there? I maintain that one must hold on to one's own place, even if one is treated cruelly or even killed.

Ordering Nehru to discourage the resettlement of Hindu refugees fleeing Pakistan, he added:

> They should not be afraid of dying. After all, the killers will be none others than our Muslim brothers.

Gandhi's comments were never as outrageous as when he spoke of violence committed against women:

> I always thought it was physically impossible to rape a woman. The outrage only happens when she succumbs to fear or is not conscious of her moral strength. If she cannot oppose the physical strength of the assailant, her purity will give the force to die before he could rape her.

He even had some advice for Hindu or Sikhs women crossing the border under threat:

> If a Muslim expresses the desire to rape a woman, she should never refuse him, but on the contrary cooperate, play dead with her tongue between her teeth. The sooner the rapist is satisfied, the sooner he will let go of her.

The Mahatma generally poured out these obscenities on an audience of devotees during semi-public 'prayer' meetings in Delhi. On 30 January 1948, at the end of such a meeting, an Indian man, Nathuram Godse, approached him, bowed silently with folded hands, and discharged his pistol in his chest. Gandhi died on the spot. The media portrayed Godse as a Hindu extremist in the grip of his passions. At his trial, in a 90-page document listing the aberrations of the past 30 years under Gandhism, he claimed to have acted on behalf of all innocent Hindus killed by the decision to create an Islamic state in defiance of the Hindu majority. He closed his deposition by singing the *Bande Mataram*. He was hanged in November 1949. In an interview in January 1998, his brother Gopal, sentenced to 18 years in prison for complicity, expressed no regrets:

> How can any sensible person tolerate Gandhi's one-sided attitude? We killed him because he was harmful to India. Our love for the motherland made us do it. Gandhi used to claim the Partition would be done over his dead body. So after Partition, when he didn't die, we killed him.

Today, the words evoking the last moments of Nathuram Godse reading his plea before his judges are banned in India.

For the new team in power in Delhi (Nehru had become prime minister in August 1947, while other Gandhi's heirs shared key appointments), there only remained to make a good impression—and, if possible, to draw the attention of the world away from the ongoing tragedy. Nehru reassured the West with his diplomatic skills; in his words, the massacres at Pakistan's border became the catharsis of a new birth, but his unflagging liberal zeal could not completely erase the facts. As a former official of the Salt March would concede: 'We accepted the Partition to avoid the civil war, but we got both—the partition and the civil war.'

Indeed, the episodic inflammation of relations between India and Pakistan—including four open conflicts—remind the world that India's dismemberment has not solved anything.

Gandhi's slim figure walking the roads of India with his pilgrim's staff, the familiar white dhoti raised on his bare legs, is engraved in the history of the 20th century. Seventy-five years after his death, his celebrity has grown to become a popular myth. The official celebration of his legend by the Indian government has found significant support even in Hollywood. Short of a substantial factual revision, Gandhian orthodoxy remains in India the embodiment of the 'Father of the Nation' while it provides to the world the profile of a 'modern-day Christ'. Yet, despite the official propaganda, the younger Indian generation remains sceptical of the Mahatma's cult, if only because modern information techniques now allow delving into the real events that preceded the partition. Furthermore, the research carried out by R.C. Majumdar in his *History of the Freedom Movement in India* provides the material for a fundamental reassessment of Gandhism from undistorted sources. In particular, it enables us to review arguably one of the most persistent myths associated with Gandhi, that of the liberator of India.

Last Creations

In the 1940s, Sri Aurobindo's life was punctuated by the physical rehabilitation of his leg, Mother's visits, meals and reading the news. He also spent three to four hours sitting in his deep armchair, eyes wide open, staring at the wall. 'Wrapped in mysterious silence,' as described by one of his attendants.

> All that was visible to our naked eye was that he sat silently, with his eyes wide open just as any other person would. Only he passed hours and hours thus, changing his .position at times and making himself comfortable; the eyes moving a little, and though usually gazing at the wall in front, never fixed on any particular point. Sometimes, the face would beam with a bright smile without any apparent reason, as a child smiles in sleep.... Occasionally he would look towards the door. That was when he heard some sound which might indicate the Mother's coming.

One can only get lost in conjectures about the meaning and scope of these absorptions among 'forces not recognised by physical reason or science'.

Towards the end of the afternoons, Mother paid him a visit. The evenings were devoted to literary work. Since the mid-1940s, his eyesight no longer allowed him to write easily; he required the help of an assistant to read and dictate his texts. He stayed awake until two o'clock in the morning, not going to bed before he was certain Mother had retired for the night.

The conversations and correspondence with the disciples had almost entirely ceased. In July 1947, he dictated a final letter on the state of his sadhana:

> My present effort is not to stand up on a high and distant Supermind level and change the world from there, but to bring something of it down here and to stand on that and act by that.

During the four annual days of Darshan, he became more active than usual. In the early afternoon, he and Mother sat down side by side in a small adjoining room while disciples and visitors filed past—they numbered 3,000 in the late 1940s. Sri Aurobindo looked each person directly in the face. His gaze continued to overwhelm many people with emotion.

Even more mysterious is what was reported by an older discipline gifted with the capacity of occult vision. He detected that, during Darshan, Sri Aurobindo was drawing into himself 'dark fumes' rising from the subconscious parts of the people filing past him. He seemed to be gathering the lowest elements of earth-nature in order to take them in and transform them.

The independence of British India in 1947 had not changed the status of Pondicherry, which remained a French colony. Sri Aurobindo hoped and worked for its reunification with the rest of India while retaining cultural links with France. He exhorted Nehru to act in that sense and received a high-power French cultural delegation headed by Maurice Schumann and François Baron, the then Governor of Pondicherry, to prepare the groundwork—this was the first time in 18 years that he met anyone external to the Ashram. In 1954, Pondicherry was reintegrated into India.

After Gandhi's assassination, many in the political class turned to Sri Aurobindo. Calls to get him out of political retirement became increasingly pressing, but all he could offer was the assurance that 'the present state of this perturbed world was necessary because certain possibilities had to emerge so that they may be grappled with and thrown out or to emerge from latency in the depths for the same purificatory purpose'.

By 1949, Sri Aurobindo devoted much time working on *Savitri*, his epic poem and most extensive literary creation, which now exceeded 20,000 lines. Through it, he meant to achieve more than a story of conjugal love conquering death:

> *Savitri* has not been regarded by me as a poem to be written and finished, but as a field of experimentation to see how far poetry could be written from one's own yogic consciousness and how that could be made creative.

Sitting in his armchair while Nirodbaran, his assistant, read the stanzas of the previous day, he dictated new passages or revised old ones. In 1950, the first volume of the poem was published by the Ashram printing press.

This period was also used to revise the texts he had published almost 30 years earlier in *Arya*. *The Human Cycle* and *The Ideal of Human Unity*, in particular, were updated to take into account the huge political changes in the world since 1920. New editions of these works were published in Pondicherry and New York.

A few new visitors were allowed to visit him. The photographer Cartier-Bresson asked for permission to attend Darshan, and then convinced Mother to let him take some pictures in Sri Aurobindo's room. The next day, he took a series of portraits, the first since 1920, and expressed his surprise: 'Sri Aurobindo did not blink once during the 10 minutes I watched him!'

In mid-1949, Sri Aurobindo began to experience difficulty urinating. A surgeon visiting for the Darshan diagnosed a dilated prostate. When he returned for the November Darshan, Sri Aurobindo reassured him: 'It is no more troubling me. I have cured it.'

However, a year later, his assistants noticed that he had become increasingly quiet. He only gave monosyllabic replies to their attempts at conversation. 'Why are you so serious, Sir?' dared his surgeon. 'The time is very serious,' he replied. Perhaps, he was referring to the Korean conflict, which threatened to break out into a third world war. At about the same time, the signs of prostatic hyperplasia reappeared. Doctors were convinced that Sri Aurobindo would use his yogic force to heal them; they were dismayed by the reappearance of symptoms.

He pursued the work on *Savitri*: 'I want to finish quickly.' This was the first time his assistant had heard him talk like that. They opened the 'Book of Fate', which depicts Savitri's strength in facing her destiny:

> A day may come when she must stand unhelped
> On a dangerous brink of the world's doom and hers,
> Carrying the world's future on her lonely breast,
> Carrying the human hope in a heart left sole
> To conquer or fail on a last desperate verge,
> Alone with death and close to extinction's edge.

Before the November 1950 Darshan, Sri Aurobindo's discomfort worsened. A second surgeon confirmed the diagnosis, and the remedy would be to remove the prostate, a relatively safe and benign operation, but Sri Aurobindo refused to turn in his body to the surgeon's scalpel. Mother approved.

A suggestion to postpone Darshan was also ruled out. More than 3,000 people had made the trip to Pondicherry; they could not be disappointed. The slow procession before the two pairs of eyes of Sri Aurobindo and Mother began.... After two hours, a soft whisper ran through the crowd, signalling a wish to speed up the pace. Everyone advanced a little faster, and the Darshan ended at 5 pm. Sri Aurobindo seemed exhausted.

In the following days, the symptoms worsened. The surgeon was recalled from Calcutta. Sri Aurobindo suffered from a mild kidney infection which an antibiotics treatment should have cured.

The next day showed a notable improvement. He regained his appetite and joked with his doctors.

> You doctors think only in terms of diseases and medicines....

In the evening, however, the patient's condition deteriorated again, and the surgeon asked permission to use a more aggressive treatment. Mother rejected the idea; Sri Aurobindo's body would not tolerate powerful drugs. The next morning, he seemed to be doing so well that the doctor asked Mother if he could return home.

Later, in the afternoon, the temperature rose to 102 degrees, and Sri Aurobindo began to have trouble breathing. Doctors insisted on performing a blood test, and the results were very alarming: 'All the signs of imminent kidney failure.' Sri Aurobindo could not eat anything. Mother made him drink a little fruit juice. She took the doctor aside:

> He is fully conscious within, but he is losing interest in himself.

The next day, on the morning of 4 December, Sri Aurobindo was much better. He went to his armchair and sat calmly.

The doctors noticed a significant improvement. One of them enquired if he was using his yogic power to heal himself. He replied negatively.

'Why not?' asked the doctor.

'Can't explain. You would not understand,' came the astounding answer. Towards noon, the breathing difficulties resumed, and the temperature shot up. Sri Aurobindo returned to lie down, then got up, and then lay down again. Inconsolable, his faithful Champaklal was at his feet. Sri Aurobindo kissed him on the cheek.

When Mother came back in the evening, the doctors asked permission to use an injection. She answered: 'I told you this is not necessary. He has no interest in himself. He is withdrawing.'

She returned at 11 o'clock, made him sip a little juice, and then left. When she came back an hour later, Sri Aurobindo opened his eyes, and they looked at each other for a long time. She left and came back around one in the morning. This time, Sri Aurobindo kept his eyes closed. 'Call me when the time comes,' she said, then left the room.

Sri Aurobindo's breathing became so ragged that the doctors plugged in the oxygen. Around 1.15 am, he sat up, inquired about the time, and asked for a drink. After a few sips of juice, he went in again. Champaklal and Nirodbaran massaged his feet while the surgeon brushed his hair. Suddenly, a tremor shook his body. He lifted his arms and crossed them over his chest. It was 1:26 am. He stopped breathing. It was 5 December 1950.

All the country's major newspapers headlined the news with abundant obituaries. President Rajendra Prasad, Prime Minister Nehru, the ministers, governors, maharajas as well as intellectuals and spiritual leaders, praised his contribution to the struggle for independence, his philosophical work, and the altruism of his spiritual practice. His death was noted in Paris, London and New York. A *Manchester Guardian* reporter hailed him as 'The most prominent philosophical thinker in modern India' and reminded the readers that he was 'a product of the West as much as of the East'.

While standing near Sri Aurobindo's body after he passed away, Mother related that she suddenly felt 'all the Supramental force passing from his body into mine'.

Filled with this force, she would pursue for another 23 years the mission Sri Aurobindo had assigned to her a few months before leaving:

> You alone can pursue the physical work. You cannot leave, you must stay.

Under her guidance, the Ashram continued to house a growing number of spiritual seekers. The Master's presence could now be felt through the Mother.

In 1968, she founded Auroville, a new international settlement a few kilometres from Pondicherry, as a 'laboratory of the new evolution'. For its inauguration, children from 124 nations and 23 Indian states mixed a handful of soil from their own country in a lotus-shaped urn at the centre of the future township. Auroville currently has about 3,000 residents from almost every country in the world.

In 1978, five years after her demise, her private journal appeared. Called *Mother's Agenda*, it is a series of 13 volumes composed of private conversations collected by Satprem, Mother's closest disciple. The record over a period of 17 years describes how Mother fulfilled the mission entrusted to her by Sri Aurobindo. It elucidates her exploration of the body consciousness and the revelation of a 'cellular mind' capable of recasting the conditions of the body and the laws of the species as the 'thinking mind' had evolved the conditions of the anthropoid. It is an initiatory document on the unravelling of the mysteries of the new species.

Epilogue

Seventy years after his death, Sri Aurobindo figures prominently in 20th-century thought. Debated by historians, philosophers, literary critics and social scientists, he is also admired, and even revered, by thousands of spiritual seekers around the world.

Although few readers were able to grasp the inward breath of *The Divine Life* or the inspiration of *Savitri*, and even less to pursue his path of yoga, his disappearance touched a large number of aspirants. As an Indian politician summed it up, 'He was the last of the great geniuses of the last century.' Vivekananda and Tagore had left before him. The survivors were not of the same caliber. It was the end of an era.

Like all legends, that of Sri Aurobindo was distorted by his admirers and detractors alike, and he was raised to the skies or vilified for acts never committed or words never spoken. The value of his achievements can only be judged by the historical and literary evidence, by estimating the nature and effects of his thought and his action. Sri Aurobindo's role in India's liberation struggle is recognised by all contemporary sources. Before him, no one even dared speak of India's independence; 20 years later, it had become a goal accepted by all.

Although his place as a leading thinker and politician is assured, Sri Aurobindo never considered his action in these areas as representing the true measure of his aspirations. As he wrote to a disciple who wished to propagate his fame:

> In my view, a man's value does not depend on what he learns or his position or fame or what he does, but on what he is and inwardly becomes.

If he refused to offer this disciple any detail on his inner life, his *Record of yoga* allows us an intimate glimpse of his activities below the surface.

Upon his arrival in Pondicherry, he considered that his real work was to bring down a new principle of consciousness—the Supramental consciousness—onto earth. In the *Record of yoga* and in his final letters, he indicated having made significant strides in this direction, although what he called 'The complete descent of the Supramental power' still eluded him. His disciples often asked him to describe the Supramental. 'What's the use?' he replied.

> How much would anybody understand? Besides the present business is to bring down and establish the Supermind, not to explain it. If it establishes itself, it will explain itself—if it does not, there is no use in explaining it.

For Sri Aurobindo, the descent of the Supramental consciousness was the key to the transformation of the individual and, eventually, society. While other yogas have the sole aim of inward liberation of the individual, he envisioned a race of human beings forming a gnostic society:

> A collective soul-power of the Truth-consciousness.

Such a society could only come into existence if enough individuals opened themselves to higher levels of consciousness, but he never believed that such a development would emerge from a popular movement or a religion.

Two generations after Sri Aurobindo's death, his work endures in his Ashram, in the international township of Auroville near Pondicherry, in centres in India, the United States, Canada, and Europe. However, beyond established groups and institutions, it is the silent practitioners of his yoga around the world who bring a concrete meaning—a body—to its vision: the appearance of a new human species on earth.

Suggested Readings

Complete Works of Sri Aurobindo

Published by the Ashram in Pondicherry, the set comprises 36 volumes in a uniform library edition, plus a reference volume with index and glossary.

Each of the volumes can be viewed and downloaded in PDF format. All PDF files are also comprised in a zip file available for download. Most notables titles in the set are:

The Life Divine
The Synthesis of Yoga
The Secret of the Veda
Bande Mataram
Karmayogin
Upanishads
The Human Cycle
Savitri
Collected Poems
Letters on Yoga
Letters on Himself
Record of Yoga

Mother's Agenda, a set of 13 volumes available in French and English from:

Institut de Recherches Evolutives, 32 avenue de l'Observatoire, 75014 Paris

About the Author

Luc Venet was born in Paris in 1943. At the age of 26, while a Mathematics teacher, he discovered Sri Aurobindo's message and visited the Ashram of Pondicherry in South India. There he met the Mother, Sri Aurobindo's long-time spiritual companion, who was 91 years old at the time. This meeting changed his life.

In 1972, he was accepted by the Mother to live and work in Auroville, the International Community she had projected a few miles from Pondicherry. He worked in publishing and built one of the the very first experimental houses in Auromodèle.

In 1977, leaving Auroville for America, he helped Satprem publish the complete set of *Mother's Agenda* in English—the day-to-day account of Mother's cellular transformation in her attempt to seek the emergence of a new humanity on earth. Luc Venet now lives in southern France.